FOOD AND BEVERAGE: COMPREHENSIVE COST CONTROL AND SYSTEM MANAGEMENT

FOOD AND BEVERAGE
Comprehensive Cost Control and System Management

KAMAL MANAKTOLA
ALOK PRASAD

KANISHKA PUBLISHERS, DISTRIBUTORS
NEW DELHI-110 002

KANISHKA PUBLISHERS, DISTRIBUTORS
4697/5-21 A, Ansari Road, Daryaganj
New Delhi-110 002
Phones : 2327 0497, 2328 8285
Fax : 011-2328 8285
E-mail: kanishka_publishing@yahoo.co.in

Food and Beverage:
Comprehensive Cost Control and System Management

First Published 2008

ISBN 978-81-7391-069-4

PRINTED IN INDIA

Published by Madan Sachdeva for Kanishka Publishers, Distributors, 4697/5-21A, Ansari Road, Daryaganj, New Delhi-110 002, Typeset by Sunshine Graphics, Delhi, and Printed at Nice Printing Press, Delhi.

Preface

There has been a long felt need among students and practicing Food and Beverage professional to have an updated perspective into the art and science of Food and Beverage Management. The book is an attempt to meet this requisite need and is a further step into the understanding of Food and Beverage complexities. This book is designed and being published as convenient textbook for students and a guide as well as a handbook for hotel professionals.

During the period of teaching in hospitality education, I have become very cognizant of the need for a Food and Beverage Management textbook suitable for by the hospitality management students as well as managers/consultants in the Food and Beverage operation.

The book has been compiled for students studying hospitality management at various levels with an aim to provide them a comprehensive knowledge of the various aspects of Food and Beverage Management and Control to effectively manage food and beverage operation and providing productivity and profits.

This book covers the syllabus of various university and institution conducting courses for diploma, degree and post-graduate programme having Food and Beverage Management as one of the essential subject. It has been observed that students use to be sporty of this subject and they feel uncomfortable while they are in real work situation. While writing this book emphasis has been laid to create interest in the subject.

The primary chapter of this book are leading towards Food and Beverage Sectors and planning of different component of food and beverage and outlet in the initial stage. As book progresses cost concept has been discussed which has been followed by different areas and activities where control is required for profitable operation (comprehensive cost control). Production control is also being a very big issue for formulating strategies for pricing and sales of Food and Beverage items.

Pricing and sales have been very diverse practice in food and beverage operation and management. Menu engineering and menu analysis can be used for interpretation of indifferent behaviour of customers/consumers of food and beverage industry.

I hope the students, teachers, hotel professionals consultants, researchers, and entrepreneurs will find this book helpful to get solution of any problems in day-to-day operation and management in Food and Beverage area. It is a great motivation and encouragement of the Kanishka Publishers, Distributors, the organization committed to higher education in hospitality, tourism and all other areas of education world wide, that this book has been compiled.

I would like to thank to my organization and it's dynamic management which has given all support that is required for completion of this work. I am very thankful to my family, colleagues and seniors who have contributed in different ways.

AUTHORS

Contents

Introduction

Maximizing profit margins and avoiding waste requires accurate knowledge of Food and Beverage control procedures. This book has been written with dual purpose of helping both students to learn correct procedures and systems as well as for professionals to reorient themselves with the updated knowledge on Food and Beverage control procedures.

Book examines and identifies varied factors which influence food and beverage costs in a food service operation. Readers would be equipped with analytical tools and techniques to enable them to interpret, to make operational decisions, to identify problems in achieving cost and quality control in a food and beverage system

This book is a must read for any food service manager who is interested in an accurate, to the point, and technologically advanced review of food and beverage cost control methods. Controlling food costs has never been more important than in today's environment. Those managers who master control procedures will succeed, and this book helps them to do just that.

Responsibility for every aspect of any food and beverage enterprise rests with management. Control, therefore, is clearly a responsibility of management. In some food and beverage enterprises-probably the majority-managers take personal charge of directing and supervising the control procedures in every phase of operations. In others, managers delegate some or all of the work to subordinates. The nature, size, and scope of operations help determine the extent to which managers can exercise direct control rather than delegate that control to someone else. In general, the larger and more complex the operation, the more likely it is that control procedures will be supervised by subordinates. Job titles for these subordinates include food controller, beverage controller, assistant manager, supervisor, and a number of others.

Throughout this text, several job titles are used for those having responsibility for supervising food, beverage control procedures. In the majority of food and beverage enterprises, one is likely to find control procedures supervised directly by managers, so that title is used most often. In larger operations, one may find food controllers and beverage controllers. Today, there are comparatively few of these, but the job titles are still useful in discussions of control principles and will appear in various chapters.

Starting point for control process would be to establish standards. Standards are defined as rules or measures established for making comparisons and judgments. In business these standards are set by management and are used for judging the extent to which results meet expectations. Several types of standards are useful in establishing control over food and beverage operations. The control process is cyclical which means it is never finished. Controlling leads to identification of new problems that in turn need to be addressed through establishment of performance standards, measuring performance etc.

Employees often view controlling negatively. By its very nature, controlling often leads to management expecting employee behaviour to change. No matter how positive the changes may be for the organization, employees may still view them negatively.

We are confident that readers would benefit immensely from this book.

1

FOOD AND BEVERAGE SECTORS

INTRODUCTION

The food and beverage service industry consists of every establishment that sells food and beverage to people outside their own homes. On about global scale it is about multibillion dollar enterprise which employees millions of people and is of vital worldwide economic importance.

Most statistics classify food and beverage service as the fifth largest industry in the United States. In this country it employs more than 8 million people. Statistics indicate that Americans eat one out every three meals away from home. The food service industry will sell them these meals.

In the late 1980s the American food and beverages service industry's total sales were estimated at more than Rs. 8000 billion, that's more than four times what it was in the mid-1970s. Some of this increase is due to inflation and increased population, but much of it is solid growth. The industry has expanded dramatically in the United States and in other nations during this century. And in the past few decades in particular, it flourishes today and its future looks bright . There are many reasons why the business lost food and beverages service which has grown in the past and will probably continue to do so in the years ahead.

Growth of the Industry

Since the beginning of humankind, some people have eaten some of their meals away from home. Cavemen and women probably wandered off sometimes away from their caves to munch fruit under or in about tree, maybe just for a pleasing change of scenery. They surely ate out when they were off on food gathering (shopping) trips. Perhaps our reasons for eating out have not changed much at that.

More formal places for dining away from home—inns and taverns—really signalled the start of the food, beverages and lodging service industry. Such establishment probably came into being when trade and commerce began. In 500 B.C. there were hosteleries in Athens where local people and visiting tradespepole could buy lavish food and drinks. Ancient Rome had restaurants England's alehouse served meats and ales in the twelfth century. In 1800 there were at least 600 restaurants in Paris. But until quite recently, "eating out" was dome by about comparatively small present age of about population. Today in America fast food restaurants have sold billions of hamburgers to millions of people. "Eating out "and the food service industry in general a rein as process of worldwide growth. About much higher proportionate percentage to the population eats out, and they eat out oftener, particularly in the United States.

Why do People Eat Out?

Today, many people cannot eat three meals a day at home as most could 100 years ago. They commute to their jobs and are too far away to return home for meals. This is especially true at lunchtime, but it includes the doughnut and coffee breakfasts at work and the dinners in town for those working late. When society was mainly rural and agricultural, people usually working near their homes and simply went home to eat. But many people have migrated from rural to urban areas. Many now work in cities and live in the suburbs.

The structure of society has changed in other ways. Many people live alone. Some men and women marry later in life and are single working people for a long period. There are also many widows, widowers, and divorced people who live alone. They all are apt to go out to eat now and then. A high percentage of women have full-time or part-time jobs. They do not have time for extensive cooking. Working men and women generally have higher incomes than ever before, and whole families go out to eat more often. Children are apt to have about say in where the family will eat, and this factor, too, has its own influence on the food service industry.

The automobile and mass transportation have made it feasible to travel to restaurants. Jets have made world travel convenient, and travel in general has shown an enormous increase. People travel for business purposes or for vacation enjöyment, and this obviously adds to instances of eating away from home.

Frozen foods and instant dinners available at supermarkets have also played a part in the growth of the food service industry. So has the women's movement. Society no longer expects women to cook. People may rely heavily on frozen quick dinners at home. Many enjoy going out for special meals or to enjoy foods prepared by chefs. The frozen dinners they can now heat and serve at home are apt to introduce people to foods that are new and different to them.

The increase in travel, the increase in mobility, and the fact that people are now much more apt to move frequently have all combined to make dinners more adventurous in their tastes in food and drink.

Fast and easy transportation, leisure time, travel, women with careers all of these plus other factors contribute to the total status of the food service industry. The percentage of the population that eats out is increasing. These percentages will probably continue to increase in the future. Because the food and beverage service industry is growing and expanding, opportunities for employment at all levels in this industry should increase.

SECTORS OF FOOD AND BEVERAGE OUTLET

There are many kinds of food service operations. They include:

1. Service restaurants
2. Self-service restaurants (cafeterias)
3. Coffee shops
4. Fast-food restaurants
5. Hotel food services
6. Private club food services
7. Hospital food services
8. College dormitory food services
9. Airline food services
10. Contract food services in factories and office buildings
11. Private catering
12. Banquet hall facilities
13. Federal institution food services

14. Public and private school food services
15. Military food services.

This does not mention them all. The list could go on.

Sectors of the Food and Beverage Service Industry

The Standard Industrial Classification indicates that there are many types of food and beverage operations. It also indicates that some operations are primarily concerned with the provision of food and drink, for example restaurants and take-always, whereas other operations are what can be called secondary operations, i.e., the provision of food and drink is part of another business, for example, welfare catering and industrial catering.

The SIC classifies the industry by types of food and beverage premises. This does not necessarily indicate the type of demand being met or the conditions under which provision is being made. For example, cafeterias may be found in motorway service stations, in airline terminals, on rail stations, in retail catering, in industrial and in welfare catering. It should therefore be understood that similar types of food and beverage operation may be found in a variety of different sectors. This identification of sectors also provides a framework for those studying the food and beverage service industry to which further studies and experience may be related.

In order to be seen in more detail each sector may be analyzed by reference to a set of variables that exist in the different sectors (Table 1.1). These variables represent elements. Which vary in particular sectors and thus provide a basis for examining the operation of

Table 1.1: Variables in Catering Sectors

Historical background	Interpretation of demand/catering concept
Reasons for customer demand	Technological development
Influences	Primary/Secondary activity
State of sector development	Types of outlets
Size of sector: In terms of outlets	Profit orientation/cost provision
In terms of turnover	Public/private ownership
Policies: Financial, Marketing,	
Catering	

outlets within specific sectors. They enable comprehensive pictures of industrial sectors to be complied, and also provide for profit whereas others are working within the constraints of a given budget, often called cost provision (e.g., welfare and industrial). Some sectors are providing services to the general public whereas others provide them for restricted groups of people.

Defining the nature of market in this way help us to understand why different methods of organization may be in operation; e.g. in captive markets customers might be asked to clear their own tables, whereas in non-captive markets this is unlikely to be successful.

Table 1.2 : Sectors of Food and Beverage Service Industry

Sector	*Purpose of Sector*	*Historical Summary*
Hotel and other tourist accommodation	provision of food and drink together with accommodation	Developed from inns. Supported by development transport and increases in business and leisure related tourism.
Restaurants inclu-ding: conventional, restaurants Specialist, Carveries, thmed and ethnic high level service	provision of food and drink generally at medium to high price with medium to through chefs wishing to start	Grew out of hotel (Escoffies/ Ritz influenced which were originally highly formal) their own business
Popular Catering		
Including: cafés, pizza, Wimpy, Grills, specialist Coffee shops, Little Chefs, steak houses	provision for food and drink generally at low to medium price with limited levels of service	Developed for ABC and Lyons concepts. Gone through various phases. Latterly American influenced
Fast Food		
Eg: McDonalds, Burger King	provision of food and drink in highly specialized Environment characterized by high investment, high Labour costs and vast Customer throughput	Grew from combination of popular catering and take-away, heavily influenced by American companies: sophisticated meal packaging and marketing

(Contd.)

Sector	Purpose of Sector	Historical Summary
Take-Away		
Including: ethnic, KFC, snacks, fish & Chips, sandwich bars food Kiosks	provision for food and drinks quickly	Developed from original fish & chips concept. Influenced by America and trends in tastes.
Retail Stores Food	provision of food and drink As adjunct to provision of Retailing	Developed from prestigious stores wishing to provide and drink as part of retailing Concept
Banqueting/ Conferences/ Exhibition	provision of food and drink on large scale,usually pre-booked	Originally associated with hotels but has now become major sector in its own right
Leisure Atteractions		
Eg: theme parks, galleries, Theatres, airline terminals	provision of food and drink for people Engaged in another Leisure pursuit	Increases in leisure have made profit from food and drink attractive to leisure and amenity providers
Motorway Service Stations	provision of food together with retail and Petrol services for Motorway travellers, Often in isolated Location	Born in 1960s with advent of motorway building. Influenced by America and became specialized because of government regulations on provision of catering, retail and petrol as well as location
Welfare		
Including : hospitals School, colleges, University, forces, Prisions,other welfare	provision of food and drink to people through social need, primarily determind by an authority Social conscience	Regulated and given substantial boost by welfare state creation in 1948 and maintained now through
Industrial Catering		
Either in-house operations or provided by catering Contrctor	provision of food and drink to people at work	Born out of regulation that better fed workers work better. Given boost in 1st and 2nd World Wars By unions wish to preserve conditions and emergence of professional contractors

(Contd.)

Sector	*Purpose of Sector*	*Historical Summary*
Licensed Trade		
Including: Public houses, wine bars, licensed clubs Members clubs	provision of food and drink in environment dominated by licensing requirements	Developed from inns; also original of steak houses, e.g. Berni in 1960s
Transport		
Including: railway, Airline, marine	provision of food and drink to people on the move	Grew out of need to meet requirements of travelling public. Originally services were mainly of high levels reflecting the type of traveller eventually changed to meet need of wide range of travelling public
Outdoor Catering (ODC)		
('off premises catering)	provision of food and drink away from home base and supplier	Developed through need to provide services at special events. The term ODC is misleading as little of this catering actually takes place outside

It is useful to define these different types of market as follows:

- General market
  Non-captive: Customers have a full choice.

- Restricted market
  Captive: Customers have no choice, e.g. welfare Semi-captive Customer have a choice before entering, e.g. marine, airline, trains, some hotels and some leisure activities. The customers could have chosen alternatives to these but, once chosen, have little choice of food and drink other that on offer.

Taking the above points into account a general summary of sectors may be drawn up as seen in Table 1.3.

Variables in Food and Beverage Operations

The list of types of outlets indicates by itself very little in terms of methods adopted and the management of them. In a similar way to

Table 1.3 : Summary of Sectors in the Food and Beverage Service Industry

Profit Orientation		*Cost Provision Resticted Market*
(Public or private ownership) (Catering, main and secondary activity)		Institutional catering Schools Universities and Colleges Hospitals, The forces Prisons
Restricted Market	*General Market*	
Transport catering Clubs	Hotels/restaurants	Industrial (own catering)
	Hotels/Restaurants	
	Popular catering	
Industrial (contract)	Pub and Wine bars	
Private welfare	Take away/Retail stores	
	Banqueting/Conferences/Exhibitions	
	Leisure attractions	
	Motorway service stations	
	ODC/Fast food	

the identifying variables for sectors (Table 1.4), variables can also be identified for outlets/operations. These variables have been identified from a variety of published sources as well as from experience. They can be separated into three groups:

1. Organizational
2. Performance measures
3. Customer experience

These groups provide for the systematic examination and inter-comparison of types of food and beverage operations through profiles of differing operations that can be drawn, based upon these variables (Table 1.4).

Table 1.4: Variables in Food and Beverage Service Operations

ORGANISATIONAL	
Service methods	*Dining* arrangements
Specialized service requirements	Nature of market
Legislative controls	Range of choice
Billing methods	Style of menu/drinks list
Checking methods	Staff working hours

(Contd.)

Marketing/merchandising	Staff organization
Control method Cost/revenue	Number of staff
Provisioning and storage methods	Opening times/service period
Production methods	Scale of operation
Clearing methods	Seating time
Dishwashing methods	Number of covers available
Type of equipment	Capacity
PERFORMANCE MEASURES	
Seat turnover/customer	
Throughput	Sales/profit per sq m (or ft)/per seat
Customer spend/average check	Sales analysis
Revenue per member of staff	Departmental profit
PERFORMANCE MEASURES	
Ratio of food and beverage sales to	Stock turnover
Total sales	Stock holding
Productivity index	
CUSTOMER EXPERIENCE	
Food and drink available	Level of service and other services
Price range/value for money	Cleanliness and hygiene
Atmosphere (e.g. decor, lighting, air-conditioning, acoustics, noise, size and shape of room, other clientele, attitude of staff)	

It should be pointed out, for example, that a restaurant may be being operated within the Restaurant Sector as a stand-alone operation. Alternatively a restaurant may be operated within say in hotel, in the Hotel Sector. Both sets of common variables will need to be examined to give a clear picture or the operation and business as a whole. In a small business the proprietor/manager would be concerned with the management of the whole business (i.e., factors indicated by applying both sets of variables). However, the food and beverage manager of an hotel would be principally concerned with the common operational variables.

The Meal Experience

The main aim of food and beverage operations is to achieve customer satisfaction. In other words, to meet the customer's needs. The needs that the customer might be seeking to satisfy include:

1. *Physiological:* For example, the need to State one's appetite or quench the thirst; the need for special foods (diabetic, vegetarian).
2. *Economic:* For example, the need for good value; rapid, fast service; a convenient location.
3. *Social:* For example, when desiring enjoyable company; going out with friends or business colleagues; attending functions to meet others.
4. *Psychological:* For example, the need for enhancement of self-esteem; fulfilling life-style needs; the need for variety; as a result of advertising and promotion.
5. *Convenience:* For example, as a result of being unable to get home (shoppers, workers) or having to attend some other event (cinema, theatre); the desire for someone else to do the work; the physical impossibility of catering at home (weddings and other special functions).

Customers may be Wanting to Satisfy Some or All of Desired Needs

It is important to recognize that the specific reasons behind a customer's choice determine the customer's satisfaction (or dissatisfaction) rather than the food and beverage service by itself. A good example is the social need to go out with friends: if one person fails to turn up or behaves in a disagreeable way, then the customer may be dissatisfied with the meal.

The customer who is not able to satisfy his/her needs will be a dissatisfied customer. The customer may, for instance, be dissatisfied with unhelpful staff; cramped conditions or the lack of choice available. These aspects are the responsibility of the food and beverage operation. However, sometimes the reasons for the customer being dissatisfied might be beyond the operation's control, e.g., location, the weather, other customers or transport problems.

In *non-captive markets* the customer has a choice of eating out opportunities both in terms of the food and drink to be consumed and the type of operation they may wish to patronize. Whilst it is true that certain types of catering operations might attract certain types of customer, this is by no means true all the time. The same customer may patronize a variety of different operations depending on the needs they have at the time, e.g., a romantic night out, a quick office lunch or a wedding function.

In *semi-captive markets* this is also important. The customers may choose, for example, a certain airline or boat or hotel based upon the identification of certain needs they may wish to satisfy. Also in *captive markets* where the customer does not have a choice of operation, there is still a need for satisfaction. For instance, it is generally recognized that better fed workers work better and that better fed patients recover quicker. 'Better fed' here, though, does not just refer to the food and drink provided but the whole experience of the meal.

From the food and beverage operator's point of view it is important to recognize that the customer's needs may vary and that food and beverage operators should be aware of factor which might affect the customer's meal experience. Much research has been carried out in recent years identifying these factors. They range from location to the acceptance of credit cards, and from attitudes of staff to the behaviour of other customers. These factors are summarized in Table 1.5.

Table 1.5: Meal Experience Factors

Factors	*Description*
FOOD AND DRINK	Range of food and drink on offer; type and variety; availability of special items; quality
LEVEL Of SERVICE	Method of service; speed of service; reliability; booking facility; acceptance of credit cards; availability of credit facilities etc
LEVEL OF CLEANLINESS AND HYGIENE	Cleanliness and hygiene of equipment, premises and staff
VALUE FOR MONEY AND PRICE	Perceptions in the customer's mind of the value of the product (not just the food and drink) related to the price one is prepared to pay at the time
ATMOSPHERE	A fairly intangible concept but contributed to by aspects such as decor, lighting, heating, furnishing, acoustics. Other customers and the attitude of staff.

Food and Beverage Service Methods

The service of food and beverages may be carried out in many ways depending on a number of factors:

1. The type of establishment.
2. The type of customer to be served.
3. The *time* available for the meal.
4. The turnover of custom expected.
5. The type of menu presented.
6. The *cost* of the meal served.
7. The *site* of the establishment.

Service staff are involved in a process or service sequence which essentially forms the link between the customer and the food production area, the stillroom, the cashiers and other departments. This process or service sequence can be summarized as a series of stages as in Table 1.6.

Table 1.6: Food and Beverage Service Sequence

(*a*) Preparation of service (which may include taking booking)
(*b*) Taking customer food and beverage orders
(*c*) Service of food and beverage
(*d*) Clearing
(*e*) Billing (which may take place at time of service, as in take away operation of later at end of a meal in the a restaurant
(*f*) Dishwashing
(*g*) Clearing following service

For each of these stages there are a variety of methods in which they may be carried out. The choice of method for the individual stage depends as much on the factors listed at the start of this section as it does on taking into account the process in which the customer is to experience.

Essentially, the customer enters a food service area, orders or selects his/her choice and then is served (the customer may pay either at this point or later). Food and beverages are then consumed, following which the area is cleared.

Using this approach, five basic types of service can be identified. These are shown in Table 1.7. In the first four the customer comes to where the food and beverages are provided, for example to the restaurant or take away. In the fifth the food and drink is taken to where the customer is, for example in guest rooms, lounges or to hospital patients.

The 15 service methods available to the food and beverage operator are identified in Table and grouped based upon the simple categorization of the food and beverage customer process (Table 1.7).

A particular service methods e.g. requires a number of tasks and duties which are under taken during the actual service of food and beverages. However, there are other tasks and duties which contribute to the service. These may be identified using the service sequence (see Table 1.6). The level of complexity of food and beverage service in terms of staff skills, tasks and duties reduces from Group A (the most complex) to Group D. Group E contains specialized forms of service.

Table 1.7 : Simple Categorization of the Food and Beverage Customer Process

Service Method	*Food and Beverage Service Area*	*Ordering/ Selection*	*Service*	*Dining/ Consumption*	*Clearing*
(*a*) **Table Service**	Customer enters in area	From menu	By staff to customer	At laid over	By staff
(*b*) **Assisted**	Customer enters in area and is seated	From menu, buffet of passed trays	Combination of both	Usually at laidover	By staff
(*c*) **Self Service**	Customer enters	Customer select own tray	Customer carries	Dining area or take away	Various
(*d*) **Single Point Service**	Customer enters	Ordered at single point	Customer carries	Dining area or take away	Various
(*e*) **Speciali-zed or In Situ Service**	In situ	From menu or predeter-mined	Brought to customer	Where served	By staff customer or customer clearing

Types of Service	*Description*
	GROUP A: Table Service
1. Waiter	
(a) Silver/English	Presentation and service of food to customer by waiting staff from food flat or dish
(b) Family	Main courses plated with vegetables placed in multi-portion dishes on table for customers to help themselves: sauces offered
(c) Plate/American	Service or pre plated foods to customers
(d) Butler/French	Presentation of food individually to customers by food service staff for customers to serve themselves
(e) Russian	Table laid with food for customers to help themselves (also sometimes confusingly used to indicate Gueridon or Butler service)
(f) Gueridon	Food service on to customer plate at side table or trolley; also may include carving , cooking and flambage, preparation of salad and dressing, and fish filleting
2. Bar Counter: Service to customers seated at bar counter (usually U-shaped) on stools.	
	GROUP B: Assisted Service
Combination of table service and self-service	
3. Assisted	
(a) Commonly applied to carvery type operations. Some parts of the meal are served to seated customers; other parts are collected by customers (also used for breakfast service).	
(b) Buffets where customer select the food and drink from displays or passed trays; consumption is either at tables, standing or lounge area.	
	GROUP C: Self-Service
Self-service of Customers	

4. Cafeteria

(a) Counter	Customers queuing in line formation pass a service counter choosing their menu requirement in stages and loading them on to a tray (may include a Carousel—a revolving stacked counter saving space).
(b) Free flow	Selection as encounter (above) but in food service area where customers move at their will to random service points; customers usually exit via a till point.
(c) Echelon	Series of counters at angles to customer flow within a free flow area, thus saving space.
(d) Super market	Island service points within a free flow area.

GPOUP D: Single Point Service

5. Take-Away

(a) Customer orders and is served from single point, at counter, hatch or snacks stand	Customer consumes off the premises (some take-away establishments provide seating.
(b) Drive-through	From take-away where customers derives vehicle past order, payment and collection points.
(c) Fast food	Originally used to describe a service at a counter or hatch where customers receive a complete meal or dish in exchange for cash or ticket; commonly used now-a-days to describe type of establishment offering limited range menu, fast service with take-away facility.

6. **Vending:** Provision of food service and beverage service by means of automatic retailing.
7. **Kiosks:** Outstation to provide service for peak demand or in

specific location (may be open for customers to order or use for dispensing only).

8. **Food Court:** Service of autonomous counters where customers may either order and eat (as in bar counter, above) or buy from a number of counters and it in separate eating area, or take-away.
9. **Bar:** Term used to describe selling point and consumption area in licensed premises.

GROUP E: Specialised (or in Situ)

10. **Tray:** Method of service of whole or part of meal on tray to customer in situ, e.g., hospitals aircraft, also used in ODC.
11. **Trolley:** Service of food and beverage from trolley, away from dining area, e.g., for office workers, in aircraft or on train.
12. **Home Delivery:** Food delivered to customer's home or place of work, e.g., 'meal on wheels', pizza home delivery.
13. **Lounge:** Service of variety of foods and beverages in lounge area service of variety of food and beverage in guest.
14. **Room:** Service of variety of foods and beverages in guest apartments or meeting rooms.
15. **Drive in :** Customers park motors vehicle and are served at the vehicle.

Food service operations require many personnel doing many types of work—cooks, waiters, waitresses, buspersons, supervisors, hostesses and hosts, dishwashers, saladmakers, and so on, including managers. The food service industry is huge, employs millions and grosses billions. That's an overview of the entire field.

If you are about food service operation manager reading this, you may be wondering why your own establishment is not effortlessly earning about fortune since your industry is about flourishing one. No business operation effortlessly earns about fortune, of course, but this is particularly true of about food and beverage service operation. The industry is prosperous, but for individual operations the food service business is very hard work and it is full of risks. The industry in general flourishes, but for the individual people who work in the industry and for each food and beverage establishment, success is about hard-won achievement.

It takes effort, knowledge, good management, good location, and sound control systems (among other things) for about food and beverage operation to succeed.

The two major reasons why restaurants fail are:

1. Lack of management skills.
2. Lack of good accounting records.

There are estimates that 80 per cent of all restaurants change ownership on an average of once every five years. Some of these make money and are sold at a profit. But many fail. Money is lost and new owners take over or the building is converted to uses other than about food service operation.

The food service industry is about high-risk business. It is possible to earn high profits. It is also possible to lose about lot of money. Because of the risk, banks do not readily lend money for restaurant venture, no matter what the state of an economy is. The individual in this industry who knows management and understands the accounting and recordkeeping involved—including the application of control techniques—has a chance of succeeding.

Successful food service management is difficult. Investing in a food service establishment is extremely risky. Competition is fierce. Many go under. Management that survives and goes on to real success is management that makes every possible effort to really control the overall operation of its food service establishment. As economies change from prosperity to inflation to recession to depression and back again into varying degrees and stages of these, sound management and sound control become all the more important. Sound marketing plans are important too. But this is not about marketing book.

This book was written mainly for owners, managers, assistant managers, supervisors, students, and anyone interested in entering or learning about the food and beverage service industry. In the following chapters we will present, and use, adapt and tailor them yourself to fit the specific needs of your own operation.

Food service operations come in great varieties. They differ in size, location, clientele, foods offered, reasons for existing, types and number of employees, market, amounts of money invested, and so on. Despite all the differences, they all do have many routines, basic objectives, structures and systems, and problems in common. They are all food service operations and they all need fundamental management controls. There are management procedures, technique, and tools that can be of sound service to all, and we will discuss them in this book. If you want to succeed in the field of food service management, it is absolutely essential for you to understand and correctly use the principles and procedures of food and beverage control.

If you, the manager of food and beverage service operation, do not exert control over your operation, something else will. That is an ominous fact about food service management or the management of most businesses, for that matter. If you do not act and maintain specific standards, your operation will have standards anyway, but almost surely not the standards you want. Your operation will be controlled by your cook, or your cashier, or your customers, or blind luck, or a lot of other factors you do not want in control and may not even know exist. If you are not in control, other people or things surely will be. The purpose of this book is to help you, the manager, see to it that you — not your cook, not luck, not your competitors — do these managerial jobs of maintaining your standards and controlling your procedures. And do them well.

FOOD AND BEVERAGE MANAGEMENT

The better organized your establishment is, the more efficiently it can run. Some time, though, efficiently is pursued relentlessly by business operation. Do not be so totally dedicated to instant efficiency that you neglect to marks plans for long-range efficiency. There have been food service managers who have achieved high menu price, low food cost, low labour cost and no customers! Their establishments may have efficient organization on paper but could scarcely be called efficient or well-organized in reality or in the long run.

The eternal business quest for sound management and real efficiency has to be tempered by commonsense. Keep your long-range goal as well as your intermediate objectives well in mind. A truly efficient operation has the means to achieve its objectives and works out some valid solution for them in advance.

There are some fundamental management concepts you can apply to your food service operation. Adapt them yourself to fit your specific needs.

Goal

A food service operation usually has one main goal—long-term profit (Exceptions to this would be not non-profit operation, such as food services in hospitals and schools, whose goal usually is to break even). Owners decide on the goal.

Objective

Owners decide objectives are decisions you make, steps you plan to take, characteristics and qualities and you try to achieve while you are in the process of working to attain your goal. Objectives are things you do to get your goal accomplished. Examples of objectives would be: type of food service (seafood, steak house, fast food), standard of cleanliness; types and quality of food; quality of service; type of atmosphere and décor, whether or not to serve liquor; type of market the operation will try to attract; and type of location that will be sought for the operation.

Means

The manager decides on the means, based on the owners' wishes. "Means" are steps you take to get your objective accomplished; Examples would include: how you organize your establishment: number of people you hire; skill levels of employees; purveyors you select to supply your food; and your methods of recordkeeping. Generally means can be defined as the total work that a manager does to see that the owner's objective are achieved and the goal of profit is attained.

Functions and Responsibilities Food and Beverage Management

The manager of a food service operation is operation for the overall, day to day functioning of the operation. The work of a manager involves long-term planning, short-term planning (forecasting), organization, directing and coordinating, hireing and training. The manager is responsible for controls. What the manager does in each of these areas will have a direct effect on the overall success of any individual food service unit.

Planning

Planning your business means plotting about course of how you intend to get to where you want to go. It means looking ahead a few days, a few weeks six months, a year maybe more. It means making short-term plans (forecasting) and long-term plans. In long-range planning you consider where you want your business to be one, two, five years or more from now, plot course of action to get there. Unless yours is an operation that is supposed to just about break even (like most hospital cafeterias and university dormitory food services, for example), your main goal is to try to make profit now and the future.

You make basic decisions if options are in your hands. Owners decide on the type of food service operation and the market the operation will try to attract. Managers decide what prices to charge and what the food, labour, and overhead cost per cent should be. Managers decide on the number of employees and what skill levels employees should have.

You will probably have to work toward many intermediate objectives en route toward the ultimate goal , which is meeting profits and getting them consistently. There are many intermediate objectives and there is one main goal you want to achieve. You plan a course of action accordingly and follow it, altering your means and objective when and if you need to.

Forecasting

Forecasting means short range plans for a short period of time. Forecasting is an important technique you should use to strengthen your chance of achieving your larger, long-range, long-time plans.

A short-range plan, for example, could be where you forecast your business for tomorrow for next week. You make a plan about prediction, for a small period of time. From your forecast you figure how much food you will need for next week, for example, and how many employees you will need, and so on. Forecasting means you do some detailed planning and figuring ahead of time.

You take time to think about next week. You figure out everything you can about what will probably happen to your business operation next week. You do ahead of time anything you possibly can to make sure that next week is a success. You use every scrap of valid information you have plus a calculated guess. You look at your records of the business your operation did last week and last month. You check your records of your business for the same week about year ago. (This impels that you make detailed records and retain them for future reference. You do, and we will discuss these records through this book.) You cannot, unfortunately, use magic to help you forecast. You do use your written records.

You keep track of conventions due in town, big football games coming up, bad weather predicted. In short, you find out everything you can about anything that could possibly affect your volume next week. Then you put your ideas and estimate into action. You buy food, decide how much of it to cook, and schedule employees for next week based on your forecast for next week.

Aim at trying to achieve correct short-term predictions. When you start making predictions, you will probably make plenty of mistakes. But you will get more accurate with time and experience. The better you do at making accurate forecasts and thus achieving a short-term objective, the easier it will be for you to achieve your long-term goal of profit.

Organizing

This should be done with objectives in mind. Organizing is where you devise the means you use to achieve objectives. Do this by figuring out the types of employee positions you need to fill, how many employees you need and what work each employee should do. Analyze and list the positions you need to fill. Another part of organization is deciding how you will group people together. In other words, decide what department you will have, who will be in charge of each, what work department should accomplish, and so on.

Directing and Coordinating

Directing and coordinating are closely related. Managers direct people and supervise the work they do. Managers also coordinate departments and general divisions of work so that work routines are set and accomplished. Managers must know how to establish and coordinate work routines so that department heads and their employees can do their jobs well. Handling people and understanding their problems and differences is about major part of management.

Coordinating means fitting activities together, considering the timing of who does what—and when—and arranging patterns of action in which people can best carry out the work you want them to do. The work of preparing food, for example, must be coordinated with the work of serving food so that individual employees can work with the best results. You coordinate each branch and type of working activity with other activities for total functioning which is as smooth, on-time, and as frictionless as you can get it.

Another main function of management should be to give clear directions and make sure that they are followed. Employees who follow directions should be thanked, complimented, encouraged and rewarded. Employees who don't should be reinstructed in precisely what the directions are, precisely how they should carry out the directions correctly, and checked to make sure they do. Some people perform well only if they have very close supervision and someone constantly telling them what to do. You want employees who do best when you explain to them the job you want them to do, then alone to do it, and they go ahead on their own and do it right and they keep on doing it right.

Hiring

You can make your work in directing and coordinating simpler if you exercise care when you hire employees. Many managers insist that only experienced personnel be hired. Others are willing to hire less experienced people and train them. Probably the best method is a combination of both. Some jobs do call for experienced people. For other jobs, many managers feel that it is better to hire inexperienced personnel. They would rather train them in the procedures they want followed and not take about chance on having to correct bad habits that experienced workers may have acquired on previous jobs.

Obviously, you should try to hire the type of person who seems suited for the position you have in mind. Figure out exactly what qualifications about person must have in order to do a specific job. It is usually best to find a person who fits the job instead of changing the job requirements to fit about person. Some people will find about particular job too easy and will be bored with it. Others would find the same job nerve-racking and too difficult. Bored employees leave soon, as do employees who are not capable of handling their jobs and thus become frustrated and unhappy. Gauge people's interests and abilities as well as you can when you hire them.

Establish procedures for hiring employees. Decide where to seek them through newspapers, employment agencies, friends of your present employees. Decide what kind of personnel forms you might need, who will conduct interviews, what criteria you will use to select new employees, and so on.

In the food service industry, dependability is frequently about much more important factor for hiring and retaining employees than the level of skill about person possesses. Everyone hired should fit the needs or your establishment and be reliable.

Many firms have found that physically and mentally challenged persons are excellent employees. Many restaurants have had about great deal of success in retaining such persons at any level their abilities indicate. Definitely consider older and retired people, too.

Training

Training is about vital part of the entire process of directing people and activities. You will have to spend about lot of time training your employees, or assign a competent employee or employees to do job of training. Training is too often delegated to a subordinate who was never trained. About great deal depends on how well training is done originally and on how good and long-lasting the follow-up supervision is.

Thorough training is extremely important. It can actually affect whether your operation flourishes or fails. It is up to managers to train immediate subordinates and to see to it that they, in turn, train those under them. The success or failure of the chain of training rests solely on the shoulders of the manager.

Control

Control is about management tool. It should be helpful to all and frightening to none. The word "control" should definitely not mean tyrannical, unfair, or authoritarian management tactics. There are employees who regard "management" and "control" at their own jobs in this light. Some of them are, unfortunately, justified.

Control should mean the methods you use to keep the operation functioning smoothly and profitably for all concerned. Managerial control, as the term is used in this book, means sensible safeguards that management sets up to help the operation succeed.

Control should mean the methods you use to keep the operation functioning smoothly and profitably for all concerned. Managerial control, as the term is used in this book, means sensible safeguards that management sets up to help the operation succeed.

Control consists mainly of three things. When you exert management control in your food service operation, you do the following:

1. *Measure:* You measure what has been done—what has taken place in about given period.
2. *Evaluate:* You evaluate how well or how badly things have gone, comparing the situations and events with your operations.
3. *Act:* You take action based on your measurement and evaluation.

Control is really your (managements) action based on your measurement and your evaluation. Managers often check situations and then decide not to act. They conclude that the situations do not require their action or intervention. The act that they have investigated and then decided not act is an action in itself. Control means that managers investigate situations, understand events, and then decide they will or will not act. Either way, they are exercising control. (Control is discussed further in Chapter 3).

Supervisors

All the things we have just been discussing are management activities. Management activities appropriate to each managerial position should be performed at all management levels, from the top executive position to the least authoritative supervisory job. They should be performed in accordance with overall organizational plans, which come from the top administrative level.

Supervisors are part of management. They have their own appropriate duties and responsibilities in some of the management functions. Supervisors should follow the overall plans of the total operation and make them work.

Supervisors should make both long-term and short-term plans. They should organize and coordinate the jobs in their own departments. They should direct and train all employees who report to them (unless someone else is assigned to do the training) and do follow-up checking on employee performance.

Supervisors should coordinate the work of their own department with the work of other departments. They should gather information about their own departments, compare the results with their department standards which have been set by management, and take action where they can to improve and tighten all activities in their departments.

In short, supervisors perform all the broad management activities we have talked about in terms of their own jobs, departments, and responsibilities. They must have authority to do all this and to enforce their decisions.

New Employees

New employees starting to work in food service operation may wonder how their own jobs relate to the overall activities of others. If they do not really understand where and why their work fits into the operation as a whole, they may shrug off their work and perform haphazardly because they conclude their own jobs are not important. It is your job (managements) to show and convince new employees that they are needed and necessary and that if their work did not have to be done you would eliminate the job. You would not have hired them if they were not needed and if their job did not have to be done. It is your job to show them how and why they are important to the operation.

The easiest way to begin to teach new employees their jobs is to give them written job descriptions of the work they are to perform. About job description should list the tools employees will work with and the duties they are expected to complete. Written job descriptions simplify training and help speed the adjustment of new workers. Job descriptions are very helpful for both employer and employee during the orientation process, when new people are being acquainted with their work and with the overall working routines of the establishment. But so not just leave it at handing them a dittoed sheet of instructions. Make sure they know who to go to for help and make sure that help is really forthcoming whenever they need it.

You decide what employees you need and what jobs need to be done. You determine this when you devise your organization structure.

Organization Structure

Organization structure means the hierarchy of planned relationships between people and between departments. An organization chart is just about chart showing the organization structure. There are lots of ways in which businesses can be organized.

Traditionally, the food service industry has been organized departmentally. Departmental organization means that persons who perform similar work are grouped together in a department. To certain extent, departmental organization means organizing employees according to their physical location in the establishment: kitchen employees in one department, dining room employees in another department, and so on. This can breakdown further—cooks in one sub-department in the kitchen, dishwashers in another sub-department in the kitchen, and so on.

Organization Charts

Shown below are two sample organization charts for two sizes of food and beverage operation. Chart 1.1 illustrates about medium-1.8 sized operation and Chart 1.2 a large operation.

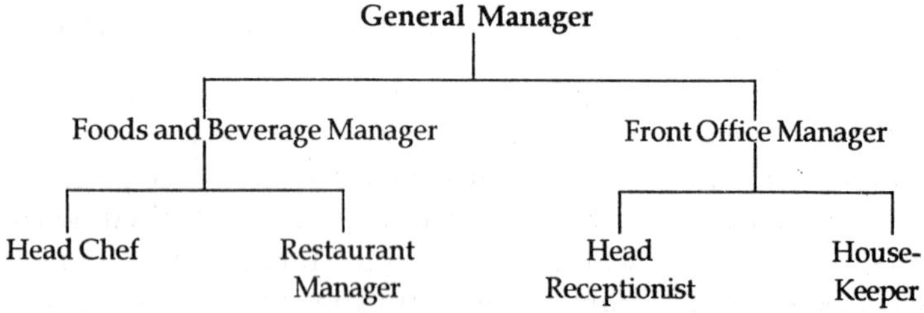

Fig. 1.1: Small Hotel Organization

Probably no food service establishment will have a chart exactly like either of the shown. These charts are set up to give you ideas. You can follow them where they apply or charts them to suit your own operation.

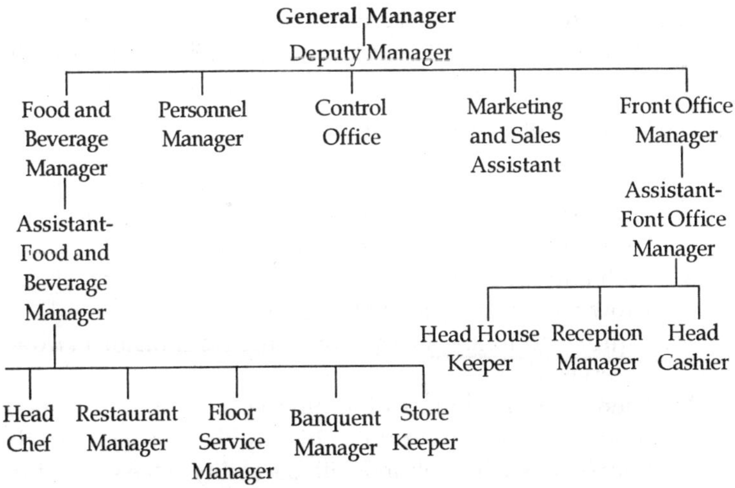

Fig. 1.2 : Larger Hotel Organization.

Every operation's charts is to be unique and about it different from any other. The bigger your food service operation is, the more you will probably need to set up more departments and go in for more specialization.

In small to medium-sized food operation, employees will probably have to be able to perform many different jobs. They will do some tasks well and some tasks not so well. But they will probably have to know how to do about lot of different jobs. In larger establishments, employees are more apt to be specialists. They may know little about the other tasks in the establishments, but they will have to know quite about their own specialities. They will probably perform fewer jobs. They may just do one job do one job – or perhaps just one small part of one job. They may take little or no part in other work in the operation.

1. In about bigger organization you need more specialization than in a smaller one.
2. In about bigger organization there is about need for more detailed measurement and control than in about smaller one.

Where an organization is large, there will be greater need for you to gather information from each area because of the sheet amount of activity going on. You make decisions and take action on this information. Know and follow the principles of good management when you do.

Principles of Good Management

1. Every business should have a primary goal. Usually, it is long-term profit. Every person in the organization should know the long-term and try to help achieve it.
2. Each employee should have only one supervisor, should know precisely who that supervisor is, and should be required to follow instructions only from his or her own supervisor.
3. There is about limit to the number of employees about supervisor can supervise. This number varies with the complexities of the job and with the ability of the supervisor. Usually, the more complex the job, the fewer employees one person can effectively supervise.
4. No now can completely delegate responsibility. Work can be delegated, but the immediate superiors at each level still retain responsibility for people who work directly under them.
5. Supervisors should not be held responsible for the work in their departments unless they have enough authority to enforce what they say and do.
6. The organization must be flexible. It must be able to adapt readily to change and adjust for the future.
7. The organization should take planned steps to provide for its continued existence and survival.

These ideas cover some of the main principles discussed in most General Management books. About lot of managers in the food and beverage industry violate some or all of them. The list above is not complete. There are other principles of management. You must cannot violate many of them for very long and stay in business.

Examine your own management ideas and your own food and beverage operation closely. Do you have about plausible goal and objectives and means of attaining them? Are they clear? Do your employees know them and under stand them? Are there too many "bosses" in your operation? Do wirers cab can come in and give employee directions that conflict with manager's or supervisor's directions? Do your employees know precisely which person's directions they are really supposed to follow? Is thereabout clear line of authority from top to bottom in your operation, and from bottom to top? Do you ask your supervisors to be responsible for areas and activities that involve more people and work than they can supervise effectively? Did you ever know about manager who made a flat to about supervisor such as: you're responsible for supervising those waiters! (or whatever the task). "Go do it!" if the supervisor goes ahead and tries to solve problems and changes the waiters' procedures, does manager them how! Him or her out and make another flat statement! You can't do that! You don't have the authority to do that! Does the show fit? Know the principles of management and use them—with about large does of common sense.

Another thing you have to do is stay flexible and adjust with the times. There is about danger that your business could eventually fill or that you could be fared out of about management job of if you are completely incapable of changing when is necessary. "If my restaurant is exactly the same this year as it have moved forward. "That is about smart food service manager's attitude. Good management includes knowing and correctly applying sound principles of management and keeping up with times.

Management Ethics

As about manager, you are supposed to direct the work of your employees. In the food service industry, you usually direct employers who handle food, beverages, and money. Your own actions and activities must be above reproach. You need about code of good ethics, and you need to follow in all in your dealings with your employees, purveyours and customers.

Employees

Dishonest employees may walk out of about food service establishment with about few hamburgers in their pockets without paying for them. They are stealing. Dishonest managers may load their cars with steaks from the establishments. Some managers have about pre-arranged subsistence agreement with the owner. If such an agreement does exits, all employees should know about it and know that it is about legitimate owner-manager arrangement.

Employees and managers who steal may feel that the food service owes them the food, beverage, or many consider that they are underpaid and that some extras are due them; and may ever; feel consciously or unconsciously self. Righteous about taking whatever they take. You cannot ask or expect your employees to be honest if you are not. You set the example of honesty personally. You will have about slim chance oftrolling left theft if you are not honest yours. Your employees will know whether you are honest or dishonest. That is a fact that's as old as the food and beverage service business.

Purveyors/Suppliers

You have to be honest and ethical in your dealings with your purveyors too. Buy from purveyors who supply you with the highest quality of merchandise and service for the price you pay. Some manager buy from the purveyor who pays them the biggest amount of money in personal kickback for choosing them. These managers set an example of dishonesty for their employees. Who will, as we said know what they are doing.

The example above touch on just about few areas of personal management ethics. Ethical (or unethical) behaviour is all inclusive and comes into play in about multitude of management activities, your own personal morals and ethics come thought loud and clear in your every work and action. If you want to control theft at all job levels, the first essential step is for you to set a personal example of absolute honesty yourself. You own pity still get employees who steal from you, no matter how pristine you are. But don't let that stop you from being scrupulous, get about better theft detection and control programme going.

Managers and middle managements personal usually have more opportunity to steal from an establishment, and they can usually do it on about bigger scale than employees in lower position. If managers are dishonest, they will fool no one, if they steal or cheat, their employees are sure that managers are scrupulously honest with them and with the food operations, they may be tempted to join them in the that, too. It is economically profitable in the long run (and, of course, right in any run) to be honest, fair and ethical in the true sense of those terms.

As about manager, you should perform organizing functions for your business so that it runs smoothly and operates efficiently. Apply general management knowledge to the specific problems of the food service operation. While you are performing these management functions and activities, your own business activates must be honest and above reproach.

2
CONCEPT OF FOOD AND BEVERAGE COST AND COST CONTROL

Fundamentals of Control

Before beginning the discussion, it will be well to point out that control really means controlling people rather than things. It should be obvious that cans of food do not disappear all by themselves, that excess amounts of liquor are not used unless a bartender allow it, that incorrect hours of work are generally not recorded except to the extent that about paymaster has incorrect information; that food is not consumed by rodents unless human beings leave that food accessible; that revenues will be missing to the exact that patrons are allowed to leave without paying for what they have consumed. In all these cases, the difficulties that can arise are the result of human action, or lack of it, and if about business is to proceed profitably according to plan, it is the actions of people that must be controlled.

The people involved may not be simply the personnel of the food and beverage operation; the concept of "people" may often include guests and patrons of the establishment, and in shoe case, intruders, who may seek to avail themselves of the resources of the establishment without the knowledge and agreement of the management. Thus locks on both the front and back doors would be two of the most basic control devices, preventing intruders from entering and probably stealing food. Beverages, equipment, and even cash during periods, when the operation is closed. Another simple control procedure is to locate the crasher near the front door in an effort to prevent customer from leaving without paying their bills. About time clock for employees, severs many purposes, one of which is to develop an accurate set of records of the numbers of hours worked by each of the hourly wage employees, and this is another kind of control. Still another good example is the bartender's use of about measuring device to ensure that each drink mixed will contain the correct amount of particular alcoholic ingredient. interestingly enough, the concept of control refers to nonhumans too. For infestation by various insect and rodent pests; loss of food to constituted unwarranted additional cost to any restaurant.

Definition of Control

Control is about process by means of which managers attempt to direct, regulate and restrain the actions of people in order to achieve desired gloats.

An obvious first step is to establish goals for the enterprise. Probably the most common goal for all private enterprises is financial success, although this is by no means the only long-range goal of business. Other might related to preserving the environment, promoting better health among the population, or aiding in the integration of minority groups into national economic life.

In order to achieve these goals, managers must set up any number of sub-goals compatible with its long-range plans. These tend to be rather more specific, and usually more immediate in nature. For example, in order to achieve the goal of preserving the environment, it would be necessary to make rather immediate plans to process or dispose of waste materials in appropriate ways. A full discussion of general businesses goals and the planning for their achievement is not within the scope of text. Rather we will restrict ourselves to about discussion of the control processes employees by managers in the hospitality industry to achieve the goal of profitable operation. Thus it will entail about discussion of how costs and sales are controlled in food and beverage operations the means employed by food service managers to direct, regulate, restrain the actions of people, both directly and indirectly. In order that costarred within acceptable bounds, revenues are properly accented for, and profits result.

Responsibility for Control

The total responsibility for the operation of any food and beverage enterprise is ultimately with management.

A number of factors, including nature and scope of operations, will distaste exigent to which the manager exercises direct control as opposed to delegating responsibility to about subordinate. In general, the large the operation, show more likely it is the one or more subordinates will supervise and direct control procedures.

For the purpose of this text, the authors will assume the existence of both about for controller and about beverage controller, each of whom be responsible for the supervision of all procedures in that single area. By the same token, we will assume that the manager himself will retain direct control over labour cost. While we clearly recognize that this is not the case in all operations, such assumptions do facilitate discussion of the principles of control. Given the variety and number of different types of food and beverage operations in existence, it would be all but impossible to pinpoint just who is responsible for what controls in which type of restaurant, and in our view such about discussion would require considerably more space than it would be worth. The important point to keep in mind that ultimate responsibility rests with management.

Objective of Food and Beverage Control

The food and beverage business can be characterized as one that involves raw materials purchased, received, stored and issued for the purpose of manufacturing products for sale. In these respects many similarities exist between the food and beverage businesses. As an example, let us look at the steps involved in the production of wood furniture.

The furniture manufacturer must determine what kinds of woods are best suited to the kinds of furniture he or she intends to manufacture and must purchase appropriate numbers of board feet of lumber at favourable prices. When the wood is delivered, the shipment must be checked to ensure that the material delivered is exactly what was ordered. Then it must be moved into appropriate storage facilities. Partly to prevent theft and partly to ensure that the characteristics of the wood will not be adversely affected by climate. The wood must then be issued in appropriate amounts for the production of various kinds of tables and chairs. During the manufacturing process, some efforts must be made to ensure that about balance exists in the production such that one table top is made for each four legs produced. When the manufacturing process is completed and the furniture is sold to customers, care must be exercised to ensure that each is properly recorded. That the correct price is charged for each piece of furniture sold and delivered, and that total dollar value of each sale is collected. A great number of similarities exists between the manufacturing industries and the food and beverage business. The motel coffee shop, the school cafeteria, the hotel dining room, the resort cocktail lounge—all these have in common with other manure materials for purchasing, receiving, storing, and issuing raw materials for the production finished products for slaw. In the food and beverage business we talk about fruits, vegetable, meat poultry, and an infinite number of other foods—fresh frozen, and canned—but these are really serving the same purpose in our business that wood serves in the furniture manufacture similarly we deal' with wines and spirits and about number of other beverages, both alcoholic and non-alcoholic which constitute the raw materials from which drinks are produced for sale here raw material must be carefully selected, always with the desired final products in the mind, and appropriate number of each must be ordered to meet expected production needs in each case, the order whom for any raw materials should be placed with the vendor who will deliver it at the most favourable price. As food and beverage items are received, they must be checked to see that the restaurant or bar is getting what it pays. For them the raw materials must be stored appropriately with respect to temperature and security, the raw food or beverage item must be made available for the production of menus items for sale.

At each stage of operation it is necessary to institute control in order to prevent development of the kinds of problems suggested earlier. Control may be accomplished in about variety of ways, and anyone who attempts to manage about food and beverage operation should be aware of the techniques and devices available for use.

The selection of particular techniques and devices depends on the nature of the difficulty to be controlled and the situation in which the difficulty exists, as well as on the management style of the individual making the selection. Thus, selection of the means of control is not always simple, and the student be aware of some of the option available.

CONTROL TECHNIQUES

The variety of control techniques available to about manager includes the following:

1. Establishing standards.
2. Establishing produces.
3. Setting examples.
4. Observing and correcting employee actions.
5. Requiring records and reports.
6. Preparing and following budgets.
7. Censuring and disciplining employee.

Establishing Standards

Standards may be defined as rule or measure established for making comparisons and judgment. In business, these standards are set by management and are used for judging the extent to which results meet expectations. There are several types of standards set by food and beverage manager that are useful in establishing control over operations. It will be important to develop about working understanding of the several kinds of standards before proceeding.

Quality standards refer to the degree to excellence of raw materials, finished products, and by extension work. In one sense, the establishment of quality standards is about grading process. Most food items are graded as to degree of excellence many of them by the United States Department of Agriculture and Management must establish a standard of quality for each item for purposes of purchasing beef. For example is general available in a number of different grades for restaurant and institutional use, and it is important to establish which grade will be used for the preparation of a particular menu's items.

Beverage items may also be differentiated by quality. For example, some spirits improve with age, and a twelve-year-old scotch whisk'y is generally considered to be of a higher quality than another is that is only eight-years old. Managements in beverage operations must determine which beverage items are of appropriate quality to ensure customer satisfaction.

Quality standards must be determined even for the work force, in some hotels and fine restaurants, highest degrees of skill are required for the production and service of elaborate menu items then would be necessary on the average roadside diner.

Quality standards refer to measures of weight or count or volume. Thus management must establish such Hardball Sign quantity standards as portion sizes for menu items and drink and, in many instances, work output for employees.

The portion size for every food items served must be clearly established. Each shrimp cocktail should contain a predetermined number of shrimp of specified size and a certain measure of sauce. As well in case, cleary identified measures of garnish. An order of a soup should be identified as to size of bowl or cup to be used. Or the size ladle to be used in dishing it out, and the quantity of garnish to be included. Entrée items must be established as being of certain number of ounces or pieces. Surrounding items such as vegetables should be served with a certain size spoon, as with peas, or be measured by count, as with asparagus spears.

In bar operation, management must establish a standard quantity (in ounces) for each short of liquor used. In many instances bars operate with standard drink recipies indicating the quantities of ingredients to be used in the preparation of a particular drink.

Quantity standards are often important in the control of labour cost as well. It is useful to know when staffing, for example, how many tables or seats a waiter or waitress can cover during a given period, or how many sandwiches a pantry man can make in an hour when planning a luncheon schedule for the staff.

In addition to quality and quantity standards, it is ultimately necessary to determine and set cost standards for operation. Cost standards are usually referred to as standard costs.

A standard cost is the agreed upon cost of goods or service used to measure other costs. Paradoxically, it is at one and the same time both realistic and ideal. For example, if one quart of liquor costs Rs. 256 to purchase, each and every ounce has a real cost of Rs. 42.60, that is the standard cost of one ounce. If the entire bottle is used to prepare drinks, each of which contains one ounce, the standards cost of each should be Rs. 42.60. However, this is an ideal, since this does not allow for spillage or evaporation, both of which are likely to occur in bar operations. Standard costs are determined in several important ways, each of which will be discussed in detail in succeeding chapters. In the case of labour; these standard costs may be determined by obtaining averages over a period of time. In the case of foods and beverage, they may be determined by actual test the samples from which has previously illustrated in the discussion of the standard cost of one ounce of liquor.

Standard costs are useful in measuring the effectiveness of an operation. As we shall see, it is possible to compare standard costs with actual costs in order to determine how effectively food and beverage materials and labour resources are being deployed in a business operation. Cost standards are necessary in cost standards control because they provide a means of comparing what we are doing with what we should be doing.

Establishing Procedures

In addition to establishing standards for quality and quantity. Food and beverage managers must establish standard procedures. Procedures are the methods employed to prepare a product or perform a job, and standard procedures are those that have been established as the correct methods, routines and techniques for day-to-day operations. As we shall see in later chapters, in order to management to achieve effective control over food, beverage and labour cost, it is necessary to establish these standard procedures at every stage of the "manufacturing" process.

Ordering and purchasing procedures must be standardized to ensure that the raw food and beverage materials are purchased in needed quantities and qualities and at favourable prices at appropriate times. Receiving procedures must be standardized so that all goods received confirm as to quality, quantity, and cost to those ordered. Standard storing procedures must be put into effect to guard against both spoilage and theft, either if which will lead to excessive costs.

Issuing must be standardized to ensure that food and beverage items are used in the order they are received, thus to preventing spoilage and the resulting excess costs. In addition, they must be issued according to carefully determined production needs to further guarding against spoilage and theft. Moreover, records of issues must be maintained in order to calculate a cost per item produce, which can then be compared to standard cost to determine the effectiveness of operation.

Production procedures must be standardized for a number of reasons. In order to satisfy customers, any given item must be produced by the same method and with the same ingredients every time it is served. In addition, it should be served in the same quantities each time, partly so that customers will not feel cheated and partly to maintain cost standards.

When standards have been instituted in each of these categories–quality, quantity, and procedure – it then becomes possible to measure each aspect of the business. The day-to-day operating realities can be compared to the standards established, significant variations noted, and changes made to bring products and practices more nearly in line with the standards set. To the extent to which realities compare favourably with the standards set, effective controls exist.

Setting Examples

Often the establishing of standards and standard procedures is not quite as formal as may be suggested in the foregoing sections. In many instances, these are really established informally when the employees in an operation follow the examples set by the manager's overt behaviour, responses to questions, and even by the manager's failure to speak or take action in some situation. In general, the behaviour of individuals in a group tends to be influenced by the actions, statements, and attitudes of their leaders. Thus by instructing personnel in the particulars of how their jobs are to be done, managers are in effect controlling; since their particular goals are presumably consistent with their long-range business objectives, their instructions reflect the standards and procedures which they expect will lead to those goals. At the same time, the manager's individual behaviour in performing any task will influence the manner in which an employee will perform that same task. If the manager who has occasion to work with employees plating food for the dining room serves excessive portion sizes, employees will be inclined to do the same when the manager is not there. Similarly, if a manager inclined to warp up parcels of food to take home for personal use, employees will be so inclined as well. And if the manager observes them doing so and fails to end the practice, the amount of food leaving the premises will usually escalate.

It must be noted that any manager must be consistent in setting examples as well as in directing, regulating and restraining employees and their actions. In far too many cases managers appear not to have long-range and short-range goals clearly in mind as they go about the business of managing, and their examples, actions, directions, and responses to employee questions do not offer a clear picture to subordinates. Such inconsistency confuses employees and has the effect of breaking down whatever control might otherwise exist.

Correcting and Observing Employee Actions

If management observes a bartender mixing drinks without measuring ingredients and fails to direct the individual to measure quantities carefully as drinks are mixed, then the bartender could reasonably assume that such work was acceptable and the manager would be missing an opportunity to control behaviour. Should the manager observe the receiving clerk receiving meats without verifying that quantities received agree with the quantity on the invoice and fail to correct the practice, the employee could not possibly know that his or her performance was unacceptable.

One of the important tasks of a manager is to continually observe the actions of all of the employees as they go about their daily jobs, to judge those actions in the light of what employees should be doing, and correct them to the extent necessary at appropriate times.

Requiring Records and Reports

Obviously the manager cannot be place at all time to observe employee actions. In smaller food and beverage operations, the owner/manager can observe employee actions to a far greater extent than can the manager of a larger operation consisting of one or more bars and dining rooms seating hundreds of people and employing hundreds of personnel. The larger the establishment the more likely it is that management observations cannot be directed but must be abstracted and inferred from a variety of records and reports. The variety and extent of these will be discussed in great detail in later chapters. One such report already discussed is the Income Statement, which summarizes cost and sales information for a particular period and from which can be determined such factors as cost-to-sales ratios of various kinds. If the ratios are acceptable to management. This implies in general terms that the performance of employees has been acceptable during the period covered by the statement. If these ratios are not acceptable, the implication is that the employees have not followed some or all of the standards and standard procedures formally or informally established. We may not be able to pinpoint specific problems from such a general report as the income statement; other more specific and more timely reports and records are often required. Some of these may be developed daily; others, weekly and monthly, as will be seen in succeeding chapters. Of significance is that the manager needs timely information to determine whether or not long -range and short-range goals and sub-goals are being met. If not, the timeliness affords the opportunity of taking corrective action.

Preparing and Following Budgets

Perhaps the most common technique for controlling business operations is the use of budgets. A budget is a realistic expression of management's goals and objectives expressed in financial terms. Stated in revenue terms, it is a forecast of sales activity and an estimate of costs that will be incurred in the process of generating those sales. By extension the budget suggests the profit that should result after the costs of producing those sales have been met and also represents a financial plan for operations for the period it covers. Large businesses establish overall financial budgets for the operation of the entire enterprise, including a number of specific budgets for specific aspects of operation—such as sales budgets, cash flow budgets, cash equipment budgets, and even advertising budgets, as well as other.

For established restaurants these budgets are prepared with the help of historical information coupled with anticipated changes in the various categories in the budget, and in the business environment as well. Thus, if federal or state legislation will affect wage rates paid to employees in the period covered by the budget in preparation, this information must be used in planning. If real estate tax rates have been increased or decreased in a particular community, this information, too, should be reflected in the budget. More difficult to deal with, but equally important, are the effects of poor weather conditions on future crops, anticipated shortages of beef due to cattlemen's reduction in herds, and general conditions in the economy that affect the size of the restaurant's clientele.

In new establishments, those that do not have previous financial statements, information from a marker analysis and from a manager's previous experience provide the best alternative sources of data for budget preparation. When on market analysis is available, or when the manager is not widely experienced in the food and beverage business, or when both of these are true, budgets are often not prepared at all, and management misses an opportunity to employ one of the most useful of all control techniques.

Establishments make maximum use of the budget as a control device when they insist that employees adhere to planned expenditures as presented in the budget. In many chain restaurants the manager is required to keep labour costs within certain predetermined bounds as presented in the budget, advertising is restricted to the budget figure, printing costs for new menus and revenue available for paper supplies are like wise set, and so forth. Any changes in the budgeted amounts must first be approved by top management.

The student should note that the use of budget as a control device requires first that the budget be thoughtfully and carefully established as the financial standard against which financial performance will be judged. When records of financial performance are available in the form of monthly income statements, among others, they are compared to the budget and differences noted. If the differences between budgeted figures and actual figures are significant, corrective action may be required and may take various forms.

Censuring and Disciplining Employees

Censure and disciplinary action are two commonly employed control techniques. For example, the manager whose financial performance did out compare favourably with budget may have this fact pointed out to him top management in any number of ways. The possibilities may range from quiet discussion to heated admonition, or from demotion or transfer to termination. On another level, an employee who has been informed as to performance standards and who then does not meet these expectation is likely to learn about it from a supervisor or manager. At first, this might be simply called to his attention in an objective and unemotional was, and he could be given an opportunity to improve performance. If that improvement is not forthcoming in a reasonable period, then admonition on a second occasion is likely to be more severe. Most responsible managers would hope that a second such occasion would be the last and would bring the necessary improvement. However, if it were not, then a manager would find it necessary to take progressively more forceful action, the final one of which would be termination. This last should normally be used only if it simply impossible to control and modify the employee's job performance. After all, if an employee was worth hiring, he or she should be worth keeping, and all suitable efforts should be made to excessive firings can be very costly, leading perhaps to such additional costs as classified advertising for new help, increasing rates of productivity, higher training costs, and others.

On the one hand, it must be understood that the object of censuring and disciplining employees is to change or modify their job performance to control performance in such a way that the job activity of each employee is consistent with the standards and procedures that management has determined are likely to enhance the standards and procedures that management has determined are likely to enhance the firm's goals and objectives. On the other hand, it should be apparent that censure and disciplinary action generally have negative connotations in the mind of employees, most of whom would normally prefer to avoid any such unpleasantness. If certain behaviour patterns – bring the negative and unpleasant rewards of censure and disciplinary action, then most employees will generally prefer to strive toward the former and to avoid the latter. The very fact that employees know that transgressions lead to unpleasantness tends to have the desirable affect to tending to make job activity conform with management's planned standards and procedures.

THE CONTROL PROCESS

From the foregoing discussion of the techniques of control, it is possible to extract and to generalize three basic steps that lie at the heart of the control process:

1. Establish standards and standard procedures for operations.

2. Measure performance and compare actual performance with established standards.
3. Take action to correct deviations from standards.

To illustrate the manner in which the control process follows these steps let us assume a restaurant, the owner of which wants to serve the finest food. In order to reach this goal the owner must establish those standards and standard procedures that will define the meaning of "the finest." In the case of one menu item—prime sirloin steak—the standard is prime, a term that specifies certain identifiable characteristics. The instructions to appropriate employees must reflect the fact that only prime beef is to be purchased for the production to this menu item. Whoever receives beef from the purveyor should check to see that it is the correct quality by examining the meat and checking for the USDA Grade stamp on the outside fat. From time-to-time, the manager must make some observations to see that meat purchased the new standards set. Among other actions this may require examining raw meat gangling in the refrigerator or sitting down in the dining room and ordering a steak. If the manager is lax, customers will often note the divergence in quality from their past experiences there, and some will undoubtedly complain; others will merely not return. If the manager finds that the beef purchased is not in compliance with the standards set, then some remedial action is calls for if the goal of offering the finest food is to be met.

It is possible to develop a set of analogous circumstances in virtually any other area of the operation where control must be instituted. Wherever control is needed in restaurant operations, it can best be accomplished by means of following these three important steps.

Two of the major areas in which control must be exercised in profitable food and beverage operations are costs and sales.

Cost Control

All we begin to discuss the areas of cost control and sales control it will be useful for the student to keep in mind that the restaurant business has as one of its primary functions the sale of food and beverage items. The process by means of which this is accomplished includes the following:

- Ordering and purchasing
- Receiving
- Storing
- Issuing
- Preparing and producing
- Selling

As each stage of this process, there are opportunities for excessive costs to develop. Two of the principal causes of excessive costs are inefficiency and waste. For example, the storage of food in refrigerators that are not cold enough, or the storage of liquor in bottles that are not tightly closed, will lead to spoilage of raw materials and hence to excessive cost. So will the preparation of an inedible beef stew or an undrinkable martini. When the stew is thrown into the garbage can or the martini poured down the drain, costs of operation are increased but sales are not. Since profit is essentially the difference between sales and costs, it is apparent that any increase in costs that does not lead to corresponding increases in sales can only have the effect of reducing profits. Clearly, management must take steps to guard against the occurrence of these excessive costs.

The process whereby managers attempt to regulate costs and guard against excessive costs is known as cost control. It is an ongoing process and involves every step in the chain of purchasing, receiving, storing, issuing, and preparing food and beverages for sale, as well as scheduling the personnel involved. Exact methods for cost control will vary from place to place, depending in part on the nature and scope of operation; but the principle behind varying methods will be constant. The obvious goal is to eliminate excessive costs for food and beverages and labour to exercise governing power over costs in all areas in order to ensure that the business will operate at a profit.

Sales Control

While the control of cost is critically important to the profitable operation of any business, cost control alone will not ensure profitability. Additional steps must be taken to ensure that all sales result in appropriate income to the business. In the case of the furniture manufacturer cited earlier, care must be taken to ensure that each chair is sold at the correct price. For example, profits will be adversely affected if a steak listed in the menu as selling for Rs. 358 is sold to a customer for Rs. 318, of the cocktail that is supposed to sell for Rs. 54 is sold for Rs. 46. Therefore, it is important in most instances to insist that employees record each sales clearly on a check.

In addition, it is useful to check recorded sales against production records to ensure that all quantities produced are accounted for. Various methods for ensuring that all portions that have left the kitchen or bar have been recorded as sales on checks.

Although it is unfortunate that not all employees are completely honest, it is a fact of life that must be taken into account in food and beverage operations. Therefore, guest checks are usually numbered to ensure accountability. Sometimes duplicate copies of the checks, clearly identified as duplicates so they are not confused with the originals, are used to reconcile kitchen production with recorded sales. When the checks and duplicates are numbered sequentially, missing numbers can be noted and investigated at once.

As will be seen in succeeding chapters, many possible systems and procedures for control exist. Some will require very little additional time or effort. However, certain others might require the hiring of additional personal, or the purchase of new equipment or supplies, any of which would add to the already overburdened cost structure.

Cost-Benefit Ratio

One additional important concept must be introduced before leaving the general subject of control and proceeding to the specific controls available to food and beverage operators: the relationship between costs incurred and benefits obtained.

The student can appreciate that all control measures bring some cost to a business, some time relatively insignificant, at other times great, and occasionally even prohibitive. A relatively insignificant cost is required to institute the simple control measure of locking the front and back doors at night to prevent burglary. The relocation of a cashier's desk to a position judged more suitable for preventing customers from leaving without paying, costs somewhat more. The establishment of a system of the time clocks presided over by timekeepers is of even greater and ongoing cost.

The establishment of a control department within the restaurant and the hiring of a food controller and a beverage controller, with appropriate secretarial and other assistance, together with all of the paper, supplies, and equipment these individuals would need, would surely entail large and possibly prohibitive sums of money.

It must be kept in mind that the purpose of cost and sales control measures are to guard against excessive costs and to ensure that all sales result in appropriate income. In other words, there must be some beneficial result to the business from the introduction of any control device, procedure, or personnel. For example, if recent telephone bills have reached unwarranted levels because of nonbusiness-related long-distance calls placed on the office telephone a simple control expenditure for a telephone lock might result inconsiderable to the establishment. In similar fashion, the hiring of a cashier to record sales and collect cash would probably go further toward ensuring that sales resulted in income than could a procedure that permitted waiters and waitresses to collect for the food and beverages they served. In each of these cases, as in all examples of incurring cost for purposes of control, the amount of such cost incurred should be exceeded by the benefits derived by the business.

Control systems and procedures generally affect many aspects of the operation, sometimes in a negative way not anticipated by the manager. For example, a system that verifies that all food going from kitchen to the dining room is appropriately recorded on checks may have the effect of slowing down service, reducing turnover, and even resulting in cold food being served to guests. By the same token, the installation of a time clock to develop accurate payroll records might cause resentment among certain long-time, loyal, and valued employees, some of whom might seek other employment rather than punch time clock.

ELEMENT OF COST AND COST GROUP

Definition of Cost

As we use the term in our discussion of cost control in the food and beverage business, cost will mean the price to the hotel or restaurant of goods are consumed or the services rendered. Food and beverage items are consumed when they have been used up, wastefully or otherwise, and are no longer available for the purpose for which they were acquired. Thus, the cost of a piece of meat is incurred when the piece is sold, or thrown away because it has spoiled, or when it has been stolen and is no longer available for the purpose for which it was purchased. The cost of labour is incurred when services are rendered, whether the person rendering the service is paid at that point or a later date.

The cost of any item may be exposed in a variety of ways in units of weight or volume or total value. The cost of meat for example can be expressed as a value per kg or as a value per individual portion. The cost of liquor can be discussed in terms of the cost per bottle, per drink or per ounce. Labour costs can be expressed in terms of an hourly wage, or a weekly wage.

Fixes and Variable Costs

Costs can be divided into several different categories, and it is necessary to distinguish between them. Fixed costs are those that have little direct relationship to the volume of business. As volume increases and decreases, those costs remain the same. Insurance premiums, real estate taxes, and depreciation on equipment are all example of fixed costs.

Directly variable costs, on the other hand, are those that have a direct relationship to the volume of business, such that every increase or decrease in volume brings a corresponding increase or decrease in cost. Food and beverage costs are good examples. Every time a restaurant sells an order of roast beef, it incurs a cost for the meat sold. Each sale of a bottle of beer at the bar brings about a monetary cost for the beer sold. Directly variable costs, then increase or decrease, or at least should increase or decrease in directly proportion to sales volume.

By contrast, semi-variable costs vary with volume but not in direct proportion of it. Labour costs are considered semi-variable taken as a whole. When a restaurant or bar is open, a basic staff must be maintained. As business increase, or volume increases, additional staffing may become necessary and desirable, but not until all present employees are working to maximum capacity at optimum efficiency. Beyond that point, new staff will be hired in numbers and at costs related to volume, but not in direct proportion to it.

Controllable and Non-Controllable Costs

Costs may also be labelled controllable and non-controllable. Controllable costs are those that can be changed without much difficulty. Directly variable costs are normally controllable. The cost of food or beverages sold can be changed for example, by varying portion sizes or by varying ingredients, or both either considered controllable. The cost of labour can be increased or decreased in the short run by hiring or laying off workers, or by increasing or decreasing working hours or, in some instance, by increasing or decreasing wages. By contrast, non-controllable costs are those that can be changed only with great difficulty, and usually not in the short run. Fixed costs are generally non-controllable. A change in real estate taxes, for example, is normally beyond immediate power of management.

Every business has certain fixed costs built into its cost structure. Such items as rent and insurance are fixed costs that are common to the structure of a vast number of business. It is necessary for sales volume to reach a certain minimal level to cover just these fixed costs. Only after the fixed directly variable and semi-variable costs of operation have been met can a business begin to operate profitable.

Because fixed costs are usually considered, at least in the short run , we will not be especially concerned with those costs that food and beverage managers have a reasonable chance of controlling. Future discussion will deal almost exclusively with directly variable and semi-variable costs – the cost of food and beverages sold, and the cost of labour.

Unit and Total Costs

It is important to distinguish between unit costs and total costs. The units may be food or beverage portions, as in the cost of one steak or one martini, or units of work, as in the hourly rate for an employee.

On the other hand, it is sometimes, useful to discuss costs in terms of totals, as in the total cost of all food served in one period – such as a week or a months or the total cost of labour for one period. These, of course, are how costs are expressed in the income statement.

Some example will be useful to illustrate the above. A restaurant cutting steaks from a strip loin purchases one strip loin for Rs. 2100.

If all of the strip is consumed in one day the total cost is Rs. 2100. However, the cost per unit, the steak, will depend on the number of steaks cut from the strip. If there are fifteen steaks cut, the unit cost is an average of Rs. 140. However, each steak will vary in cost because it is not normally possible for a butcher to cut all steaks exactly the same weight. In the food and beverage business we usually deal with average unit costs, rather than actual unit costs. Nevertheless, it is necessary to know unit costs for purposes of pricing and determining unit profitability. Total costs, including those that appear in income statements, are normally used for broader purposes, including overall relationships between costs and sales, as will discussed later in this chapter, and for determining overall profitability of operations.

It is significant to note that as business volume changes, the effects on various costs change. Let us assume that a restaurant has a fixed cost for rent of Rs. 80,000 per month. If there were 2,000 customers served during a period of one month, the average unit rental cost to the restaurant would be Rs. 40 for each customer served. If in the succeeding month the number of customers increased to 4,000, the total fixed cost for rent would not change, but the fixed cost per unit (customer) would be reduced from Rs. 40 to Rs. 10.

The same analysis may be some with variable costs. The variable cost for the steak described above was Rs. 140 per unit. If 2,000 customers in a given month order steak, the total variable cost would be Rs. 2,80,000 at Rs. 140 average unit cost per steak. If in the following month 4,000 customers ordered steak, the variable cost per unit (the steak) should remain Rs. 140, while the total variable cost for 4,000 steaks increases to Rs. 5,60,000.

While the foregoing illustrates behaviour with increase in business volume, the same relationships hold true as business volume decreases. Table 2.1 illustrates the above behaviour of fixed and variable costs per unit and in total. It is important to understand these relationships when dealing with cost-volume-profit analysis and the calculation of break-even points.

It must be noted that not all will agree with this. The point must be made that actual variable costs tend to decrease as volume increases. Labour becomes more productive with greater time utilization, and food purchasing at greater volume can reduce cost.

Table 2.1: Cost Behaviour as Business Volume Changes

	Unit Cost	*Total Cost*
Fixed Cost	Changes	Does not change
Variable Cost	Does not change	Does not change

Historical and Planned Costs

Two additional cost concepts are important for a deeper understanding of cost control. First, the definition of cost, it's implication that all costs are historical, that is, that they can be documented through such records as invoices, wage rates, and contractual agreements, such as a lease. These documents are used for various purposes, such as establishing unit costs, menu prices, and total wages for past periods. Generally, when we speak of costs we are using the term in this historical sense. However, cost control is a management tool, and it is not sensible for management merely to wait until historic costs for any period are available. Hence, planning is always a vital function of management and in order to be effective, a manager must often use historical costs to infer what costs will be or should be for a coming period. Thus, historical costs are necessary for effective planning.

Costs fluctuate considerably in the food and beverage business for several reasons:

1. Most food costs change seasonally, depending on supply and demand conditions;
2. Inflation has been evident in the economy especially in the past; and
3. Legislated minimum wage rates and negotiated labour agreements also affect labour costs over time. Management must somehow keep these anticipated, though not necessarily accurately predictable, changes in mind when planning for future costs. For example, many banquet functions are booked substantially in advance with menus and prices agreed on. Anticipated, yet in exact changes in cost must be factored in the agreed on prices if adequate profits are to be derived.

Cost to Sales Ratio: The Cost Percentage

Raw rupees figures for directly variable and semi-variable costs are seldom, it ever, of any particular significance for control purposes. Because these costs vary to some extent with business volume, they become significant only when expressed in relation to that volume with which they vary. We calculate costs in rupees and compare those costs to sales in rupees. This enables us to discuss the relationship between costs and sales, sometimes described as the cost per rupee of sale, but more often as the cost percentage, or the ratio of costs to sales. The formula common to the industry that we will use throughout this book is:

$$\frac{\text{Cost}}{\text{Sales}} = \text{Cost per rupee of sale}$$

The division problem implicit in the formula always results in a decimal answer, and any decimal can be converted to a percentage by moving the decimal point two places to the right and adding a % sign. For this reason, the formula is often written as:

$$\frac{\text{Cost}}{\text{Sales}} = \text{Cost\%}$$

This formula can then be extended to show the following relationships:

$$\frac{\text{Food Cost}}{\text{Food Sales}} = \text{Food Cost\%}$$

$$\frac{\text{Beverage Cost}}{\text{Beverage Sales}} = \text{Beverage Cost\%}$$

$$\frac{\text{Labour Cost}}{\text{Total Sales}} = \text{Labour Cost\%}$$

Let us assume the income statements for the Rush Hour Inn and the Graduate Restaurant. In the case of the Graduate Restaurant, food costing Rs. 26,76,000 ultimately resulted in sales of Rs. 89,20,000. In order to determine the percentage of sales represented by cost, we divide the cost by the sales, as in the preceding formula, and multiply the resulting decimal answer by 100 in order to convert it to a percentage.

Rs. 26,76,000/Rs. 89,20,000 = 0.3 × 100 = 30 %

Thus we learn that the food cost percentage, or the cost-to-sales ratio, in the Graduate Restaurant over the past year has been 30 per cent. This tells us that 30 per cent of the income from food sales over the year has gone to cover the cost to the food sold. Expressed another way, the cost of food sold represents Rs. 12 out of each Rs. 40 in sales. Following the same formula, we may now take the figures for food costs and food sales from the income statement of the Rush Hour Inn and calculate the food cost percentage, or cost per rupee of sale, for purposes of comparison.

Rs. 58,24,000/Rs. 1,66,40000 = 0.35 × 100 = 35 per cent.

So in the case of the Rush Hour Inn, the cost per rupees of sale is Rs. 1,400 and the food cost percentage is 35 per cent.

Cost percentage are useful to management in at least two ways. They provide a means of comparing costs relative to sales for two or more periods of time, and they provide a means of comparing two or more operations. When comparing cost percentages for two or more operations, it is important to note that the comparisons can only be valid if the operations are similar. Thus, comparisons are often made between two fast-food restaurant with similar products; but one could not compare a French restaurant with a local diner and expect the comparison to be meaningful.

A comparison of the figures that will reveal some useful information now can be established for our two restaurants in Table 2.2.

Table 2.2

	Rush Hour Inn	*Graduate Restaurant*
Food sales	Rs. 1,66,40,000	Rs. 89,20,000
Cost of food sold	Rs. 58,24,000	Rs. 26,76,000
Cost per Rs. of sale	.35	.30
Food cost percentage	35%	30%

It is only at this point that the figures can begin to take on some real meaning for us and that we can begin intelligently to compare them. Significantly, we learn that one of the principal differences between the two restaurants lies in the fact that the food cost per rupee of sale is Rs. 2 higher in one. Expressed another way, we can say that the cost to sales ratio for food is 5 per cent higher in the Rush

Hour Inn. It is not untill we have converted the raw rupees figures to this form that we have any useful way of comparing them.

Because food is a variable cost, it will increase and decrease with sales volume. It would not be possible to establish useful comparisons between operating periods for one restaurant or between comparable restaurants (as in a chain, for example) unless were to work with the cost percentages, or the costs per rupee of sale. Since cost control figure in the hospitality industry are more commonly expressed in terms of the cost percentage, we will deal with percentage figure in this text. In addition, because rupee figures in real restaurant operations seldom result in round numbers, we will express our percentages in tenths of one per cent, for example, 35.9 per cent or 36.2 per cent. This, too, is common to the hospitality industry, and permits a greater degree of accuracy. After all, in the case of the Rush Hour Inn, one-tenth of one per cent of sales is Rs. 1,66,40,000, which is a considerable quantity of real rupee.

Using the formula above, it is now possible to establish a chart comparing the to restaurants from the point of view of costs as percentages of sales.

It is both interesting and significant that the variable, controllable costs for the Rush Hour Inn are higher in every case. Only the fixed costs, which are essentially not controllable, are the same.

Table 2.3

	Rush Hour Inn	*Graduate Restaurant*
Food cost as a % of food sales	35.0%	30.00%
Beverage cost as a % of beverage sales	30.0%	25.0%
Combined food and beverage costs as a % to total sales	34.5%	29.5%
Payroll and related expenses as a % of sales	35.0%	30.0%
Overhead as a % of sales	30.0%	30.0%

INDUSTRY-WISE VARIATIONS IN COSTS

As percentages of sales, the costs for food and beverage operations vary considerably. Some of the factors contributing to these variations would include type of service, location, price structure and type of menu.

In very broad terms, there are two types of restaurants:

- Those that operate at a low margin of profit per item served, and depend on a relatively high volume of business to make a profit.
- Those that operate at a relatively high margin of profit per item, and therefore do not need to rely on such a high volume of business in order to show a profit.

It is apparent that if the two were to have any menu items in common, the price would tend to be lower in the first category.

The following examples of the cost structures of hypothetical restaurants in each of these two categories are intended to serve only as illustrations of relative costs. The examples should not be taken to imply either that these are standards for the industry or that and particular restaurant should have the illustrated cost structure. The cost structure for each individual restaurant must be determined for that restaurant alone. The obvious point being that as percentages of sales, costs must always total less than 100 per cent if the operation is to be profitable.

Restaurants that depend principally on convenience foods—the so-called fast-food operations—are generally in the first (low margin) category above. Because of relatively lower menu prices, the food cost percentages in such establishments tend to be higher. Because they are often able to operate with less highly skilled, highly paid personnel, and often with fewer personnel, they are able to offset the high food cost percentage with a low labour cost. A typical cost analysis for such a restaurant might be as seen in Table 2.4.

Table 2.4

Sales	100.0%
Cost of food	40.0%
Gross profit on sales	60.0%
Cost of labour	20.0%
Profit before overhead	40.0%
Overhead costs	30.0%
Profit as a % of sales	10.0%

Restaurants in the second (high margin) category tend to depend less on convenience foods and to cater to customers who are looking for fresh foods, often prepared gourmet-style, and core service. This type of food preparation and service usually requires a greater number of personnel who are more highly skilled and often better paid. This tends to keep the cost of labour higher than in the first example, but the food cost percentage in such establishments will tend to be lower, partially because of higher menu prices. An analysis of the costs for such a restaurant might look like this:

Sales	100.0%
Cost of food	25.0%
Gross profit on sales	75.0%
Cost of labour	35.0%
Profit before overhead	40.0%
Overhead	30.0%
Profit as a % of sales	10.0%

It is important to note that operations in the first category require numbers of customers to achieve a given rupee volume of sales. In the second example partially because of higher menu prices, fewer customers are required to reach a given rupee volume. In general, it is possible to achieve a profit with fewer customers if menu prices are high.

In the two examples cited above, profit as a percentage of sales is shown a 10.0 per cent. We must emphasize that these figures are not to be taken as industry standards, or even as necessarily desirable standards. There are some experts who feel that 25.0 per cent profit is desirable, and others who feel that a lower percentage of profit will help ensure customer return and lengthen the business life of a restaurant. The percentage of profit for any restaurant must lead on other factors, such as return on investment, the risk of being in business as opposed to other forms of investment, the return one might get in some other business, and a whole range of considerations involving the competition. In the last analysis, cost and profit determinations must be made on an individual establishment basis.

Now that we have taken a brief look at the types of costs involved in food and beverage operations and have found that some of them are controllable, it is time to take a closer look at what we mean by control and at what factors must be established before management can institute systems for keeping costs under control. However, before we do so, it will be useful to arrive at a working definition of a word that we have taken for granted thus far: sales.

3

PURCHASING, RECEIVING, STORING AND ISSUING CONTROL

FOOD PURCHASING

Introduction

The primary purpose for establishing control over purchasing is to ensure a continuing supply of sufficient quantities of foods. Each of the quality appropriate to intended use, purchased at the most favourable price. Although it is not the job of the food controller to purchase foods, or even to assign responsibility for their purchase, he does become involved in the purchasing process to the extent that his responsibility is for setting up the control procedure. Under the direction of management, he sees that appropriate standards for quality and quantity are set and that procedures are established for meeting these standards.

Cost will be governed to be a great extent by purchasing policies and techniques. Therefore, it will be useful to discuss purchasing in some detail from the point of view of food controller, covering four principal characteristics of effective purchasing control:

1. Responsibility for purchasing is fixed.
2. Standards of quality are established.
3. Needed quantities are established.
4. Purchases of food are at the most favourable prices.

Duties/Responsibility

Responsibility for purchasing can be delegated to any one of a number of persons in restaurant operations, depending on organizational structure and management policies. It is not uncommon to find the owners or managers taking the responsibility in some establishment, while in other, either the chef or the steward may be assigned the purchasing duties. In some hotel operations, foods may even be ordered by some individual in the office of the purchasing agent.

In order to facilitate discussions, we will arbitrarily fix responsibility for purchasing the necessary foods with the steward. This should not be taken to mean that the authors believe that this responsibility should always be given to the steward; on the contrary, the determination of who should be assigned this responsibility must be based on situations and conditions existing in each individual restaurant operation. The important point to be made here is that for control purposes, the authority to purchase foods, and the responsibility for doing so, should be assigned to one individual. One individual can then be held accountable for operating the system of control procedures established by the food controller.

Kinds of Foods to be Purchased

The types of foods to be purchased for any operation may be divided roughly into two categories: Perishables and Non-perishable. Because several significant differences will be presented in the techniques and procedures for the purchase of them, it will be useful at this point to differentiate between them.

Perishables are those items, typically fresh foods that have a comparatively short useful life after they have been received. Various kind of lettuce and fresh fish, for example, begin to lose their quality very quickly, some meats and cheeses will retain their quality for somewhat longer periods, but they too will begin to lose their quality far sooner than, say, a can tomato puree. Perishables, then, should be purchased for immediate use in order to take advantage of the quality required at the time of purchase. If a steward is careful always to purchase the best quality available for intended use them it would be wasteful and costly not to make use of that carefully selected quality.

Non-perishables are those food items that have a longer "short life." Often referred to as groceries or staples, they may be stored in the containers in which they may be received, often on shelves and at room temperature, for weeks or even months. They do not deteriorate quickly, at least as long as they are kept in sealed containers. They are typically purchased and stored in jars, bottle cans and boxes; and the storage area in which they are kept, called a storeroom, would resemble the shelves of supermarket to the layman.

PURCHASING PROCEDURE

If a restaurant is to produce products of consistent quality, it must use raw materials of consistent quality. Therefore, it is important that the food controller, in cooperation with other members of the management team, draw up a list of food items to be purchased, and list in appropriate detail those specific and distinctive characteristics that will best desirable that the desired quality of each. These carefully written descriptions are known as standard purchase Specifications. These specifications are often based on grading standers established by the federal government, or in some instances, when federal grading standards are considered too broad. specifications are based on grading standards common to the appropriate commodities market. However, the restaurant is not restricted to these possibilities. Many knowledgeable individuals writes specifications that are far more precise, and thus more useful for indicating to purveyor the exact quality desired. Once these standards purchase specification have been written and agreed upon by the management team, they are often duplicated and distrainment of the restaurant. Table 3.1 give examples of standard purchase specifications.

Standard purchase specification, if carefully prepared, are useful in several ways:

1. To force the management team to determine exact requirements in advance any commodity.

Table 3.1: Standard Purchase Specifications

Strip lion	Bone-in 10″cut. USDA Prime, upper half. Range #2 minimum 14 kg., maximum 16 kg. One-Half to three-quarters of an inch fat except for scam fat.

(Contd.)

	Moderate marbling, light red in colour to slightly dark red. New York cut, chilled upon delivery. Free from objectionable order, deterioration, and evidence of freezing or defrosting.
Flounder	Whole, dressed, fresh day of delivery (grey sole) Minimum 2 kg, maximum 4 kg. Fish should be twice as long as is broad, with oval body. Flesh should be firm and elastic, meat should be white and slightly translucent, colour should be bright and clear. Gills should be free from slime and reddish-pink in colour, and scales should adhere tightly to the skin. No stale odours of ammonia. Yield of 40 per cent to the fillet. Delivery to follow day to order.
Grapefruit	Florida. Medium to large; 3-3/4" in diameter. Light yellow in colour; approximately 12 to 14 sections; oval to round. Thin-skinned, tender, delicate flesh. No visible spotting or bruising on skins. Medium acidity and sweetness, faint bitterness. Packed 36 to a crate. Delivery to follow day after order is placed.
Canned peaches	Yellow, cling halves-canned, US Grade A (Fancy), heavy syrup. 19-24 Brix, minimum drained weight, 66 ounces per # 10 can. Count per # 10 can: 30 to 55 Quote by dozen # 10 can. Federal Inspector's certification of grade required.
Asparagus tips, frozen	Tips large, all green, frozen Us Grade A (Fancy). Packed in 2-1/kg. Cartons, per case. Must be delivered 10 °F or below, quote by pound net. Federal inspector's certifications of grade required.

2. They are often useful in menu preparation, in that it is possible to use one cut of meat, purchased according to specifications to prepare several different items on the menu.

3. They eliminate misunderstandings between the steward and purveyors if they are circulated.
4. Circulation of specifications for one commodity to several purveyors makes competitive bidding possible.
5. They eliminate the need for detailed verbal descriptions each time a commodity is ordered.
6. They facilitate checking food as it is received.

Quantity Purchase

Although purchase specifications can be established at one particular time and merely reviewed and updated on occasion, quantity standards for purchasing are subject to constant review and revision, often on a daily basis. All foods deteriorate in time, some more quickly than other, and it is the job of the food controller to provide a system that will ensure that only those quantities are purchased that will be needed immediately or in the relatively near future. In cooperation with the steward, the food controller does this by instituting procedures for determining the appropriate quantities of each item that should be purchased. These procedures are based principally on the useful life of the commodity.

For purchasing purposes, foods are divided into the two categories previously discussed, perishables and non-perishables. The procedures for determining quantities to purchase vary somewhat and will be discussed separately.

Perishables

The very nature of perishable commodities suggests the importance of continually using up those already on hand before purchasing additional quantities. Therefore, the purchasing routine must provide for determining amounts already on hand. Decisions also must be made as to total quantities needed. Once these have been arrived at, the difference between them is the correct amount to order.

A basic requirement of the purchasing routine is that the steward take a daily inventory of perishable. This daily inventory may be an acute physical inventory in some cases. In others, it may be only an estimate based on physical observation. For example, the steward would probably count the actual number of ribs of beef but might only estimate the quantity of cases of lettuce.

A very important and useful tool for the steward to use in taking this daily inventory is a standard form called the "steward's market quotation list", illustrated in Table 3.2. This form, generally available from stationers who cater to the hotel and restaurant industry, is a listing of the most common perishables, arranged by types, with several blank lines provided for the special requirements of each restaurant. (Restaurants that offer menus so specialized that this particular form is useless are well-advised to devise their own and have them duplicated.)

In order to take the daily inventory of perishables, the steward will usually go through the refrigerators and freezers with the form in hand and, next to the appropriate items on each category, fill in the column on the left, marked "on hand" after completing this survey, the steward has a relatively accurate inventory of perishable commodities.

The next step in the routine involves determining anticipated total needs for each item, based on future menus, and often on experience as well. Depending on the restaurant, these figures for total anticipated needs are determined sometimes by the chef, sometimes by the steward, and often by the two working together. Two heads are usually better than one. It is helpful to write this for total anticipated needs in the "article" column, just after the name of the item in question.

Following this determination, the steward enters the difference between total anticipated needs and the amount on hand in the "wanted" column at the right. This difference is the amount that should be ordered to bring supply upto the total quantity required.

It must be noted that there are exceptions to the rule from time, as, for example, when the opportunity arises for purchasing a four-month supply of non-perishable commodity at a substantial discount.

Nonperishable

While non-perishable commodities do not present the problem of rapid deterioration, they do represent considerable amounts of money invested in material in storage. It is obvious that cash tied up in non-perishable commodities is not available to meet other operating expenses to the business. Therefore, one goal of the

Table 3.2 : Steward's Market Quotation List

On Hand	Article	Wanted	Quotations OM	MP	JM	On Hand	Article	Wanted	Quotations OM	MP	JM	On Hand	Articles	Wanted	Quotations FF	HF
	BEEF						**PROVISIONS**						**FISH**			
	Corned Beef						Pig's Knuckeles Fresh						Carp			
	Corned Beef Brisket						Pigs' Knuckless Corned						Codfish, Live			
	Corned Beef Rump						Pig, Suckling						Codfish, Salt Boneless			
	Corned Beef Hash						Prok, Fresh Lion						Codfish, Salt Flake			
	Beef Chipped						Pork, Larding						Eels			
	Beef Breads						Pork, Spare Ribs						Finan Haddie			
	Butts						Pork, Salt Strip					12lb	Flounders 32	20	1.25	1.20
	Chuck					5lb	Prok Tenderlion	10	15lb	1.20	125		Flounders			
30lb	Fillets						Sausages, Corned		1.10				Flounders, Fillet			
	Hip Short						Sausages Frankfurter						Fluke			
	Hip Full						Sausages, Meat						Haddock			
	Kidneys						Shoulders Fresh						Haddock, Smoked			
	Livers						Shoulders Smoked					30lb	Halibut			
	Lion, Short						Shoulders Corned						Halibut, Chicken			
40lb	Strip 70	30lb	2.55	2.45	2.50		Tongues						Herring			
	Shell Strip						Tongues, Beef Smoked						Herring, Smoked			
	Ribs Beef						Tongues, Fresh						Herring, Kipered			
	Shins						Tongues, Lambs						Kingfish			
	Suet, Beef						Tripe						Mackerel, Fresh			
	Tails, Ox												Mackerel Spanish			

(Contd.)

On Hand	Article	Wanted	Quotations OM	Quotations MP	Quotations JM	On Hand	Article	Wanted	Quotations OM	Quotations MP	Quotations JM	On Hand	Articles	Wanted	Quotations FF	Quotations HF
	VEAL						**POULTRY**						Mackerel Salt			
10lb	Breast 30	20lb	2.75	(2.60)	2.65		Chickens						Mackerel, Smoked			
	Breast						Chickens, Roast						Perch			
	Feet						Chickens, Broilers						Pickerel			
	Fore Quarters						Chickens, Broilers						Pike			
	Hind Quarters						Chickens, Supreme						Porgies			
	Head						Cocks						Pompano			
	Kidenys						Capons						Redsnapper			
	Legs						Ducks						Salmon Fresh			
	Liver						Ducklings						Salmon, Smoked			
	Lions						Fowl						Salmon, Nova Scotia			
	Racks						Geese						Scrod			
	Saddies						Goslings						Shad			
	Shoulder						Guinea Hens						Shad Roes			
	Sweet Breads						Guinea Squabs						Smelts			
							Pigeons						Sole, English			
							Poussins									

(Contd.)

On Hand	Article	Wanted	Quotations JP	Quotations BP	On Hand	Article	Wanted	Quotations JP	Quotations BP
	VEGETABLES					**FRUITS**			
	Estragon					Dates			
	Egg Plant					Figs			
	Garlic					Gooseberries			
	Horseradish Roots				5lb	Grapes 5 lb			
	Kale					Grapes			
	Kohirabi					Grapes, Concord			
1 crate	Lettuce 2	1 Crate	(12.50)	13.10	5lb	Grapes, Malaga			
	Lettuce, Ice Berg					Grapes, Tokay			
	Lettuce, Place				½ Box	Grapefruit	1 box	(9.50)	7.25
2 bunches	Leeks 2					Grapefruit			
	Mint					Gauvas			
3 bunches	Mushrooms 3				1 Box	Lemons			
	Mushrooms Fresh					Lemons			
	Okra					Limes			
½ bag	Onions 1	1 Bag	6.75	6.90		Limes, Florida			
	Onions, Yellow					Limes, Persian			
	Onions, Bermuda					Muskmelons			
	Onions, Spanish				1 Box	Oranges			

(Contd.)

On	*Article*	*Wanted*	*Quotations*		*On Hand*	*Article*	*Wanted*	*Quotations*		
			JP	*BP*				*JP*	*BP*	
	Onions, White					Oranges				
	Onions, Scallions					Oranges				
	Oyster Plant				¼ CME	Peaches	125½	1	12.00	12.50
2 bunches	Parsky 1					Peaches				
	Parsnips					Pears				
	Peppermint					Pears				
	Peas, Green					Pears, Alligators				
	Peas					Pineapples				
	Peas					Plums				
	Peppers, Green					Plums				
	Peppers, Red					Pomegranates				
	Potatoes					Quinces				
	Potatoes, Bermuda					Rasperries				
1 Box	Potatoes, Idaho					Strawberries				
	Potatoes, Idaho					Strawberries				
	Potatoes, Sweet					Tangerines				
	Potatoes, New					Watermelons				
	Potatoes, Yams					Watermelons				
	Pumpkins									

purchasing routine for non-perishable should be to avoid excessive quantities on hand additional benefits to be derived from reducing quantities on hand include the elimination of some possibilities for theft, the reduction of storages space requirements, and possibly the reduction in number of personnel required to maintain the storage area.

Fixing labels on shelves is one important step that should be taken in every storeroom to identify permanently the location of each item maintained in stock. In the way no item will ever be found in two or more different locations at one time. When items appear in several different locations, there is tendency to order additional quantities in the unwarranted belief that the stock is running low. Moreover, when locations are identified, it becomes easier to find things when regular personnel are on duty or when personnel change.

For the convenience of stewards, there is a form available from stationers that list non-perishable, just as the steward's market quotation list itemizes perishables. Widely used, however, since lists of groceries are not as universally applicable from restaurant to restaurant. A great number of stewards prefer to make up lists of contents of their particular storerooms and to have them inexpensively duplicated. These serve the same purpose. To list amounts to be ordered and competitive prices.

While there are a number of specific systems for maintaining grocery inventory at appropriate levels, most are variations on the following methods.

Periodic Order Methods

Perhaps the most common method for maintaining stores inventories at appropriate levels is the so-called periodic method. Which, by contrast with methods for order in perishables, permits comparatively infrequent ordering. Because non-perishable items have long shelf life than perishables, it is both possible and desirable to order the less frequently, thus leaving the steward free to attend to perishables, which typically require considerable time. When this method is followed, a steward will normally establish with the advice of management periods for ordering purposes. On a regular basis – once every week, or every two weeks, or even once each month, depending the policies of management as to the amount of money to be tied up in inventory the stewards reviews the entire stock of non-perishable items and determines how much each to order to ensure a supply sufficient to last until the next regularly schedule order date. The calculation of the amount of each item to order is comparative simple:

   Amount required for the upcoming period
- Amount presently on hand
+ Amount wanted on hand at the end of the period to last until the next delivery
= Amount to order

For example, in a certain restaurant ordering once a month, one of the items ordered might be 2 and half cans of sliced pineapple, packed twelve cans to a case. The item is used at the rate of ten cans per week, and delivery normally takes five from the date an order is placed. If the steward in this establishment found fifteen cans on the shelf, anticipated normal use of forty cans during the upcoming period of approximately four weeks, and wanted fifteen cans on hand at the end of the upcoming month, the calculation would be

   40 cans required
- 15 now on hand
+ 15 to be left at the end of the month
= 40 to be ordered on this date

However, since orders are normally placed for this item in cases rather than in cans, it is likely that the steward would round the order up the next highest purchase unit and that the order placed would be for four cases consisting of forty-eight cans. While this rounding procedure may appear to lead to over purchasing, in fact the steward is subtracting quantities on hand at the beginning of each period before placing the orders, and thus any such small over purchases are likely to be used up at the beginning of the next period. Additionally, the order the next period is, in effect, reduced by the amount of the small over purchase in the current period.

The student might well ask how the steward knows the requirements for the upcoming periods. Storerooms have hundreds of items, and it is impossible for a person to know without records how much is needed of most items. Fortunately, the steward is aided by the salespersons, in addition, many establishments keep appropriate records of amounts used. Smaller establishments typically rely on salespersons to keep track of previous orders. The steward can then look on the storage shelf to make an approximate calculation of the amount used by subtracting what is remaining from what was ordered. While this is probably a better method than having no knowledge of usage, it is unreliable because it fails to take into account the amount on hand at the beginning or any period. Nevertheless, this method is very common in the food and beverage industry. One additional note: If an establishment orders every time a salesperson calls, the order period will vary from item to items as salespersons do not call with the same frequency.

A more systematic method of determining usage requires that certain additional steps be taken. A desirable first step is to enhance the utility of shelf labels by including additional information on them. For example, if the label were somewhat larger than standard size, it would be feasible in many establishments to record the quantities added to and taken from shelves right on the label. When used in this form, labels become known as bin cards, an example of which is shown in Table 3.3 as each delivery is received and placed on the shelf, both the date and number of units so placed is entered

Table 3.3 : Bin Card

Item : Pineapple Slices *Desired Ending Inventory : 15*

Date	*In*	*Date*	*Out*	*Date*	*Out*	*Date*	*Out*	*Balance 15*
10/1		10/2	2	10/3	2	10/4	2	9
		10/5	2					55
10/6	48	10/5	2					

on the bin card. As quantities are issued for use, those dates and amounts are recorded as well. There are more spaces provided for items issued that for items received far the obvious reason the purchases are comparatively infrequent, but issues may be daily. A balance column is provided in order that a steward may determine and enter amounts on hand at any desired time, such as when a salesperson called or when the periodic ordering date arrived. At such times, it is quite simple to determine approximate usage by looking on the card for the balance on hand on the date the last order was placed, adding to that figure the number of units placed in shelves when the last order was received, and subtracting the balance currently on hand. The result will be approximate usage in the most recent period, regardless of the length of that period. The assumption is made that this quantity was used productively, although this may not always be the case, and should be considered in determining the amount to order for the next period. When such a system is followed, it is normally wise to compare the balance on the bin card with the number of units of the item actually on the shelves in order to be sure that all items issued have been suitably recorded. If discrepancy exists, the balance shown on the bin card will not be entirely reliable in measuring actual usage during the period, and the missing items, presumably issued, must be added to the derived usage figure to achieve a more accurate figure.

If the amount used on the preceding period were the amount ordered for the coming period, the strong possibility exists that the establishment would end the coming period with no units of that item left on the shelf. Since this might make it impossible to produce certain items on the menu, or might make it necessary to secure some emergency supply in order to carry on to the next delivery date, most restaurants that follow this periodic method establish the amount that should be on hand at the end of any period and that should be sufficient to last until the next delivery is received. Once established, this is known as the desired ending inventory, and is entered on the bin card. Both delivery time and daily usage for that time must be used in determining the desired ending figure. Furthermore, it is advisable to add on to this figure some carefully considered amount as a safety factor, in case of delay in delivery. In many cases this safety factor may also include some amount to be kept on hand in the event that business volume in the coming period rises above normal levels.

It is important for anyone planning to enter this business to realize that none of the amounts mentioned in the preceding paragraphs should be determined and then never again re-evaluated. After all, many changes occur in usage from period to period, and the steward or manager who fails to take changes into account is taking risks needlessly. For example, as the weather and menus change, some foods will be used in greater quantities. If demand for some items increases, usage is likely to increase as well; the converse would also be true. Thus, before ordering, it is normally advisable to compare usage in similar periods in preceding years. If menus and sales volume have changed as well, these, too, must be taken into account.

Perpetual Inventory Method

The perpetual inventory method, while better for control purposes than the periodic, is not as widely used. This is because its successful use requires that specialized personnel maintain rather complete and accurate records and because none but larger establishments can normally justify the maintenance of such personnel. However, because some larger operations, particularly those in chain organizations, do employ these methods, students should be aware of their underlying purposes, and the procedures necessary for their successful implementation.

The primary purposes of the perpetual inventory system are to ensure that quantities purchased are sufficient to meet anticipated need without being excessive and to provide effective control over those items that are being stored for future use.

This method requires the use of perpetual inventory cards, such as that illustrated in Table 3.4. These cards, while similar to the bin card illustrated in Table 3.3, include some additional information and are used rather differently. One very important difference is that the perpetual inventory card is not normally affixed to the shelf on which the covered item is maintained but is typically kept outside the storeroom and maintained by persons who do not work in the storeroom. The amounts of food purchased are recorded on the appropriate cards, and as items are issued for use, those amounts issued are similarly recorded. If the amounts recorded accurately reflect the movement of items into and out of storage, then it is possible at any given time merely to consult the perpetual inventory card to determine how much of an item is in stock at the moment. This system makes it possible to compare balances on the perpetual inventory cards with actual items on shelves to determine if any items are not accounted for.

The additional information, including the name and address of the supplier, as well as the most recent purchase price for the item,

Table 3.4: Perpetual Inventory Card

Item	*Pineapple Slices*	*Cost*	*Rs. 394 per 12 cans case*
Size	#2 ½ can	Par Stock	32
Supplier	ABC Co.	Reorder Point	15
	18 120th st.		
	N.Y.C.		

Date	*Order # in*	*Balance*	*In*	*Out*	*Balance*
10/1	#222-24			2	15
10/2				2	13
10/3				2	11
10/4				2	9
10/5				2	7
10/6			24		31
10/7					
10/8					

facilitate the ordering of additional quantities of the item. Two additional terms used on the card, par stock and reorder point, are also of considerable use in facilitating purchase, and require further discussion.

The reorder point is, quite simply, the number of units to which the supply on hand should decrease before additional orders are placed. Thus, if the reorder point for a given item is twenty-two cans, then no order for that item should be placed until the supply, as shown in the balance column, has reached that number. On order to establish a reorder point for any item, it is necessary to know both normal usage and the time needed to obtain delivery. Furthermore, it is advisable to include in the calculations a certain additional amount to allow for delivery delays and for possible inventory method is the equivalent of the desired ending inventory in the periodic method and may be calculated in the following manner. If normal usage is two cans per day, and it takes five days from date of order to get delivery, then the basic number needed is ten cans. However, because delivery may be delayed, or because usage may increase for unforeseen reasons, or because both of those possibilities may occur at once, it is advisable to increase that amount by approximately 50 per cent, thus establishing a reorder point of fifteen cans. Under the periodic method, the desired ending inventory would similarly be calculated as fifteen cans.

The perpetual inventory card also provides for a par stock figure for each item in stock. While it is generally acknowledged that par stock is a number of units related to usage and the time needed to get delivery, there is no general agreement on an exact definition of the term. Since the term is used in a variety of ways in the industry, the student should be aware of some of its more common uses. In some places, the term par stock is taken to mean a maximum quantity of a given item that should be on hand after the most recent order has been received. In others, it means a normal quantity which should be on hand at all times. Still another possibility is to treat par stock as a range defined by maximum and minimum quantities between which the actual quantities on hand should vary.

For purposes of this discussion, we will take par stock to be the maximum quantity of any item that should be on hand at any given time. That maximum quantity can be determined only after careful weighing of the following considerations:

1. Storage space
2. Limits of inventory valuation prescribed by management
3. Desired frequency of ordering
4. Usage
5. Purveyors' minimum order requirements

Because storage space is limited for all but a few most fortunate operators, it is obviously necessary to calculate the maximum amount of space available for all non-perishable storage and then to allocate wisely the use of that space. For example, with those items normally purchased in comparatively large packages, such as bulk flour and sugar, it may be necessary to restrict space to that required for the storage of only a one week supply.

To the extent that management chooses to restrict the amount of cash invested in inventory, it becomes necessary to restrict the amount of any item that one can maintain on hand. If the cash for meeting payroll and for paying outstanding bills is in comparatively short supply, then management will often choose to reduce the size of inventory and direct rather more frequent ordering of smaller quantities. In some cases, it is possible to accomplish this by restricting only the purchase of the more expensive items in the inventory, without effecting any change in purchase procedures for the less costly commodities.

Obviously, some schedule of desired frequency must be set up by management. In addition, while the foods involved are typically referred to as non-perishable, some are, in fact, rather more perishable than others, and this account.

Determination of par stock should always take into account the relative quantities of an item used, which may change over time. If anticipated consumption of an item is expected to be high in a given period, then the par stock should be higher than at, say another time or season when consumption is rather low.

Because a considerable number of purveyors prefer to items in standard wholesale purchase units, such as cases and fifty-1b. bags, the minimum order requirements of purveyors must be taken into account as well.

Once all of the foregoing have been considered and a par stock has been established for each inventory item and has been entered on the appropriate card, ordering becomes a rather simple and straightforward matter. When the reorder point for any item is reached, the amount to order is determined by subtracting average daily usage times number of days required to get delivery from the par stock. The difference is the proper amount to order, but this figure must be rounded to the nearest standard purchase unit. Thus, in Table 3.4, when an order for twenty-four cans was placed on the first of the month, the amount to order was determined by (1) cans; (2) subtracting that ten cans from the reorder point of fifteen cans to determine that five would be left in stock on delivery date; and (3) subtracting that five from the par stock of thirty-two to determine that the proper order would be twenty-seven cans. However, since this item comes packed twelve cans to the cases totalling twenty-four cans were ordered, upon delivery, the stock is returned to thirty-one units, or approximately to par.

The final determination of routine—whether one of these two procedures or some variation—must be based on the needs of the individual operation, and the policies established by management. The important point to be made is that the purchasing procedure must take into account the need for determining on an ongoing basis the quantities of each commodity that will be adequate for anticipated demand. It must guard against overpurchasing increases the possibilities for overproduction and consequent waste. In the case of non-perishable, over purchasing clearly increases the possibilities for theft; it may increase the need for personnel, and it certainly ties up unwarranted amounts of money in inventory.

The final determination of routine — whether one of these two procedures or some variation — must be based on the needs of the individual operation, and the policies established by management. The important point to be made is that the purchasing procedure must take into account the need for determining on an ongoing basis the quantities of each commodity that will be adequate for anticipated demand. It must guard against overpurchasing — the purchasing of unneeded quantities. In the case of perishables, over purchasing increases the possibilities for spoilage, and for theft; it may increase the need for personnel, and it certainly ties up unwarranted amounts of money in inventory.

Because all of these are the very conditions that control systems are established to guard against, it is obviously important to set up procedures for determining appropriate quantities for ordering.

Once we have established purchase specifications so that we know what quality to buy, and inventory procedures so that we know what quantity to buy, it is time to discuses the question of price. Since it is normally desirable to buy commodities of the appropriate quality in adequate quantities at the lowest possible price, it is desirable to ensure that the steward will purchase foods on the basis of competitive prices from several possible suppliers.

SOURCES OF SUPPLY

The availability of sources of supply will vary considerably from location to location. Major cities, for example, tend to offer a greater number of possibilities, both in terms of different categories of suppliers and number of suppliers in each category. On the other hand, isolated areas offer few possibilities, and it is sometimes true that establishments in remote areas must be content with what they can get. In general, depending on ownership policy, availability of suppliers, and general market conditions, food service operators look to suppliers who fall into the following general categories:

- Wholesalers
- Local producers
- Manufacturers
- Packers
- Local
- Retailers
- Cooperative associations

In most instances, the restaurant operator will deal with several of the sources of supply to obtain the necessary foods. For example, it is possible that a restaurant might turn to a local producer for dairy and bakery products, a packer for canned meats, a wholesaler for fresh meats, a different wholesaler for canned fruits and vegetables, and a local farmer for eggs. In recent years there has been a tend for wholesalers to diversify their product lines in an attempt to better meet the needs of their restaurant customers. In some instances, they are able to supply virtually all of the food-related needs of a restaurant. In general, one will deal with as many as may be necessary to ensure the supply of foods of appropriate quality at the lowest prices.

COMPETITIVE PRICES

In order to be sure that purchases are made at the lowest favourable price, it is necessary for the steward to secure prices from several competing suppliers for each commodity we intends to buy. The procedures differ for perishables and non-perishables.

Perishables

Because prices for perishables often fluctuate daily, it is necessary for the steward to telephone several different suppliers of the same commodity to ascertain current price each time an order is to be placed. Assuming that copies of specifications have previously been sent to each, the steward can be assured that each supplier is quoting on commodities of comparable quality. It will be noted that the steward's market quotation list, shown in Table 3.2, provides four columns for price quotations on each commodity with provision at the top of each column for the name of the supplier. Ideally, the steward will obtain prices from at least three suppliers for each item, and select the lowest price. In reality, other things also should be taken into account, such as different delivery times from supplier to supplier, the manager's possible preference for one dealer over another, the reliability of the dealers in sending foods that adhere to specification, and so forth. Once prices have been obtained, the steward makes it selection of the supplier to be used and calls that dealer to place the order. Normally it is placed with the lowest bidder. As the order is placed the steward circles that particular price quotation next to the item to be supplied. Thus, when all perishables have record of prices, quantities, and suppliers. As we shall see in the next chapter, this list will be valuable for checking purposes when the food is delivered.

Non-perishables

Procedures involved in securing competitive prices for non-perishables are somewhat different. It is usual that the steward will deal with fewer sources of supply in the case of non-perishables. It is often possible to obtain price lists from wholesale supply houses, each of whom may be able to supply most of the groceries the steward intend to order. It is possible to compare prices and make selections at greater leisure than in the case of perishable. Although the steward will normally select the lowest price consistent with quality desired, exceptions are to be noted here as well. For example, if dealer A were offering all but one item at a lower prices than dealer B, and dealer B's price for that one item were only two rupee per can lower, the steward would be likely to place his order for twelve cans with dealer A in spite of the higher price, the difference being only a matter of Rs. 9.60. The expenditure would be more than justified by the simplification of the ordering. In addition, it is possible that dealer B might not accept an order as small as twenty-four cans of a single item because the profit might be more than offset by the cost of making the delivery.

CENTRALIZED PURCHASING

No discussion of purchasing procedures would be complete without some mention of the existence of centralized purchasing system, widely used by chain operations, and occasionally established by small groups of independent operators with similar needs. Under a centralized purchasing system, the requirements of individual units are relayed to a central office, which determines total requirements of all units and then purchases that total, either for delivery to the individual units by the dealer, or for centralized delivery. This last method obviously requires that a whole system for distribution be maintained and operated by the organization doing the centralized purchasing. There are both advantages and disadvantages to these centralized systems, which should be understood by anyone involved in food management.

Advantages

1. Foods and beverages are purchased at a lower price due to volume purchasing.
2. It provides a better opportunity to obtain desired quality because purchaser has a greater choice of markets.
3. Goods can be purchased to the exact specifications of the purchaser.
4. Larger inventories can be maintained assuring a more constant supply to individual units.
5. Greater control over dishonesty of individual unit food purchasers can be maintained.

Disadvantages

1. Unit must accept the standard item in stock and has little freedom to purchase for its own peculiar needs.
2. Units cannot take advantage of local "specials" at reduced prices.
3. Menus usually must be more standardized and limit the freedom of the individual unit manager to change a menu.

Finally, it should be noted that decisions as to whether or not to become involved in centralized purchasing systems are normally made by top management, and not by food controllers. However, there are times when food controllers may be called upon for advice and opinions, and they should understand what is involved in centralized purchasing.

STANDING ORDERS

Although it is desirable for needed quantities to be carefully determined each time orders are placed, stewards commonly make arrangements with certain purveyors for the delivery of goods without specific orders. These arrangements are known as standing orders, and typically take one of two forms.

One arrangement calls for the delivery of specific numbers of certain items each day; for example, twelve loaves of bread. The number would remain constant unless specifically changed by the steward.

The second arrangement usually calls for the replenishing of stock each day up to a certain predetermined number. For instance, the steward might arrange with a dairy supplier to leave sufficient quantities of bulk milk each morning to bring the total supply upto a predetermined figure, such as twenty gallons.

While these arrangements are convenient, they do present a number of possibilities for both waste and excessive cost to develop.

In summary, any system of food control must address itself to the question of purchasing. Controls must be established for purchasing if the food control system is to be effective. Poorly controlled purchasing procedures may lead to reduced sales if the restaurant constantly runs out of food, or excessive costs if the restaurant overpurchases perishables, or purchases perishables of improper quality for intended use. The procedures discussed in this chapter have as their goal the establishment of control over costs, the elimination of excessive costs inherent in over purchasing, which leads to spoilage, waste and increased risk of pilferage. As we have seen, special procedures must be established to control the purchasing of perishable and non-perishable.

PURCHASING SPECIFICATION

Any food service establishment that purchases food in quantity should definitely use written specifications. Specification should be down in writing the standard you want in a product according to the specific use you intend to make of the product.

A specification sheet or card should contain:

1. The name of the product.
2. The use you intend for this product.
3. The grade or quantity you want.
4. The basic unit (gallon, pound, case) on which price are quoted.

5. Any and all specific factors necessary to describe and identify exactly the item you want.

Product	:	Roast-ready Beef Rib
Use	:	Rib Roast
Grade	:	A
Price Unit	:	Rupee
Other	:	# 110 Rib Roast-ready Boneless, Tied

Chart: Purchase Specification Card

Ideally you should have an individual purchase specification sheet or card for each item you purchase. Some specification may be only a phrase or line. Others may be quite detailed. Put all the information on the purchase specification necessary to insure that you will get the product you want.

You do not put the purchase price or the quantities you want on purchase specification sheets. Quantities will vary and prices can change, but you seldom change the specification. You determine the quantity according to how much you need, and it will vary from day- to-day. When you order steaks, for example, quality and detailed specification factors will be the same regardless of how many steaks you want.

There is good information on meat purchasing in The Meat Buyers Guide . This booklet gives you descriptions and photographs of variety of meat items. It is helpful for anyone who writes meat specifications. If you use The Meat Buyers Guide, all you have to do is write the number and title of the item as it is listed and purveyors will know exactly what you want.

Specification Must Be Written

A few years ago, if you had asked employees responsible for purchasing for a food service operation if they used specification, they would probably have said: "Oh, sure. I couldn't do any purchasing without them." But if you had asked them to show you a copy of their specifications, sheets, chances are they would have said: "A copy? I don't have anything in writing. I keep it all in my head." Times have changed. This will not work any more.

No one should rely just on memory when it comes to purchasing for food service operation. The person or person-in-charge of your purchasing should put all specifications in writing. This is essentially for transmitting purchase specifications to other people and departments concerned with purchasing. Written purchase specifications are an important part of overall food control.

There are two main reasons why you should have purchase specifications in writing:

1. The purchaser cannot possibly remember all details.
2. If the purchaser is absent from the establishment, whoever takes the purchaser's place should have specifications in writing so that purchasing can continue exactly according to standards. If purchase specifications exist only in one person's head, that is the only person who can use them.

Specification should be prepared in quintuplet (or more). The copies should be distributed as follows:

1. One copy kept by the purchasing agent.
2. One copy to the manager to keep him or her informed of everything ordered by the purchasing department.
3. One copy to the chief (who should have helped prepare the specifications).
4. One copy to the receiving clerk, who uses it as a receiving guide for standards.
5. One copy to each purveyor who will fill specifications.

If you work with your purveyors, they can usually give you some good suggestions and help you write more effective specifications, which in turn makes it easier for the purveyors to fill your orders faster and more efficiently. It is very important to you to be on excellent terms with your purveyors. Make up good specifications for their sake and yours. When your purveyors, receive, clear, easy-to-understand specification sheets from you, it is much easier for them to follow your instructions and get you what want.

RECEIVING

If great care is taken to establish effective controls for purchasing, but no attention is given to receiving controls, all earlier efforts may be wasted. After all, the ordering of specific quantities and optimum prices constitutes no guarantee that the commodities ordered will actually be delivered. Either by accident or design, purveyors may be quote, or all three. Receiving controls, therefore, have as a primary purpose verifying that quantities, qualities, and prices conform to orders placed.

The Receiving Cleark

In our discussion, we will assume the existence of a receiving clerk who will be assigned by management, the full responsibility for receiving food deliveries and carrying out the control procedures set up by the food controller. In larger operations, particularly those with complete food control systems, this is often the case. In smaller operations, which deem the payroll expense of a receiving clerk unwarranted, food deliveries may by received by any one of several individuals, including the owner, the manager, the chef, or the steward. Although we use the title of receiving clerk here to facilitate discussion, we are aware that others do receive deliveries. The point to be made here does not involve the title of the person doing the receiving, that does not much matter.

The person who is receiving has several duties, including checking quantities delivered and unit prices, which is comparatively easy, and at the some time checking for quality, which is rather more difficult, requiring more knowledge and experience.

In order for the receiving clerk to check deliveries thoroughly, certain supplies and equipment must be available.

1. A permanent copy of all standard purchase specifications.
2. Appropriate equipment, such as platform scale, hanging scale, and hanging racks.
3. Certain paper forms, tags, rubber stamps, and related office supplies, the importance of which will become apparent later in the chapter.

The receiving clerk also must have a thorough understanding of the control procedures themselves in order to carry them out effectively. Effectiveness in complying with the receiving routine must be checked from time-to-time.

Because the receiving procedure does take a certain amount of time to follow, it is helpful for manager to arrange staggered delivery times with purveyors, beginning as early as possible in the day. The staggering of delivering time gives the receiving clerk a better opportunity to comply with routines. The early delivery times maximize preparation time available for those foods to be used on the day delivered.

The Invoice

All food deliveries should be accompanied by an invoice should accompany all food deliveries, which is another word for a bill. A typical invoice form is illustrated in Table 3.5. This is usually presented to the receiving clerk in duplicate by the person making the delivery, who will expect the receiving clerk to sign and return

Table 3.5 : Invoice

Market Price Meat Co.
300 Market ST.
New Delhi

Date
June 11

To

The Graduates Restaurant

____
____
____

Quantity	*Unit*	*Description*	*Unit Price*	*Amount*
30	Kg	Strip Steak	818	2,940
10	Kg	Breast of Veal	104	1,040
				3,980

the second copy, thus acknowledging to the purveyor that the establishment has received the commodities listed. The original is, in effect, a bill that must be paid and must be routed to the bookkeeper or other individual when has responsibility for paying bills. This rounding procedure will be dealt with later in this chapter.

Invoices not listing prices should be discouraged. Prices should be checked on receipt of the goods. Otherwise, an opportunity exists for the purveyor to bill at the wrong prices by accident or by design.

The Invoice Stamp

It is generally good practice to provide the receiving clerk with a rubber stamp to be used on all invoice. This invoice stamp, a suggested form for which is illustrated in Table 3.6 used for number of reasons.

1. It provides verification of the date on which food has been received.
2. It provides for the signature of the clerk who has received the food and vouchers for the accuracy of quantities, qualities, and prices.
3. It provides for the steward's signature, thus acknowledging that he/she is aware that the food has been delivered.
4. It provides for the food controller's verification of the arithmetical accuracy of the bill.
5. It provides for signatory approval of the bill for payment by an authorized individual before a cheque is drawn.

Table 3.6

Invoice Stamp	*Date*
Received________________________	
Steward________________________	
Price and________________________	
Extensions Verified______________	
OK for Payment_________________	

Receiving Procedure

Although exact procedures and techniques for verifying deliveries will vary from establishment to establishment, procedures for receiving control should have the following characteristics:

1. Quantities delivered should be the same as those listed on the invoice and should be the same as quantities listed on the Steward's Market Quotation List or Steward's Staple List.
2. Quality of the food delivered should conform to the standard purchase specifications for each item delivered.

3. Prices on the invoice should be the same as those circled on the Steward's Market Quotations List and the Steward's Staple List (Refer Table 3.2).

Any exceptions to have these three rules should be noted at once and appropriate steps taken. Sometimes this will involve returning inferior foods with the delivery truck. At other times it may involve changing the quantities listed on both copies of the involved and having the delivery man initial both copies. For purposes of this discussion, it is important only to note that each variation should be attended to at the time and place of delivery.

Once deliveries have been checked in the light of the foregoing, it is recommended that foods be moved to appropriate storage areas as quickly as possible, with those that will most quickly deteriorate at room temperature being put away first. The spillage and theft that may readily occur between receiving and storing foods can be major cause of excessive cost. Therefore, the food controller should check from time-to-time to be sure that foods are being moved to storage area at optimum times.

The Meat Tag

In the majority of restaurants, meats, poultry, fish and shell fish constitute the most costly group of goods on the menu. Because in this comparatively high cost, establishments with complete food control systems set up special controls for these items. The receiving clerk tags each package or piece received before it is placed in storage. In general, the rule followed is that items typically purchased to be sent to the kitchen for immediate use are not tagged; those that are typically held in inventory for one or more days before use are tagged.

A meat tag (Table 3.7) is usually printed on heavy card stock for durability and is perforated for convenient division into two parts. The tags are purchased from any number of stationers catering to the industry, and are numbered sequentially, with the number appearing on both parts. They are used in numbered order. All information is filled in by the receiving clerk, except the date of issue, which cannot be filled until the meat is issued to the kitchen for preparation. The receiving clerk fills out the tag, detaches the smaller part, and sends it to the food controller. The receiving clerk of meat, or *(b)* sending it to the steward. Because there are advantage and disadvantages to both approaches, there is no general agreement as to which is preferable, and decision as to which procedure to follow are often made by the food controller on the basis of practicability in a particular establishment.

Table 3.7 : Meat Tag

No. 20624		*No. 20624*	
Date Record 6/12		*Date Record 6/12*	
Item	: Strip steak	Grade	: Item: Strip steak
Weight	: 15 kg @ Rs. 98	Weight	: 15 kg @ Rs. 98
Dealer	: XYZ	Dealer	: XYZ
Extension	: Rs. 1470	Extension	: Rs. 1470
Date issued	________________	Date issued	________________

ABC and Co. N.D. Stock form : 9247

Receiving Clerk's Daily Report

Larger operation with complete food control systems will require that foods typically purchased for immediate use be charged to cost as received. The balance will be included in inventory and charged to cost as issued. In food control, all foods that are charged to cost as issued are called Stores, and all foods charged to cost as received are called Directs. An understanding of the difference between the two, as well as working definitions for both, will be increasingly important in future chapters.

Directs are those foods that, due to their extremely perishable nature, are purchased on a more or less daily basis for immediate use. The quality of these foods tends to demise quickly, and if they are not used very soon after the time of purchase, they will become unusable for the purposes for which they were intended. Foods that typically fall into this category are fresh fruits and vegetables, fresh baked goods, and most dairy products. Ideally, the quantities of each purchased on any given day should be sufficient for that day alone. Therefore, since they should be purchased for immediate use, they will be included in food cost figures on the day of delivery. The working definitions will be that Directs are those items that will be charged to food cost as received.

Stores, on the other hand, are those foods that, while ultimately perishable, will not significantly diminish in quality if they are not used immediately. They can be half in storage and carried in inventory for a day or so, or in some instance for considerable periods. Meats, for example can be maintained for reasonable periods of time if stored under proper condition. So too, can those grocery items that are purchased in cans, bottles and boxes. These are all items that are purchased based on anticipated needs, not necessarily immediate, and that will be kept in inventory until they are needed. When the need arises, they are released from inventory, and issued to the kitchen. Since we have seen that cost occurs when food is used. These items will be included in the food cost figures when they are issued for use. The Working definition will be that stores are those items that will be charged to food cost as issued.

It is possible to go into long, elaborate discussion—even arguments—about the category into which any given item should be placed. Unquestionable, there are differences from restaurant to restaurant. There are some place for example, where fresh fish is included with Directs, because it is purchased for use on the day of delivery. Other places may buy whole fish, which are cleaned and otherwise prepared for use the following day, and thus include fresh fish with Stores. Such discussion serves no useful purpose within this context. It is sufficient to say that the food controller in each establishment must make those decision individually on the basis of use and then must consistently include each item in the reselected category.

When food is received, most larger establishments require the receiving clerk to complete a form listing all items received on a given day, fully divided by purveyor, and listed in the order received. One form is called the Receiving Clerk's Daily Report items received, the form provides for the division of costs into three categories: Directs, Stores and Sundries, which are non-food items such as paper supplies and cleaning supplies, the cost of which is not a part of the cost of food.

By the time all deliveries of the day are in, preferably as early in the day as possible, the receiving clerk will have stamped and signed all invoices and entered each on the receiving sheet. The sheet with the invoices attached should then be sent to the steward him to sign the invoices, and then routed to the food controller who will check the arithmetical accuracy of each invoice. When the checking has been completed, the controller sends the receiving sheet and the invoices on the accounting department, where the figure will be entered in the purchase journal.

However, while the food controller still has the receiving sheet, one very important total figure is recorded, the total cost of Directs. Because Directs are charged to the food cost as received, the food controller will need this figure in order to compute the daily cost of food sold. When we reach the chapter concerned with computing daily food cost, it will be important to keep in mind that the daily cost Directs comes from the receiving sheet:

- In some establishment the food controller will not be concerned with arithmetical accuracy, because the accounting department will verify all bills prior to payment.

In smaller establishment that do not have complete food control systems, many or all of the foregoing steps will be skipped, and the invoices are merely given to a bookkeeper by the person receiving the deliveries. However, this will preclude a number of important possibilities for effective control. For example, such simplification will make it virtually impossible to compute daily food cost. We will see that operating without knowledge of the daily food cost may be somewhat risky, and possible a great disadvantage.

We have seen then, that the purpose of establishing control procedures for receiving is to ensure that the establishment is receiving food in the quantities ordered, in the qualities specified, and at the prices quoted. These steps are basic, and should be common to all food service operation, regardless of size. More complete system control, operated as they are with greater number of personnel and more equipment and procedures for checking, obviously offer greater measures of protection, but do so at greater cost. However, even the small owner-operated restaurant should take the basic steps to guard against excessive costs that may develop from the receiving of improper quantities or qualities, or the charging of improper prices.

Control of Storing, Issuing and Transfers

Efforts to control costs by instituting the standards and procedures discussed in previous chapters can be largely wasted if excessive

Table : 3.8

Receiving Clerk's Daily Report				*No. 1: Date: June 2000*			
					Purchase Journal Distribution		
Qty.	*Unit Description*	*Unit Price*	*Amount*	*Total Amount*	*Food Direct*	*Food Store*	*Sundries*
30	Market Price Meats	98.00	2,940.00				
30	lbs Strip Steak	104.00	1,040.00				
10	lbs						
				3,980.00		3,980.00	
	Ottman Meat						
15	lbs Pork Tenderloin	44.00		660.00		660.00	
	Jones Produce Fruit						
1	Crate Lettuce	500.00	5.000				
1	Bag Onion	270.00	270.00				
1	Box Gapfruit	380.00	380.00				
1	Crate Peaches	480.00	480.00	1,630.00	1,630.00		
				6,270.00	1,630.00	4,640.00	

costs develop between the time goods are received and the time they are used in production. Although not responsible for the actual storing and issuing of foods or for the transfer of any items to any other part of the unit or to another unit (in the case of chain operation), the food controller does have the responsibility to ensure that standards and procedures are establish that will minimize the possibilities for each unwarranted costs.

Before discussing specific causes and remedies for excessive cost to develop while foods are in storage, it is important to emphasize that the receiving area should never be considered a storage area. Foods, especially perishable foods, should be moved to appropriate storage area speedily and in appropriate order. The shelf life of most perishable items is considerably reduced if they are allowed to remain on a warm receiving platform for any length of time, and of course the possibilities for theft are increased.

STORING CONTROL

The principal causes of excessive costs while food is in storage are spoilage, pilferage (the industry term for theft), and wasted labour. The problems that lead to these causes should be understood by the food controller and should serve as guides in the establishing of appropriate standards and procedures. In general these problems may be divided into four categories, each of which will be discussed in this chapter:

1. Condition of facilities and equipment
2. Arrangement of foods
3. Location of facilities
4. Security

Conditions of Facilities and Equipment

The factors involved in maintaining proper internal conditions include temperature, storage containers, shelving and containers, of these may lead to spoilage and waste.

Temperature

One of the key factors in the storing of foods, particularly perishables, is temperature. Food life can be maximized by storing it at the correct temperature and humidity. The food controller should check the temperature gauges on the refrigerated storage facilities occasionally to see that the appropriate temperatures are being maintained. The temperature listed below are generally accepted to be optimum for the storage of the foods indicated.

While these temperatures are acceptable in very general terms, there are numerous exceptions. Banana and potatoes for example, should be stored at higher temperatures. For specific temperature for storage of any particular commodity.

- Fresh Meats: 34 to 36 degree F.
- Fresh Prduce: 34 to 36 degrees F.
- Fresh Dairy Products: 34 to 36 degrees F.
- Fresh Fish: 30 to 34 degrees F.
- Frozen Foods: -10 to 0 degrees F.

If temperatures are permitted to rise above these levels, shelf life is shortened, and the risk of food spoilage is increased for perishables.

Temperature also can be important in keeping nonperishable. Storage facilities for staple commodities should usually be room temperature approximately 70 to 72 degree F.

Storage Containers

In addition to maintaining foods at proper temperatures, care must be given to storing them in appropriate containers. In the case of staples most, but not all, purchased in airtight containers. Some, however, are purchased in unsealed containers, often paper bags, boxes, and sacks, which are susceptible to attack by insects and vermin. Whenever practicable, such commodities should be transferred to tight, insect proof, containers.

Shelving

For perishable foods, shelving should be slatted to permit maximum circulation of air in refrigerated facilities. For non-perishables, solid steel shelving is usually preferred. At no time should anything be stored on the floor.

Cleanliness

Condition of cleanliness should be endorsed in all storage facilities at all times, in refrigerated facilities, this will prevent the accumulation of small amount of spoiling food, which will give off odours and may after other foods.

Arrangment of Foods

The factors involved in maintaining appropriate internal arrangement include rotating stock, fixing definite location for each item, and keeping the most-used items readily available.

Fixing Definite Location

All items should always be found in the same location, and attention should be given to ensuring that new deliveries of the items are stored in the same location. Separate frailties for storage of different classes of foods should be stored with fish, cheese, or other foods that five off odours, because their shells are quite porous and will absorb flavours from other foods. Fish should always be stored in separate facilities.

Rotation Stock

It is very important the food controller take steps to ensure that older quantities of any item are used before any new deliveries. This is known as the First In First Out Method of stock rotation, commonly called FIFO in the industry.

Availability According to Use

It is usually helpful to arrange storage facilities so that most frequently used items are maintained closest to the entrance. Although it has no effect on spoilage and theft, it does tend to reduce the time required to move need foods form storage to production, and thus tends to reduce excessive labour costs.

Location of Storage Facilities

Whenever possible, the storage facilities for both perishable and non-perishable commodities should be located between receiving areas and preparation areas, and preferably close to both. A facility will have the effect of:

1. Speeding the process of storage and issue
2. Maximizing security
3. Reducing labour requirements

Security

Food should never be stored in manner that permits pilferage. This is another reason for moving foods from the receiving area to storage as quickly as possible. Once it is stored, attention must be given to maintaining appropriate security at all times. In the case of a storeroom for staple commodities, the room should never be left unattended. Employees should not be permitted to remove items at their will. It is typically for a storeroom to be open at specified times for specified periods well-known to the staff, and otherwise closed to enable the attendant to perform other duties.

It is sometimes advisable to establish separate control procedures for steaks, liquor, and other high-cost items.

Dating and Pricing

It is desirable to date items as they are put away on shelves, so that the storeroom clerk can be certain of the age of each item and make provision for use before spoilage sets in. Of particular concern are those items that are infrequently used. The storeroom clerk should visually check the stock frequently to ascertain which items are beginning to get old and then inform the chef so that items can be put on the menu before they spoil.

In addition, all items should be priced as goods are put away, and the cost of each container should be clearly marked on it. Following that procedure will greatly facilitate issuing because the storeroom clerk will be able to price requisition with little difficulty. If items are not priced as goods are put away, the storeroom clerk will waste considerable time looking up prices when goods are sent to the kitchen.

ISSUING CONTROL

Directs were defined as those foods charged to cost as purchased and stores as those carried in inventory and charged to cost as issued. From the point of view of a food controller, that distinction becomes particularly important in a discussion of issuing procedures. Its importance will become increasingly apparent as we approach the disunion of the calculation of food cost.

Directs

Directs are charged to the food cost as purchased on the assumption that the quantities of these perishable items are for immediate use. In effect, these foods move directly from the receiving area to the kitchen, where they are used immediately to meet the production needs of the day. Although this is not strictly true in every instance, it does simplify the maintenance of cost records. In order to determine the cost of Directs for any given day, the food controller merely looks at the receiving sheet for the day and takes the total figure in the direct column. If these perishables are being purchased in reasonable quantities, the cost of Directs may be artificially high on one particular day, when leftover quantities are used up but are not reflected in cost for that day.

For all practical purposes, then Directs are "issued" to the kitchen the moment they are received, and no further record is kept of particular quantities of particular items. If there is waste or spoilage, or even pilferage, it will be reflected in an excessively high food cost figure, which will beat investigation.

The alternative to considering Directs issued ads purchased would be to follow as issuing procedure such as that described below for Stores. It will be readily apparent that such a procedure for Directs would probably involve greater amounts of record keeping than should seems warranted to most establishment.

Stores

The food category known as stores was previously described as one consisting of *(a)* staples and *(b)* tagged items. When purchased, these foods are considered part of inventory until issued for use and are not included in cost figures until they are issued. Therefore, it follows that records must be kept of uses in order to determine the cost of Stores. For control purposes, some system must be established to ensure that no Stores are issued unless the kitchen resumed; submit lists of the item and quantities needed.

The Requisition

A requisition, illustrated in Table 3.9 is a form prepared by a member of the kitchen shaft listing the items and quantities needed from stores. Each requisition should be received by the chef, who should check to see that each item appearing is genuinely required in the amount listed. The requisition is then approved and signed by the chef. It is next given to the storekeeper, who fills the order. Whenever practical, it is advisable to require that these requistions be submitted in advance to enable the storekeeper to prepare the order without haste. In some places, it has been found quite practical to insist on requisitions being submitted the day before food is needed. This has the desirable effect of forcing kitchen personnel to anticipate needs and plan for the following day's production.

It is also desirable, in many instances, to set define times for the issuing of food by the storekeeper, who, after all, has a number of other duties to perform, including keeping the storerooms and refrigerators clean, maintaining stocks of samples on shelves, rotating stock, and doing considerable paper work. Some operations have achieved good results by restricting the times for issuing food two hours in the morning and two in the afternoon. Naturally, such decision must be left to management in any particular operation.

Table 3.9 : Requisition

	Supply Main-kitchen Department	*Date*
Quantity	*Description*	*Cost*
6	#10 Cans Green Peas	
50	Lbs Sugar	
40	Lbs Ground Beef	
6	Lions Pork	
	Charge to: ....Dept.	
	Chef	

The Pricing Requistion

After stores have been issued from the appropriate stockroom, refrigerator, or freezer, it is the responsibility of the storekeeper to list on each requisition the cost of listed items, and to determine the total rupees value of the foods issued. This information is necessary for a daily determination of food costs.

Meat and Tagged Items

As meat are issued, the tag is detached from each price and the rupees value recorded on the requisition. If one listing requires the issuing of several pieces of meat, the tag are attached to the requisitions.

Staples

The unit cost of each listed item must be entered and multiplied by the number of units issued in each case. This is called extending the requisition. The unit cost will come from one of the following depending on the system in use:

1. The unit cost of each item in market on each container as it is stored, making of units issued in each case. This most recent purchase price is always entered as prices change.
2. A perpetual inventory card for each item has indicated on it the most recent purchase price.
3. The storekeeper keeps a index card for each item and usually has the purchase price of each in from constant use.

While it is generally agreed that the first method is preferred, it unquestionably involves considerable labour and consequently is costly to maintain. Therefore, while preferred, it is not the method in general use. More often than not, price come from the storekeeper's head. Although this system needs least time and labour many operations have found the resulting inaccuracies have on significant effect over the long run.

Once the values of tagged items have been entered and the unit costs of staples entered and expended, each requisition is totalled. At the end of the day, with meat ages attached, all requisitions are sent to the food controller.

It should be pointed out that on the following morning the food controller will have figure available for the principal components of a daily food cost:

1. Cost of Directs from the receiving sheet.
2. Cost of stores from the requisition with meat tags attached.

Food and Beverage Transfers

In our discussion thus far we have assumed that a restaurant purchases, receives, stores and issues food for use in which all production is accomplished. By doing some we have ignored, quite purposely, the existence of a number of possible complication, which it will be useful to consider at this point. For example, even in smaller restaurant, food production in the kitchen may require the use of certain beverage items, such as wines and liquors, not purchased specifically for kitchen use conversely, in many establishments some food items are purchased in certain knowledge that they will be used at the bar for drink production. Whole oranges and lemons, as well as heavy cream, are good examples of this possibility. In addition, in some of larger hotel and motel operations, more than one kitchen may be in operation and it may be necessary or desirable from time-to-time or even regularly to transfer food from one to another. Transfers may occur in chain operation, where one unit may produce such items as baked goods for other units, or where one unit in the organization, running short of needed items, may be encouraged to secure them from another unit.

Since one of the goals in food control is to determine food cost as accurately as possible, and to match food cost with food sales, it is necessary in many which instances to maintain records of the cost of the food transferred. When the amounts involved are relatively insignificant, and have little appreciable effect on cost and on the cost to sales ratio, they may be, and usually are, disregarded. But when the amounts become somewhat larger and have rather more significant effect, records of some type must be developed.

Intraunit Transfers

Food and beverage transfer the bar and the kitchen frequently occur in operations of all sizes. Many kitchens use such beverage items as wine, cordials, brandy, and even all for the production of sauces, parfaits, certain basked items and rarebits. Occasionally, these items are purchased by the food department for use in the kitchen, kept in a storeroom until needed, and then issued on requisitions directly to the kitchen. In such cases additional records are not required: the quantities and values listed on the requisition are sufficient to permit accurate calculations of cost.

However, in most instances when these beverage items are needed in the kitchen, appropriate amounts are secured from the bar. After all, if sufficient supplies are already being maintained that at bar. It makes little sense to maintain additional quantities for species use in food production.

The same may be said of certain food items in the Direct category used by bartender in drink production: if supplies of oranges, lemons, limes heavy cream, and eggs are already available in the kitchen, it makes little sense in most operations of purchase specific supplies of these items for exculsive use at the bar. It is far simpler merely to secure the needed items from the kitchen. When it is far simpler desirable to achieve a high degree of accuracy in determining costs to match with sales, records of those transfer between the food the beverage departments must be memo, illustrated in Table 3.10. As transfers are made, items and amounts are recorded on such memos by authorized individuals, when these memos have been completed, they may be sent to the food controller, who may use them to adjust food cost figure to achieve greater accuracy, and then routed to an accounting office, where the appropriate entries may be made in the financial records.

Kitchen to Kitchen

In some hotel and motel operations with more than one kitchen and dining room in operation, it is common practice to determine food costs for each separately and to match the costs for each operating unit with the sales generated by that unit. Where some food items are transferred from one kitchen to another, higher degrees of accuracy in determining food costs may be acthieved by keeping records of items and amount so transferred. In cases where, for example, one unit closes earlier than another, and cooked foods may be conveniently transferred from a closing unit to one that will remain open until a later hour, it would be possible to achieve a higher degree of accuracy in determining costs for each unit by crediting cost for the early closing unit for the value of the items transferred and by adding the same amount to the cost for the later closing unit.

Table 3.10 : Food/Beverage Transfer Memo

From : Bar | Date:
To : Mainkitchen

Quantity	*Description*	*Unit Price*	*Amount*
1	Qt ....Sherry	Rs. 75.60	Rs. 75.60
	Bottle Red wine for Cooking	Rs. 55.60	Rs. 55.60

Sent By: | Rs. 131.20
Received

Even in cases where items are not transferred as above but are merely returned to a central kitchen or commissary for reissue to the same or to other units on succeeding forms makes possible more accurate determination of food costs, and consequently or cost-to-sales ratios for operating periods.

Inter-Unit Transfers

The two examples that follow illustrate the problems of inter-unit transfers, and effect of such transfers on food costs.

There are a number of instances of small chains that produce some items, baked goods, for example, in only one unit, and then distribute those items to other units in the chain. If the ingredients for the baked goods come from the regular supplies of the unit in which the items are produced, then some record must be made of the cost of the ingredients used. Failure to do so would result in the food cost of the producing unit being overstated by the value of the ingredients used, and the food costs of the receiving units being understated by the value of the foods they receive, in addition, if the matching principle is to be followed, and if food sales are reported separately for each unit, then food cost figures which do not include the cost of all those foods sold, including the baked goods from another unit, cannot be said to be truly matched with sales. Under such conditions, if one of the goals of management is to match costs and sales with a reasonably high degree of accuracy, it is necessary to use the transfer memo or some similar form to record the value of ingredients used in the production of finished produced for transfer to other units.

With such records availed, it is possible to credit cost of the producing unit. Appropriately increasing the food cost figures of the receiving units may pose more of a problem. If each unit receives as equal share of the goods produced, then one could simply divide the cost of the goods produced and credited to the producing unit by the number of units to which items had been transferred, and increase the food cost of each by one equal share. However, if total produced for distribution to the various units is not divided among them in equal shares, then some more equitable means for apportioning cost must be found. One possible means of dealing with this problem is by recording the values of transferred items at standard costs.

Another problem involving the value of foods transferred from one unit to another may be found in those chain organizations that permit or encourage unit managers to use foods from other units when their own supplies run low and when additional purchases are precluded by time. When units are comparatively close to one another and offer identical menus, occasions may arise when one of the units nearly exhaust the supply of some important item and does not discover this shortage until some time in the day when it is clearly too late to purchase an additional amount. In some organizations, items are borrowed and returned within a day or so as a matter of course, and no complications arise as long as all borrowed items are appropriately returned. However, not all cases are quite so simple, as, for example, when a perishable item borrowed by one unit does not appear on the menu again for some considerable period of time. Rather than maintain records over long periods in order to ensure the return of borrowed items, it is often simpler to record such transfers of foods on transfer memos, and to use the information so recorded to increase the cost of the unit that has borrowed, and correspondingly to decrease the cost of the supplying unit.

An interesting problem that may arise in connection with this procedure is the extent to which it influence some managers purposely to maintain short supplies of some high cost and perishable items. If the organization permits one to secure needed supplies from other units at the same prices one would pay in the market, some managers will be encouraged to reduce the possibilities for excessive costs due to spoilage and pilferage in their units simply by maintaining adequate supplies. Under such conditions, it might be desirable to establishment, a price for transfer purposes somewhat higher than the current market price in order to discharge managers from taking advantage.

It is quite probable that there are in this industry a reasonably large number of transfers of the various types discussed above, but it is equally probably that a large number of these involle comparatively small amounts of food of relatively insignificant value. Consequently, because the amounts involved are usually negligible in most places, records are often not used. However, if and when the amounts become significant, provision must be made for maintaining adequate records to ensure that good cost figures include the cost of beverage used in food preparation, and exclude the cost of food items sent to the bar for beverage preparation, and that food cost figures for one unit of a larger organization include the cost of food items sold in that unit. In every case, to the extent the feasible, the cost of items sold in department division, per unit should include the cost of all items reflected in sales figures.

Monthly Inventory/Stock Taking of Food

In most business establishments, including food and beverage operations, one universally accepted practice is the taking of a physical inventory. It done at the close of an accounting period, typically after the close of business on the last day of a calendar month. In our discussion here we will be concerned only with those dealing in food and beverage item purchased primarily for the purpose of making and selling food and beverage products.

The process of taking a physical inventory requires that one physically count the actual number of units on hand of each item in stock, and record the number of units in the appropriate place in an inventory book, such as that illustrated in Table 3.11 in some other place. It is normally considered good practice to list the items in stock in a book specially for that purpose, and to list them in the same order in which they are maintained in stock, rather than in some other order as such alphabetically. This facilitates a producer that can be long and tedious, depending on the number of commodities in the inventory.

To take the physical inventory in a storeroom, for example, it is common for two people to undertake the job, one to count the unit or shelves, and other to record the amount in the inventory book. If the storeroom is arranged as suggested above, it is possible for the two to being in one logical spot in the storeroom and to work their way through it in order, finding items on shelves in the same order in which they are listed in the inventory book.

Once the quantities are determined for each item, total values also can be calculated for each. In order to do this, it is necessary to record the unit cost for each commodities, which is then multiplied by the number of units of each in the physical inventory. Once the total value of each commodity has been determined, these total can be added together to determine the total rupee value of the inventory.

This rupee figure is known as the closing inventory valuation for the next period.

One of the principal difficulties with the above procedure is determining unit costs or values for each item, since all purchases are not made at the same price. It is not uncommon for the price of any one item in the inventory to change several times during the course of month. The determination of what value to assign to units remaining in inventory at the end of month raise the question of which, if any, of the various prices should be assigned to the unit item for purposes of inventory valuation.

There are at least five possible ways of assigning values to units of commodities in inventory, each of which will be illustrated below. Because each provides a different answer to the question of inventory value at the end of any given period, it is advisable for the student to become familiar with these approaches, any one of which might be selected by management as appropriate for use in a particular establishment, give a particular set of circumstances.

Table 3.11: Store Room Inventory

Month of	*September*							
Articles	*Qt.*	*Price*	*Am.*	*Qt.*	*Price*	*Am.*	*Qt.*	*Price*
Brought forward								
Tomato Paste # 2 ½ cans	16	960	153.60					
Tomato Paste # 10 cans	6	59.60	357.60					
Tomato Puree # 10 cans	18	51.60	412.80					

Because it would be unwieldy and possibly confusing to illustrate each of the five by attempting to treat a complete set of inventory figures, we will restrict ourselves to only one item in the stores inventory of a particular restaurant, #10 cans of fruit cocktail. Records from the restaurant for a certain month reveal the following:

Opening inventory on the 1st of the month	:	10 cans @ Rs.	94	=	Rs. 940
Purchased on the 7th of the month	:	24 ″ ″	100	=	2400
Purchased on the 15th of the month	:	24 ″ ″	104	=	2496
Purchased on the 26th of the month	:	12 ″ ″	92	=	1104

A physical inventory on the 31st of the month showed that twenty cans remained in stock. From this we may deduce that fifty cans were consumed in the course of the month in this manner:

	Opening inventory 10 cans	
+	Purchased during the month	60 cans
=	Total available for use	70 cans
–	Closing inventory (Number of units still available)	20 cans
=	Amount consumed (number of units no longer available)	50 cans

Because both the value of the opening inventory (Rs. 940) and the purchases of this item (Rs. 6,000) are known, it is also possible to add both values together to determine the value of the total number of units available, or Rs. 6,940. It should be obvious that it is possible to determine the value of the amount consumed only if one can somehow determine the value of the number of units in the closing inventory and then subtract it from the value of the total available. the following are five accepted ways of assigning these unit values.

Actual Purchase Price

Perhaps the most reasonable approach would be to value the remaining items—those in the closing inventory—at actual purchase price. However this can be done only if the units are marked with those prices. If the cans are marked with actual purchase prices, totalling their value is obviously a simple clerical job requiring no more complex procedure than addition. Hence, it is possible to determine the value of the 20 cans as:

4 @ Rs. 94	=	376
12 @ Rs. 92	=	1104
4 @ Rs. 104	=	416
20	=	1896

Latest Purchase Prices

If actual purchase prices are not marked on the cans, an alternative procedure is to assume that stock has been properly rotated during the period and that the units remaining on the shelf are in fact those most recently purchased. In many cases, these are not valid assumptions, but we will make them for purpose of discussion.

In order to establish a value for the closing inventory under this method, it would be necessary to know that the latest purchase on the twenty-sixth of the month was for twelve cans and that the next previous purchase on the fifteenth was for twenty-four cans. With that information available, it is possible to determine the value of the twenty cans as:

12 @ Rs. 92	=	Rs. 1,104
8 @ Rs. 104	=	832
Total = 20	=	1,936

If cans were not marked, an alternative procedure would be necessary.

Most Recent Purchase Price

In the absence of appropriate records, when number of units received on particular dates are not known, a common practice is to use the most recent purchase price in valuing the closing inventory. One justification for this approach is that if it were necessary to replace the remaining cans, the cost of replacement at the present moment would be likely to be the latest price at which the items were purchased. If this method were followed, as it frequently is in the food and beverage business, the value of the closing inventory of this item would be:

20 @ Rs. 92 = Rs. 1,840

However, if there were no particular assurances that the stock on the shelves had been properly rotated during the month, this would not be the safest possible course, since it rests largely on the assumption of rotation.

Weighted Average Purchase Prices

Where no certainty exists that stock had been rotated, and where large quantities of goods are involved, it would be possible to determine a weighted average purchase price by multiplying the number of units in the opening inventory and in each purchase by their individual purchase prices, adding these values to determine a total value for all units together, and then dividing by the number of units involved. By following this procedure, the weighted average value of one unit could be determined by dividing seventy units into their Rs. 6,940 total value, which yields Rs. 99.20, therefore, the value of the closing inventory would be:

20 @ Rs. 99.20 = Rs. 1,984

It should be apparent that, while this procedure makes logical sense on paper, in fact it is rather cumbersome and far too time-consuming to be used in most food and beverage operations.

Earliest Purchase Prices

In certain specialized circumstances, particularly in periods of high inflation, and when management chooses to minimize profits on financial statements in order to decrease income taxes, it is possible to maximize cost by minimizing the value of closing inventory. If management directs that costs are to be kept at a relatively higher level in order to minimize profits, this can be achieved in times of rising prices by valuing the units remaining in inventory at the close of a period at the earliest purchase price. By following this procedure with the current example, the value of the twenty cans would be:

10 @	Rs. 94	=	940
10 @	Rs. 100	=	1,000
20	Total	=	1,940

It should be carefully borne in mind that a food controller does not normally determine the method to be used in valuing inventories. Although he or she may contribute to discussion of the question, the decision would probably lie with the firm's accountant. Additionally, once the decision is made, it cannot be changed capriciously: various accounting conventions and Internal Revenue Service regulations preclude simple change.

Comparison of Methods

If the prices of goods purchased were fixed, the selection of method for valuing a closing inventory would be of no importance; all methods would yield the same figure. However, in a period of fluctuating prices—which, after all, describes most period in our business—the selection of one method over another may bring a significantly different result. A comparison of the values of the twenty cans in closing inventory described above illustrate this point:

Value based on actual purchase price	:	1896
Value based on most recent purchase price	:	1840
Value based on weight average	:	1984
Value based on earliest purchase price	:	1940

Using the lowest established value, Rs. 1840, as a base, there is a difference between the highest value and the lowest value in this particular case of 7.8 per cent and while the rupee differences for this one example do not appear to be particularly great, there would be a significant difference in rupees if one were dealing with an entire inventory.

Monthly Food Cost Determination

With the information available from our discussion in this and previous chapters, it is now possible to calculate the cost, cost-to-sales ratio, or actual cost percentage of operation for any establishment, regardless of the size and the nature and complexity of the control procedures in effect.

In relatively small operations, where numbers of personnel are few (and control personnel are probably nonexistent), it is possible to perform the food cost calculation once each month, typically at the end of the month, provided some basic bookkeeping records are available indicating purchase and sales and provided some kind of inventory figure is determined each month. The accuracy of the calculation will vary considerably with the extent and accuracy of the bookkeeping records, but the calculation is within the realm of possibility.

In larger operations that employ some or many of the control procedure discussed in previous chapters, which thus have information recorded and available on a daily basis, the cost percentage can be calculated both daily and cumulatively for all the days in any given period.

The techniques for daily and cumulative costing will be discussed in further chapter. In this chapter, we will restrict our discussion to monthly cost determination for those food service establishments that have neither the records nor the desire to calculate daily cost.

By the following formula discussed in a previous chapter:

Cost / Sales = Cost%

It is possible to determine the food cost percentage for any period, provided one has some basic records giving figures to use for doing the calculations. We will assume, for the moment, that every operation maintains some basic records of daily sales in order to be able to file the tax returns required by law. If daily sales records are maintained, then the total sales for any month can be determined by adding together the daily sales for the period. Determining cost is a bit more difficult, but it can be done if records are kept of all food purchased, and if an inventory is taken monthly. With these records available, the cost of food can be determined by following the basic formula:

Opening inventory	(food on hand the first day of the month)
+ Purchases	(both directs and stores)
Total available	(total value of all food available for sale)
- Closing inventory	(food on hand the last day of the month)
= Cost of food	(includes waste and pilferage)

This procedure provides a method for determining the cost of food, which can be compared to sales for the period, in order to arrive at a cost-to-sales ratio, or a cost percentage. As an example, assume that the records of a certain restaurant reveal the following figures for the month of march:

Opening inventory	Rs. 80,000	
Food purchases	Rs. 2,40,000	(Direct and Store)
Closing inventory	Rs. 1,20,000	
Food sales	Rs. 6,00,000	

Given these figures, it is possible to determine the cost of food by the formula above:

Opening inventory	Rs. 80,000
+ Purchase	Rs. 2,40,000
Total available	Rs. 3,20,000
–Closing inventory	Rs. 1,20,000
= Cost of food	Rs. 2,00,000

Once the cost of food is known, the cost percentage can be calculated by using the formula cited above. Therefore,

$$\frac{2,00,000}{6,00,000} = 3.33\%$$

This is the same as saying that the cost of food has been Rs. 13.32 per Rs. 40 of sales.

However, it must be emphasized that the Rs. 2,00,000 figure above represents the cost of food issued but not necessarily the cost of food consumed. If there have been transfers between the kitchen and the bar, for example, adjustments must be made to take the value of the transfers into account. Similarly, if there have been transfers from units in chain to other units in that same chain, these two must be totalled and used to adjust the cost figures of all concerned. In some hotel operations, where separate cost records are kept for the several food outlets in one hotel, certain similar adjustments must be made for food items transferred from one operation to another. And transfers including the intraunit transfers of cooking liquor and food to bar (Direct), and the interunit transfers of such items as baked goods, are not the only possible adjustments to food cost figures, in order to achieve more accurate food costs, many operations make one or more of the following adjustments.

Grease Sales

In many establishments, particularly those that butcher meats on premises, raw fat is one of the byproducts of kitchen operation. Many of these places save the raw fat and sell it to rendering companies, which convert it to industrial fats and oils. The sale of this fat at so much per pound results in income to the establishment, which is generally treated as a credit to cost.

Steward Sales

In some hotels, and occasionally in restaurants, employees are permitted to purchase food cost from the establishment for their own use. Employees will sometimes take advantage of this possibility for special family occasions when, for example, a cut and grade of meat might be desired that was typically not available in local supermarkets. When steward sales are permitted, the resulting income is considered a credit to cost, reducing periodic cost by the value of the raw foods sold to employees. The cost of these foods would be wrongfully in cost figures were procedure not followed.

Gratis to Bars

There are many establishments where the kitchen is expected to produce various hot and cold hors'doeuvres that are given away at the bar. Since the purpose of this is to promote beverage sales, it seems logical to reflect the cost of the hors d'oeuvres in the cost of operating the beverage department, and to credit food cost their value.

Promotion Expense

In cases where the owner or manager of the operation has occasion to entertain persons who may bring in business, food is consumed but sales revenue is not increased because no one pays the cheque. If management seeks food cost figures that are as accurate as possible, it becomes necessary to credit food cost for the value of foods so consumed and to charge their cost to another account, such as promotion expense.

When the above are taken into account, the monthly determination of cost of food consumed takes the following form:

Opening Inventory		
+ Purchases	=	Total available for sale
– Closing inventory	=	Cost of food issued
Add:		Cooking liquor transfers from other units
Subtract:		Food to bar (Direct)
		Transfers to other units
		Grease sales
		Steward sales
		Gratis to bars
		Promotion expense
		Cost of food consumed

While use of the above expanded formula will yield the cost of food consumed, it must be noted that not all of the food consumed results in increases in sales revenue. In most establishments, employees eat on premises as matter of course, and are not charged for the food they consume. Therefore, to determine the cost of food sold, it is necessary to subtract the cost of employee meals from the cost of food consumed.

Cost of Employee Meals

While there are numerous ways of dealing with the cost of employee meals, the four techniques that follow serve to illustrate those that are probably most commonly employed by food service operators.

One approach involves separate issue requisitions, which requires that employees be given food other than that which is prepared for customers. All food used in the preparation of employee meals must be issued separately and listed on requisitions, which are kept separately from all other requisitions used by the establishment. When the food issued is so listed, the requisitions may be coasted in the normal way, and thus the cost of food for employee meals determined. This approach is perhaps best suited to those establishments which are large enough to maintain a separate preparation area and separate dining room for employees. Thus it may be seen in some of the largest hotels, but in few restaurants.

A somewhat more common approach is for the manager to direct the chef to prepare specific meals that will cost no more than a certain amount per employee. This amount will be credited to food cost for each employee, and it is then necessary only to keep some reasonable record of the number of employees who are fed each day. This number, multiplied by the pre-established cost per meal will give the cost of employee meals for the day.

Because it is very difficult in some establishment to keep a record of the number of employees who are fed each day, management will sometimes take the simple course of telling the chef that food cost will be credited for a specific number of rupees per day to cover the cost of all employee meals, regardless of the number who actually eat. It is then up to the chef to estimate the number who may eat and either prepare food that will not exceed the cost guideline or offer employees fo od prepared for customers that does not exceed the permissible cost.

Another technique requires that all employees who eat record their selection on cheques that resemble guest cheques used in the dining room. the menu price is recorded next to each selection. employees are not asked to pay these checks, which are totalled for the month. The total is then multiplied by the average food cost per cent in recent period to arrive at a reasonable cost figure for employee meals for that period.

By means of one of these techniques, or some other alternative, it is possible to determine the cost of employee meals. When this has been determined, it may be deducted from the cost of food consumed to determine cost of food sold, the figure that should be used for establishing the cost-to-sales ratio, or cost per cent. To the extent that some operators fail to take employee meals into account in food cost calculations, they are overstating cost and distorting the food cost per cent.

Using all of the above adjustments, the calculation of cost of food sold in the month of March for the restaurant previously described is as follows:

	Opening Inventory		Rs. 80,000.00
	+ Purchases		2,40,000.00
	Total Available for sale		3,20,000.00
	- Closing Inventory		1,20,000.00
	Cost of food issued		2,00,000.00
Add:	Cooking liquor	8,000.00	
	Transfers from other units	10,000.00	18,000.00
		Sub-total	2,18,000.00
Subtract:	Food to bar (Direct)	2,720.00	
	Transfers to other units	13,960.00	
	Grease sale	1,080.00	
	Steward sale	480.00	
	Grates to bar	2,880.00	
	Promotion expense	880.00	22,000.00
	Cost of food consumed		1,96,000.00
Less:	Cost of employee meals		12,000.00
	Net cost of food sold		1,84,000.00
			or Rs. 1,228 Per dollar of sale

Using the sales figure of Rs. 6,00,000 previously given, food cost per cent is 30.7, 2.6 percentage point lower than it appeared to be before the adjustments were made.

Although this information is interesting, it is not as relevant as when it is compared with figures for similar periods. Such comparisons are facilitated when current and past figures are recorded side by side on reports to management.

Reports of Management

Once food costs and cost percentages have been determined, they can be reported to management. The nature of the report must be determined separately for each individual establishment or chain, based on the information needs of management as well as food controller's ability to supply it. When the food control system is somewhat complex, more detailed information can be furnished. In such instances, management is better informed, and thus better equipped to make decisions.

Although management reports differ from place to place, a reasonable number have some points in common. For this reason, it will be worthwhile to generalize these points of commonality and to illustrate several types of reports that some establishments might find useful from the comparatively simple to the more complex.

In some smaller establishment, where are few formal control procedures and no specific control personnel, it is often impossible to prepare formal reports more frequently than once a month. These monthly reports are based on information furnished by an accountant, who often prepares them between the first and tenth days of a month for the preceding month. The figures are taken solely from the accounting records of the business and indicate the food cost and food cost percentage based on purchases and inventory, as illustrated previously. Simple report forms are available from stationers, however, reports to management should always be based on management's need for information, not on the availability of a particular form. If no appropriate form exists, it is not difficult to devise one that will meet the needs of a particular operation.

The form illustrated in Table 3.12 is possibly one of the simplest that might be devised for reporting to management.

Current figures are in the first column, and the figures for the previous year are in the second. When both are available, side by side, it is possible to compare them and to make a judgment about the relative effectiveness of current operations. Thus, if the 31 per

Table 3.12

	July 19 × 2	*July 19 × 1*
Food sales	6,00,000	56,000
Net cost of food sold	1,84,000	1,73,600
Food cost per cent	30.7%	31%

cent cost-to-sales ratio for the same period last year had been acceptable to management, it is likely that the 30.7 per cent figure this year would also be acceptable, provided there had been no significant changes in menu or operating procedure and no significant drop in sales.

In some instances, particularly when figures for previous periods have been unacceptable, it is possible to judge the effectiveness of changes made with the goal of improving performance. If, for example, comparisons were made between two consecutive months, as in Table 3.13, it would be possible to tell whether changes instituted because of unacceptable results for one month had the desired effect in the following month.

Table 3.13

	July 19 × 2	*July 19 × 1*
Foods sales	Rs. 6,00,000	Rs. 4,80,000
Net cost of food sold	Rs. 1,84,000	Rs. 1,82,400
Food cost per cent	30.7%	38.0%

If the cost-to-sales ratio of 38.0 per cent in June had been considered unacceptably by management, and changes were instituted to bring about a reduction in the figure for July, it would be possible to make some judgments about the effectiveness of the changes. In the instance cited, it is possible that the reduction in the cost percentage from 38.0 to 30.7 per cent would be considered acceptable and the procedural change judged effective, so that it would become a permanent part or the procedures used daily in the future.

The cost percentage may be measured of the effectiveness of the business. It will be useful to compare it to similar measures of effectiveness for other month. If the cost percentage for this month is approximately, the same as it has been in other months, and if the cost percentage was considered satisfactory in other months, then the chances are that it also will be considered satisfactory now, providing there has been no significant change in menu or purchase prices. However, if there has been some major change, if the cost percentage is considerably higher or lower this month, we would probably want to discover the reasons for the change. Once the reasons are known, steps presumably can be taken to ensure that it will or will not happen again.

Operating figures and comparisons between them are a little like sightings taken by mariners. No one sailing a ship across several thousand miles of ocean would dream of setting a course on leaving port, and not taking various kinds of readings during the voyage. Anyone who did that would be likely to find himself some considerable distance from his destination at the end of the voyage. During the voyage, readings are taken frequently to determine the location of the ship. Then comparisons are made with a chart of the course to determine how far the ship is off course, and corrections are made to bring the ship back to the course set for it. The more frequently this is done, the closer the ship will stay on its original course. If readings are taken infrequently, the ship will have strayed considerably of course, and considerable time and money may be lost in coming back on course. In the food business, monthly readings on the course of the business are usually too infrequent. The business can stray quite far of course during the month and can be brought back into line only at considerable difficulty and expense.

The difficulty with the relying on the cost percentage calculation is that it is often impossible to determine why changes occur from month to month. One cannot always look over a period of three of four weeks with any degree of accuracy, unless significant records are available. It is hard to recollect what happened two or three days ago, let alone what happened weeks ago, when causes cannot be determinate, it is almost impossible to effect changes.

In addition, it is too late for any changes in methods and procedures to have any beneficial effects on what happened during the period that has passed. If the cost percentage for March was disaster, we must still live with the results of March for ever. The best we can hope is that change we make will effect significant improvements in April.

In recognition of this, many establishments operate with daily or weekly reports, with varying degrees of complexity. In general, the more frequent the reports and the more detailed the information rendered, the better will be the opportunities for management to control events and to ensure that the events conform to objectives.

For those reason, many larger restaurants prefer to have cost percentage and other operating figure calculated more frequently, often on a daily basis. The man agree who can find out what happened yesterday has a better opportunity to get at the causes and direct necessary changes immediately, because the cause of problem can be better located when no great time span exists between the problem and the considerations of its causes.

Inventory Turnover

Sound food management demand that sufficient supplies of food be available when needed. However excessive amounts on hand leads to (1) spoilage, because food must be held too long before being used; (2) excessive capital tied up in inventory; (3) higher than necessary labour cost to handle the greater amount of food; (4) greater than necessary space allocated to storage; and (5) unwarranted opportunities for theft.

Large establishment need greater storage space and more food in storage than smaller ones. All foodservice establishments have slow periods during the year when less food than normal is needed on the premises. Thus it is impossible to establish a set number of food items that should be in the storeroom or a set rupee valuation for food in inventory. However, management must in some way determine that appropriate—but not excess level of food are kept in inventory.

One commonly accepted method is to calculate how often inventory of food on hand has been ordered and used during a period of time. For example, if one were to order sufficient food to last one full year, most reasonable people would agree that the amount was excessive and would lead to waste, inefficiency, and greater than necessary costs. On the other hand, if one were to order enough food to last only one day reasonable people would agree that greater amount should be ordered and that savings could result by purchasing in larger quantities. Somewhere between the two extremes is an idolized amounts of food to have on hand for a specific period. This amount will vary from place to place and will be determined by many factors including the amount of cash available for such purposes, the available for storage, and the time necessary to revive food once it is ordered and we will use that range as our guide.

To measure how often food has been ordered as used, food operations have historically calculated the frequency of turnover of the food in inventory. For example, if a restaurant orders and uses an inventory two times each month, inventory turnover of twenty-four years would result in and is in approximate agreement with our guide. One should note that all food is not turned over during the prescribed period of time. Perishables will turn over daily, and some canned items will turn over much less frequently.

Calculations are typically made when physical inventories are taken once each month. The formula for this calculation is as follows:

$$\text{Average inventory} = \frac{\text{Opening Inventory} + \text{Closing Inventory}}{2}$$

for the month

$$\text{Inventory turn over} = \frac{\text{Food Cost for the Month}}{\text{Average Food Inventory}}$$

for the Month

Putting actual figures to the equation, the inventory turnover for Restaurant A might look like this:

Opening inventory = Rs. 2,26,000

Closing inventory = Rs. 2,14,000

Food Cost = Rs. 3,96,000

$$\text{Average inventory} = \frac{2,26,000 + 2,14,000}{2} = \frac{4,40,000}{2}$$

$$\text{Inventory turn over} = \frac{3,96,000}{2,20,000} = 1.8$$

If each month's results were the same, the total for the year would be 21.6 times each year, or once every 2.4 weeks, slightly greater than our guide of once everyone or two weeks.

The astute student will question the accuracy of the average inventory figure calculated above, for there is an assumption, perhaps an invalid one, that the opening and closing inventory figure used truly represent levels of inventory during the month, and that is not always and perhaps might not typically be case. It is possible for inventories to be at a much higher figure during the month, no ordering taking place the last week of the month and the ending figure a result of a planned usage of food to bring inventory to a desired level. This does happen frequently. But the only alternative would be to take a physical inventory more frequently. A procedure that in itself is costly.

BEVERAGE PURCHASING, RECEIVING, ISSUING AND STOCK TAKING

The primary purposes of establishing beverage purchasing controls are to ensure that an appropriate supply of ingredients for producing beverage products is maintained on hand, that the quality of each is appropriate to intended use, and that is purchase and the optimum price. As with all control, the key is the establishment of standards and standard procedures.

There are basically three different types of alcoholic beverage: wines, spirits and beer. The extent of the need for each must be determined before any purchase decision can be made. Needs will differ from place to place to place depending on clientele and inherent differences in the nature of operations. Some neighbourhood bars will cater to customers whose taste will run primarily to domestic beer, inexpensive wines, and comparatively few whiskies. On the other hand, cocktail lounges serving an upper middle income business clientele may offer imported beer, a great assortment of spirits, and possibly a few fine wines, while some relatively expensive restaurant may specialize in the finest of imported wines. And those are but a few of the infinite number case, it is of particular importance to define customer tastes carefully in an attempt to eliminate the purchase of beverage that will be not sell. The purchase of beverage involves the outlay of cash for merchandise that must be carried as inventory until sold the operation is open and control procedures are in effect, it will be possible to identify slow-moving at best. It is of the utmost importance to restrict initial purchases to items that will meet customer tastes.

Purchasing Responsibility

The nature and size of an operation will often dictate the assigning of responsibility for the purchasing of beverage to a particular individual. In smaller, owner-operated establishments, the responsibility will naturally to the owner, in others, it may be held by the manager, in some particularly larger operation, the responsibility for purchasing is delegated to a purchasing agent, or a steward, or even a beverage manager. The job title of the individual responsible for purchasing of little consequence.

The important point is that one individual should be held responsible and accountable for all beverage purchasing. For control purposes, it is necessary to assign the responsibility to someone who is involved in either the preparation or sale of drinks.

Quantity Purchasing

Purchasing is simplified in part by the nature of beverage packaging. All beverages are purchased in sealed containers of one sort or another and can be successfully stored in those containers for comparatively long periods if proper conditions of storage are maintained. So long as bottle and kegs remain sealed, their contents will not rapidly deteriorate when stored in facilities to proper temperature. Storage life will very from and indefinitely for use on day received, as it often the case with food. Once purchased beverage are held in storage until needed. Therefore, purchasing may be done on a periodic basis. The frequency beverage purchasing depends on may be done on a including management policy with respect to tying up money in inventory, as well as availability, delivery schedules, and the numerous and differing regulation imposed by various state and local government. In many establishments, purchasing is done monthly, some time early in the month, and is based in part on the physical inventory taken at the close of the preceding accounting period.

In addition to establishing a periodic ordering schedule, it is important to make some determination of quantity of each item that will be needed between ordering dates. This should be based on experience. If a perpetual inventory system is in use, the figures that reflect experience are readily available. If perpetual inventory not in effect, reference can be made to past invoices or bills. The purchases reflected on the invoices may be used to infer quantities used with some degree of accuracy. This however, would be a laborious process at best and should be undertaken only as a last resort. Because it is usually desirable to issue bottle from inventory to a bar from requisitions, as discussed later in this chapter, it would be preferable, in the absence of perpetual inventory, to make reference to bar requisition for preceding months to determine levels of use for each items kept in stock.

It is desirable to maintain perpetual inventories of stocks, and the best method for determining quantities to order is tied to such a system. Perpetual inventory cards or books will often show a desired par stock for each item, which is a kind of idealized quantity that should be on hand. This will often be equal to approximately 150 per cent of the quantity customarily used during a period. In addition, maximum minimum figure may be given. The maximum will reflect management's determination of the limit to which the number of units on hand may be increased. The minimum will be in effect, a reorder point, in many establishments, the rule is that no item is to be unless and until the quantity on hand approximates or reaches the reorder point. In an effort to establish control over purchasing, it is usually desirable for the beverage controller to work with the manager to establish realistic recorder points for all items in stock.

Quality Purchasing

Alcoholic beverages used by and may be divided into two classes according to use: call brands and pouring brands is used one is that used only if specifically requested by the customer. A pouring brand is one that is used whenever the customer does not request a call brands. If a customer orders, "Scotch and soda", in just those words, he or she should be given the pouring brands, the brand the management has fixed as the one always to be used in such circumstances. One on the other hand, if the customer orders specified brand of scotch with soda, he or she is always given the call brand, the one specifically requested (if it is available). The usual practice is to designate one low to medium period brand in each category of spirits as the pouring done, all other brands became call brands. The selection of pouring brand is an important first step in the establishment of standards. Although this is usually done by management, it is important that the beverage controller recognize its significance, and check to see that the selection has been ,made, as well as to see that the proper brands are being used at the bar.

Purchasing Procedure

Whenever practical, it is advisable to establish a purchasing routine that requires the use of formal written purchase orders. In larger establishment, such as hotels and chain restaurants, formal purchase requests serve as the basis for ordering.

In a large hotel, the purchasing routine might be the following. The wine steward, the person in charge of maintaining the beverage inventory and stock room, would make up a purchase request such as that illustrated in Table 3.14. Just after the first of the month.

These are prepared in duplicate, and the original would be forwarded to the purchasing agent in the accounting department. The purchasing agent in some places is required to secure the written approval of management on the purchase request before placing any orders.

Table 3.14 : Purchase Request Form

Qty.	*Item*	*Unit Size*	*Supplier*	*Unit Price*	*Total Price*
12	Old Crow	Qt.	A. & C. Suppliers	Rs. 260	Rs. 3,120
6	Beefeater Gin	Qt.	A. & C. Suppliers	Rs. 216	Rs. 1,296

Requested by__________ Approved by __________

Beverage Pruchasing

The orders placed are recorded on purchase order shown in Table 3.15 made up in quadruplicate. The copies are distributed as follows: the originals sent to the firm from which the beverage have been ordered; a second copy is sent to the wine steward to confirm that the orders have been placed; a third copy is sent to the wine steward to confirm that the orders have been placed; and can determine the correctness of the quantities and drinks delivered; the fourth copy is kept by the purchasing agent. Obviously not all establishments follow purchasing routine that are so detailed. Nevertheless, written records reduce misunderstanding some written record of purchases, preferably on a purchase order, in order to make comparisons with the goods delivered. When written purchase orders eliminate disputes concerning brands ordered, quantities ordered, prices quoted and delivery dates. Because the purchase of alcoholic beverage involves the outlay of considerable amounts of cash. It is wise to establish systems such as the purchase order method to reduce or eliminate the possbilities for error.

In many establishments, salespeople call on the wine steward, and it is common for purchase requests to be made up the wine steward on the basis of these meetings. If some states, special discounts may be offered by dealers from time to time, and when informed of these these by a salesperson, a wine steward can frequently save a considerable amounts by taking advantage of them. In addition, in locations where fluctuating prices are possible. this kind of procedure enables the wine steward to list a quoted price on the purchase request. By listing the name of particular dealer, in states where this is possible, some of the work purchasing agent is simplified.

Receiving

One useful technique in establishing control over beverage receiving is to require that deliveries be made at times when the receiving clerk can deal with them exclusively. It is undesirable, for example, for a clerk to receive beverage deliveries while receiving highly perishable food items. Pilferage is one of the most common causes of excessive beverage cost, and goods left unattended on a receiving platform create needless possibilitittes for such pilferage.

Table 3.15 : Purchase Order

H.H. Hotel

New Delhi

Date__10/1_____

M A. & C. Suppliers

Please ship the following supplies

VIA Your Truck.

Qty.	*Unit*	*Item*	*Price*	*Amout*
12	Qt.	Old Crow	Rs. 260	Rs. 3,120
6	Qt.	Beefeater Gin	Rs. 216	Rs. 1,296
				Rs. 4,416

Ordered by___________

It is particularly important that a clerk receiving beverage items have information detailing what item are expected. This information can be furnished on copy of the purchase order, and in fact, this is usually the simplest practical method in an establishment of any size. The receiving clerk can then check the invoice against the purchase-order to see that they agree as to quantity, brand label, and price, any exceptions should be noted as directed by management and attended to in the manner prescribed. The receiving clerk should have a list of procedures to quite detailed; in small restaurants there may be no written list, but a rule that the manager is to be called if there is any problem.

A principal function of a receiving clerk is to see that the items listed on the invoice are actually received in the quantities noted. The invoice is a bill, and the establishment will be held accountable for payment of the amount indicated on it. Therefore, it is important to guard against the possibilities of being billed for items that are not received, and receiving clerk is responsible for checking to see that it does not happen. In order to accomplish this, the clerk must carefully count, sometimes weight, all items received. In case of wines and spirits delivered by the case, he should open each case, and see that each contains the requisite number of properly labelled items, each case unit, or bottle should be sealed. Any broken units should be returned for credit with the seal intact.

The Receiving Clerk's Daily Report in a Larger Establishment

Once deliveries have been received and checked, each invoice must be written up on a receiving report. This receiving report will eventually make its way to the accounting department and will serve as the basis for making entries in the purchase journal. It will serve several other important purpose as well. Before it reaches the accounting clear listing of beverages received was at *(a)* the beverage controller can compare the received and ordered beverages, and *(b)* the information can be easily transferred to inventory record by the wine steward and controller. In order for the control system to be accurate and effective, it is important that the receiving sheet be completed carefully by the clerk before the find of each day.

The most useful receiving report is one specifically designed for beverages. The beverage receiving report can take any of several forms, one of which is illustrated in Table 3.16.

Because the beverage receiving sheet is an accounting document, the specific make-up of the sheet will vary considerably from place to place, depending on the nature and degree of complexity of the accounting practices in effect. However, it is generally desirable to establish a separate receiving report for beverages and then to design a report form tailored to the needs of an individual establishment. In the case of beverages received, it is generally good practice to require not only that the receiving clerk sign a daily report, but that the wine steward sing it as well, thus acknowledging receipt of the beverage items listed on the receiving report.

Table 3.16: Beverage Receiving Report

		#	*#*	*Unit*	*Unit*	*Case*	*Total*
Distributor	*Item*	*Units*	*Cases*	*Size*	*Cost (Rs.)*	*Cost (Rs.)*	*Cost (Rs.)*
BCD, Ind	Gin (White by)	24	2	Qt.	190	2,280	4,560
BDC, Ind	Vodka (Holka)	12	1	Qt.	182	2,184	2,192
Fey, Ind	Fey	24	2	Qt.	58	6,96	1,392

Distribution

Wine	*Sprits*	*Ale*	*Beer*	*Mixers*
	Rs. 4,560			
	Rs. 2,184			
	Rs. 1,392			

Storing

It is necessary to move all beverages received away from the receiving area as quickly as possible. Alcoholic beverages are always highly susceptible to pilferage, and it is often impossible for the receiving clerk to keep watch over quantities of them for more that a very few minutes. Therefore, the wine steward should be notified of deliveries at once in order that removal of all beverage items to secure storage can be arranged at once.

Security is one of the key elements in establishing control over the storage of beverages of all kinds. Whether alcoholic or non-alcoholic, all beverages should be stored in securely locked areas to eliminate the possibilities of pilferage. Each bottle represents a cash investment ranging from a few cents for mixers to several dollars for premium spirits and fine wines.

Keys to beverage storage areas must be carefully controlled to guard against unauthorized personnel gaining access to the various wines and spirits. An excellent practice is to have only two keys for each lock. One is kept by the wine steward; the second is kept locked in a safe to which only top management has access. In some establishments, security is further tightened by the installation of special locks that record, on a paper tape in the lock, the time at which it is opined and re-locked. These time locks pinpoint the opening of storage areas at odd hours by unauthorized personnel. in any case, it is usually advisable to change locks on the beverage storage facilities from time-to-time to oddest the possibility that duplicate keys have been made. It is particularly important that locks be changed when personnel changes occur among those who have had access to keys.

Storage Facilities

It is desirable that beverage storage facilities be located in an area reasonably close to bars in order to reduce the amount of time required to distribute the supplies. In addition, it is usually desirable to locate the storage facilities in an area where the entrance is readily accessible and under continual observation. This helps to reduce the security problem as well as to facilitate the issuing of supplies.

Internally, the storage area should be kept free of debris that can pile up as the result of emptying cases and stocking shelves. Cases should be completely emptied once opened. All units in case should be stored on the appropriate shelf and the empty carton removed at once. Control must be exercised to ensure that some personnel do not remove cartons that are not completely empty.

In addition, appropriate temperature controls should be established. These will vary considerably with the kinds of beverages stored. It is desirable to store alcoholic beverages other than wines at room temperature to minimize the chances of deterioration. Wines must be stored at very carefully controlled temperatures as a general rule, red wines should be stored at about 55° F. White wines and sparkling wines should be stored at a lower temperature, if possible. Depending on the nature and extent of the Wine stores, both purpose sometimes can be accomplished in the same storage facility by means of professionally installed equipment for cooling and circulating air, and by storing items that must be kept cooler on shelves closer to the floor. Wherever and whenever possible, ales, beers and mixers should be stored at lower temperature near 40. In the case of ales and beers purchased in kegs, this is often necessary for the prevention of spoilage. Where only bottled items are stored its ice used to bring the items to proper serving temperature.

The physical arrangement of the storage area is important. It should be laid out so that like items are kept together. All gins, for example should be kept in one area, rye whiskies in another, and Scotch whiskies in a third. This kind of arrangement makes it much simpler to find an item when needed. It is helpful, too, for a floor plan of the storage area to be affixed to the door, so that authorized personnel can easily locate items when they are requested. One way of ensuring that items will always be found in the same location is to institute the use of bin cards such as that illustrated in Table 3.17.

Table 3.17: Bin Card

Item Old Crow				*Stock Number 165*			
Date	*In*	*Out*	*Balance*	*Date*	*In*	*Out*	*Balance*
10/1			4		2		
10/3		1	3		2		
10/7		1	2				
10/11		1	1		2		
10/12		4	5		–		

The bin card, a standard form available from appropriate stationery suppliers, is affixed to the shelf, serving as a label. It lists pertinent information concerning each item, such as type of beverage, brand name, and bottle size. It also may include provision for a certain number used to identify the particular item on the shelf. In some establishments, each beverage item is assigned a code number from a master list and that code number is recorded on the bin card. In many instances, the number is stamped by a mechanical stamping device on each bottle received. This technique serves several purposes.

In the case of wines, many of which have names that are not easily pronounced or spelled by the individual unfamiliar with the languages of the countries of origin, it simplifies the ordering by both customers and employees. In many instances, wine lists are printed with bin numbers. This is frequently a boon to wine sales, which can be highly profitable.

In the case of alcoholic beverages, is provides a measure of control as will be more apparent after. The number stamped on each bottle as the property of the establishment. Thus as employee cannot claim a bottle as his personal property if one is found in his possession. In addition, empty bottles can be checked for numbers before they are replaced by full bottles to ensure that no one is bringing empties in from out side and using them to get bottle from the establishment stores.

His own perpetual inventory record of quantities on hard. By using this card carefully to record for all items in stock the number of units received as they are placed on the shelves, and the number of units issued as they are given out, the wine steward has a way of determining the balance on hand without resorting to counting bottles. In addition, the wine steward who maintains such records carefully has a way of determining that bottle are missing to that this important fact can be brought immediately to the attention of management.

Table 3.18: Illustration of Beverages Code Number

Sample Numbering Code for Wines Spirits and Beers	
American whiskies	: 100 series
Blended rye	: 100-139
Straight rye	: 140-149
Bourbon	: 150-179
Sour mash	: 180-189
Important whiskies	: 200 series
Scotch	: 200-249
Canadian	: 240-249
Irish	: 250-259
Other	: 260-269

(Contd.)

Sample Numbering Code for Wines Spirits and Beers

Gins and vodkas	: 300 series
Gins: domestic	: 300-329
Important	: 330-349
Vodka	: Domestic 350-379
Important	: 380-399
Rum and brandies	: 400 series
Rum	: 400-4449
Brandy	: Domestic 50-459
Important	: 380-399
Cogan act	: 480-499
Cordials and liquors	: 500 series
Red Wines	: 600 series
White wines (still)	: 700
Sparkling Wines	: Red and white—800 series
Beers and ales	: 900 series

Inventory Control

For control purpose, it is important that records of beverage stocks be maintained by someone other than the wine steward or bartender responsible for maintaining the stores. These records should be maintained on an ongoing basis, and should reflect both additions to stores because of purchases, and deductions from stores based on issues to operating bars. It is an indispensable feature of the beverage control system.

Perpetual inventories may be an indispensable feature of the beverage control system able as standard forms from stationers. A sample of the perpetual inventory card is shown in Table 3.19.

One of card or one sheet should be maintained for each item in stock. Where numbers are used, it is typical to find the perpetual inventory maintained in code number order. The number of units received are entered from the receiving clerk's daily report or from the invoices attached from requisitions. Since items are received in quantity and issued in units, more space is provided for issued that for purchases. This type of record would be used in an operation with one bar. In a hotel or restaurant with multiple bars, the perpetual inventory more likely would be found on a card such as that illustrated in Table 3.20.

Table 3.19 : Bin Card

Code # 153	Bottle Size Qt. 2.19			
Item Old Crow	*Unit Cost Rs. 2420 Par Stock 4*			
Date	*Received*	*Issued*	*Issued*	*Balance*
10/1	–			4
10/3	–	1		
10/7	–	1		
10/11	–	1		
10/12	4	–		5

Table 3.20 : Bin Card

Code : # 153		*Size : Qt.*				
Item Old Crow	*Unit Cost Rs. 2420 Par Stock 8*					
Date	*Received*	*1*	*2*	*3*	*4*	*Balance*
10/1						6
10/4		1		1		4
10/10			1			3
10/11	4					7
10/12		1				6

In such establishment, each bar would be assigned a number, and requisitions would be prepared separately for each. By means of the card illustrated, separate records could be maintained of issues to each bar. It is particularly useful to have such records when the need arises to pinpoint problems, such as missing bottles.

When the beverage controller maintains a perpetual inventory, it is possible to spot check the number of items on shelves from time-to-time during the month, to guard against loss and to ensure that the sins steward is securely maintaining the supply.

The forms illustrated are used for the purpose of maintaining records of number of bottles on hand. Some establishments maintain records that reflect inventory values as well. This is done on a separate form and is usually handled by the accounting department, although it might be done by the beverage controller in some places.

When a perpetual inventory is maintained, it is possible to determine whether bottles are missing by simply checking the stocks on the shelves from time-to-time during the month. It is common for a beverage controller to check several items in this way every few days. When any discrepancy between inventory records and bottle on shelves occurs, immediate investigation into causes is begun, and appropriate remedial action is taken.

At the end of each month, standards accounting practice requires that a physical inventory be made of the stocks on hand. Typically, it is the responsibility of the beverage controller to take this physical inventory, often with the assistance of the wine steward. This monthly inventory is usually recorded in bound inventory book. After the total number of units in each category is recorded, that number is multiplied by the unit cost to determine the rupee value of the units on hand. It is useful to compare inventory to find any discrepancies. Where the physical inventory shows fewer of bottles on hand than there should be according to the perpetual inventory, immediate investigation should be made to reconcile the difference. Sometimes these differences are the result of improper counting of items on shelves; sometimes they are the result of improper maintenance of perpetual inventory records from receiving sheets and balance requisitions. Either of these bookkeeping errors is easily remedied. However, when the difference cannot be traced one of these causes, it is probable that items unaccounted for used have been stolen. Management should be informed at once, in order for appropriate steps to be taken.

When bin cards and perpetual inventory cards are separately maintained, the first by the wine steward and the second by the beverage controller, it is often possible to determine errors merely by the comparing entries on the cards, and where a difference exists, by checking back to the appropriate receiving sheet or requisition.

Issuing

Because beverage stores are all considered inventory, cost does not occur until beverage items are issued for use. Therefore, partly to maintain physical control over bottles, and partly to determine costs, it is of the greatest importance that no bottle be issued from stores without a written requisition signed by an authorized person, often the head bartender. A very simple form of requisition is illustrated in Table 3.21.

The dated requisition is filled out by an authorized individual who determines quantities needed at the bar and who sings the form. When the requisition is filled by the wine steward, he or she sings the appropriate line indicating that the items listed in the quantities shown have been issued. When the items are received at the bar, the

Table 3.21 : Requisition

Date 10/5

Quantity	*Description*	*Unit Cost*	*Total Cost*
1	Old Crow		
1	J & K		
1	C.C.		

Requisitioned by ________

Issued by________

Received by ________

bartender on duty (who may or may not be the person who ordered the items initially). After the delivery of the items to the bar, the requisition is returned to the wine steward, who fills in the unit cost of each items and extends the requisition by multiplying the unit cost by the number of units issued to find total cost of each. A grand total is then entered at the bottom for the cost of all items issued.

In many establishments a futher means of control is established by requiring that each requisition be accompanied by empty bottle from the bar, such that the issuing of the units listed in effect replaces quanities that have already been used by the bartenders. When this system is used, it is possible to maintain a par stoack at the bar. For example, Five bottles of particular brand of scotch might consitute the par stock for that item. When one bottle was emptied, the bartender would put it aside until the end of the night, at which time it would be listed on a requisition form, which would be left for the first bartender on duty in the morning. The morning bartender would see to it that the empty bottles were delivered to the wine steward together with the requisition on which they were listed. The wine steward would check each bottle against the requisition and replenish the bar stock before the beginning of business. This would have the effect of bringing the stock at the bar back upto par. Such a system term ensures constant and well controlled supply of beverage items at the bar. In addition, spot checks of par stocks against the par stock list can be made from time to time ensure that items are not missing from the bar. This affords an additional measure of control.

In establishments that operate more than one bar, it is important that separate requisitions are prepared for each, in order that each may be controlled separately.

Basically there are three kinds of bars:

1. Front bars, where bartenders serve the public face to face.
2. Service bars, where customer orders are related to the bartender by waiters and waitresses who serve the drinks to the customer.
3. Special purpose bars, usually set up for one particular event, such a banquet.

The par stock at a bar differs somewhat from par stock in storeroom. Par stock at a bar should be listed in exact qualities for each type and size of items kept in stock. For example, the stock of gin should be listed according to brand names; it should include bottle size for each, as well as exact number of bottles that should be at the bar at all times. One particular brand of gin, stocked in quart sizes, might have a par stock of find five bottles of that particular brand on hand. Not all would necessarily be full, but at least the number of bottles would be under control. In addition, it would be possible to replenish the supply daily by exchanging a full bottle for each empty bottle turned in by the bartender, and those maintain the par stock at all times.

It is obvious that par stocks for bars will vary greatly from bar to bar in every case. However, the par stock figures should be related to quantities used and should be varied from time-to-time as customer demand varies. Drinks may go in and out of fashion for seasonal as well as for other reasons, and it is normally demand without being overstocked with any particular item. In addition, since storage space at a bar is relatively limited, it is usually desirably to limit the quantity of any time to the supply necessary to meet no more than two days demand.

In the case of front bars and service bars, it is possible to establish par stock for each bar. However, this is not possible in the case of special purpose bars. These present unique problems. When these bars are set up, sufficient stocks must be issued to carry the bartender through the banquet. Typically, the quantities issued are greater than needed, and the remainder must be exercised to ensure that no mishandling of bottles occurs, which would lead to errors. Special banquet requisitions are often used, which make provision for all bottles issued, whether consumed or returned. An example is illustrated in Table 3.22.

Table 3.22: Banquet Bar Requisition

Function : Lions Club　　Bar Tender
Location : Green Room　　Date

Item	*Quantity*	*Original Issue*	*Additional Issue*	*Return*	*Con-sumed*	*Unit Cost*	*Total Cost*
Scotch	2	2					
Gin	2	2					
Vodka	2	2					
Bourbon	1	1					
Canadian	1	1					
S. Vermouth	1	1					
Dry Vermouth	1	1					

Requisition by : ________________
Issued by : ________________
Received by : ________________
Returns Checked by : ________________

Such requisitions are often made by the banquet manager, particular hotels. They are given to the wine steward, to issue the items listed to the bartender or babying time for the bar to be set up for the event. Provision is made for recording additional issue that may be required. At the end of the event, it is desirable that some other individual such as the beverage controller, check that all full, empty, and partially used bottles are accounted for. When this is done, it is possible to charge to cost the correct amount for the quantities actually consumed, and to return unused quantities to stock. Perpetual inventory and him card entries are made from the consumed column on the banquet requisition.

It is establishment, where most wines are sold by the bottle, additional procedures are instituted for control purposes.

In some establishment, small stocks of the most popular wines are maintained at a front or service bar to eliminate the need for going to the wine cellar each time a front or service bar to eliminate the need for going to twine cellar each time a bottle is ordered. Once the bottle of wine is taken from a bar and served to a customer at a table, it is effectively away from the control of the bartender. The bartender may not have an empty bottle to turn in with his requisition on the following day bring his stock up to par.

Therefore, many establishments maintain additional control over full bottle sales by requiring that a form be filled out each time a bottle of wine is delivered to a table. One example is illustrated in Table 3.23.

Table 3.23: Bottle Sales Slip

Date 10/5	Table # 8	Check # 1230		
Code #	*Description*	*Quantity*	*Size*	*Cost*
620	Chateau Latour	1	Full	Rs. 720

Served by ________
Issued by ________

Such a form is useful in hotel that serve full bottles of both wines and spirits to guests in their rooms. It is also useful in situations where par stocks of wines are not maintained at the bar, and each bottle must come directly from the wine cellar. The full bottle sales slip serves as a requisition in such instances. When such forms are used, it is important to require that each be filled out completely by the server before the bottle is issued to guard against potential problems. When completely filled out, the form provides an excellent means for verifying each sale. It is possible to check each against the guest check number indicated and to hold the server accountable for errors.

4

FOOD AND BEVERAGE PRODUCTION CONTROL

Food Production Control

A major key to successful food cost production is good organization proper organization makes food production easier and more efficient. During recent year there has been a definite change in kitchens organization.

In the past, large establishment had executive chef and smaller establishment had working chef-in-charge of running their kitchen. In recent years there has been a trend towards having a food production supervisor run the kitchen, particularly in institutional food service.

Old time chefs were skilled craftspeople. They had eventually worked in to jobs as kitchen chefs because they knew how to prepare all the items the establishment wanted prepared. Today's food production supervisors may the people who have only a limited knowledge of food preparation and cooking but who know techniques of management. They use management skills to schedule and plan work in the kitchen.

No matter who runs your food production—executive chef, old time general cook, food supervisor—your food production department must be well organized. The chain of command should be carefully planned by you and the head of your food production department. Authority and responsibility should be clearly defined so all kitchen personnel understand their duties and know who their immediate superior is.

We looked at organizational chart for different type of food service operation. You will have to make up and use your own organization chart. You will not find readymade chart that precisely suit your food service operation. Setup and organizational chart and chain of command and make sure that every one understands it.

Today the trend is toward simpler menus. Many cooks are not as skilled now in all aspects of food preparation as cook were few years ago. They don't have to be, but they must be able to do a good job of preparing the items the food service operation will sale.

The degrees of skill necessary for cooks will vary from one food service operation to another. In an operation that uses a lot of convenience food, or food prepared in a commissary, cooks will not have to be as skilled as they would in food service establishment that prepare all of their own food item from scratch. When you plan your own menu and food production, do not loose sight of what type and degree of cooking skill your cooks will need to do the job.

The most important rule to remember in food production is: if you want good food to come out of your kitchen, you have to buy good food to begin with. The production area is where food items are actually prepared and produced. The items you buy and use should be of the correct quality for the food you want prepared and appropriate for your own recipes.

RECIPES AND FOOD

Standardized Recipes

Over the years, many articles have appeared in food industry trade journals on the importance of standardized recipes are and extremely important tool you should use in your food production control. Virtually all food service opration can use standardized recipes and/ or standardized procedures in food production.

Get recipes from any source you wish—quantity cook books, cook books for the home, magazines—and make them standardized yourself. A standardized recipe, is a recipe that you have worked out and set up formally in terms of yield and quality for use in your establishment. When you have your recipes standardized, your cook should stick to them exactly unless you and they working together decide you ought to adjust them. If you do change them, then stick to new ones exactly.

A standardized recipes should:

1. All ingredients, including spices.
2. Exact quantities of everything.
3. Method of preparation for everything.
4. Size of portions.
5. Total number of portions to be obtained from recipes.

The name of all spices should be included in each recipes, but it is probably a good idea to list just approximate amounts of them. Cooks should test foods as they are preparing them and adjust final seasonings to test. Strength and flavour of spices can vary with brand and age. For example, a new beef base for soup could be saltier than the previous brand. If cooks don't test the soup but just add the same amount of salt called for in the standardized recipe, the soup may be too salty. Your standardized recipes should be flexible when it comes to amounts of spices. Final seasoning of all foods should be done to taste.

Write All Recipes Down, Standardize Them and Follow Them

Some old-time chefs can present problems if they will not be flexible in cooking methods. You might even find one who will refuse to reveal "secrets" about a favourite recipe. You certainly cannot standardize a recipe if you cannot even start by writing it down accurately. Perhaps by working diplomatically with such chefs you can convince them that it is important that you know each recipe. If you cannot convince chefs that you must have standardized recipes written down and followed for all the foods they prepare, you may have to find new chefs.

One big advantage in having standardized recipes is that it permits you to train new cooks in exactly how you want items prepared. If you do not have standardized recipes, cooks will probably prepare items the way they did in the last place they worked. Maybe the food will be better than your own recipe produces. Maybe it will be worse. The point is, you should control the recipes so that your food is consistently good and you know what it costs.

Make sure that your recipes do produce good food. Your establishment's recipes should be followed accurately and should produce the quality you want. Some dishes (Beef Stroganoff, for example) can be prepared many different ways by different food service operations across this country—and across the world, for that matter—but everyone still calls the dish "Beef Stroganoff" (or a, translation thereof). It is important to you that any cook in your food operation, including a new one, prepare it exactly the way you want it prepared and use exactly the ingredients you want used. Use standardized recipes and make sure they are followed.

To illustrate this point, let us say that one day your relief cook makes your cream soup for the first time. You taste it and you do not like it; it is not nearly as good as it is when your regular cook makes it. You complain to the relief cook: "What's the matter with the soup? Did you follow the recipe? This sure doesn't taste like it does when the regular cook makes it." Your relief cook answer: " No, it sure doesn't. I followed the standardized recipe exactly. I just used milk like the recipe says. The regular cook always uses real cream." Of course the regular cook's soup tastes better! It tastes better but it is costing you more to make it than you had planned and set a cost for. If you are not aware of the higher food cost cooks can cause by altering standardized recipes and if you do not charge your customers more for soup made with cream instead of milk, it will definitely raise your food cost and cut your profit for the soup.

You definitely need standardized recipes and they have to be followed. Soup is, of course, just one item—just one very small example of what we are talking about. Consider the large number of food items you produce and sell every day, week, month, year. Slight changes made in recipes without your knowledge or your planning in controlling costs and setting prices can mount into tremendous increases in your costs.

To return to our soup example, go ahead and use cream if you want to. Put cream in your standardized recipe. Plan on it, cost it, and price the soup so that guests pay accordingly. The point is, base your costs and your selling prices on your standardized recipes, have good recipes, and make sure the recipes really are followed.

One reason why standardized recipes are recommended is that they list all ingredients and quantities, which means that you can figure the cost. To find out what each portion you produce is costing you, divide the total cost of the ingredients by the number of portions the recipe yields.

A standardized recipe should also give very clear directions for preparation and should spell out cooking methods. It should state amounts of all ingredients and how the item is to be put together and prepared—braised, broiled, boiled, simmered. It should give temperatures, times, and anything that needs to be done while the food is cooking (cover it, uncover it, add water, stir). It is important to make all preparation and cooking directions detailed and explicit so they are easy to use and a substitute cook can use them with no trouble. If meat should be boiled vigorously, for example, or simmered gently, a recipe should say so. For just one example, meat boiled vigorously will not be as tender as the same meat slowly simmered. High heat causes connective tissue in meat to contract quickly. Slow simmering causes a gradual break-down of connective tissue. Different meat products with different uses and different yields result from different cooking methods. Your standardized recipe should give very detailed and specific instruction so you get just the result and the quantity and quality you want.

Occasionally, there will be mistakes in the written standardized recipes. Or perhaps the recipe was written correctly but your cooks think it could be improved with different ingredients or quantities or cooking methods. Cooks should call these things to the attention of your food production supervisor. They should change and correct a recipe together. The food supervisor should be aware of any resulting changes in the cost of the item and should tell you so you can adjust the menu price if necessary. If a standardized recipe is altered in any way, you must know so you can alter your costing and pricing accordingly.

Hot Foods

It is not enough just to prepare food properly. You must provide proper care and safe sanitation procedures for the food after it has been prepared and while it is waiting to be served to guests. Hot foods should be kept constantly hot and cold foods constantly cold-right up to the moment the guests eat them. Sometimes guests probably wonder whether their food is meant to be hot or cold. Often it is in between and not appetizing.

Hot foods that are not served immediately after preparation should be kept in a steam table or in a bain marie (a pan resting in hot water) or under infrared lights. The steam table can be heated by either moist heat or dry heat, whichever you prefer for your food service operation.

The temperature at which hot foods are held is very important. Hot foods must be held at temperatures above 140°F. At temperatures above 140°F, most harmful food organisms will be killed. At temperatures from 140°F down to 40°F, harmful organisms can grow. To prevent serious germ growth and possible danger to guests, you must keep hot food at a temperature above 140°F. Foods being kept in the steam table should be checked periodically with a thermometer. Buy thermometers from your local food service equipment dealer. Employees should regularly check the temperatures of foods with thermometers and make sure that correct heat is always maintained.

Aside from the very important factor of germ control, the temperature of the hot food is also an important factor in taste and appeal to your guests. If food is supposed to be hot, guests want it hot. Taste studies have shown that when the temperature of hot food falls below 120°F, guests consider the food cold and distasteful. It is extremely difficult to get food to the guest while it is still at a temperature of at least 120°F if the steam table is holding the food at only 120°F or less.

Holding Foods

Frequently, you will have foods cooked and all ready to be eaten but will have to keep them ready until someone orders them. Some foods hold up better than others if there is a delay. In general, the less time any food item is held, the better it will be. Ideally, a steak should be taken off the broiler, put right onto a plate, and served to the guest immediately. Creamed items (like chicken a' la king) may have to be held in the steam table.

Many foods do not hold up well at all if they are not eaten soon. Green frozen vegetables tend to breakdown and lose their colour if you keep them in the steam table longer than half an hour. Try to cook small batches of green vegetables at a time and avoid keeping them in the steam table very long.

Proper planning by the cooks can help prevent the necessity of holding foods too long. Instead of one pan or pot for cooking vegetables, they should use two or three. As they take one small cooked batch off the stove, they should put another batch on to assure a small but continuous supply. They should also have two containers for the steam table so they do not mix freshly cooked green vegetables in with green vegetables that have been held in the steam table for even a short time. There is a noticeable colour difference when freshly cooked green vegetables are mixed in with the old. First use all the food already in the steam table. Then put in all the food just cooked. From a sanitation standpoint, this is a good idea for all cooked foods that are held for a time—not just green vegetables.

Cold Foods

We have said that it is important for you to keep hot food hot. That is the way guests, want it. And it minimizes the danger of organism growth. The same factors apply to cold foods. Keep cold food cold because that is the way guests want it. And really cold temperature can reduce the danger of organism growth. Ideally, cold foods should be served at a temperature of about 40°F. Salads should not be much colder than that, though, or they can freeze. If you hold cold foods at temperatures of close to 40°F, it retards the growth of organisms.

Cold foods should be served cold and the—should be served on cold plates. Salads put on plates still hot from the dishwasher can turn soggy. Icecream or gelatin put on plates still hot from the dishwasher can turn into disasters.

Put plates for cold food in a refrigerator ahead of time—overnight if you can—so they are really chilled. Many food service operations that feature self-service salad bars have special refrigeration units right at the salad bar for chilling plates. Some of these units keep plates so cold that they almost hurt the hands. That's good and cold! Salads and other cold foods are much better if they are served on cold plates.

Portion Control

"Portion control" includes everything you do to control the exact size of a portion. There are three ways of doing portion control:

1. Buy items already pre-portioned.
2. Buy items in bulk and portion them yourself ahead of serving time.
3. Portion items at the last minute as you serve them.

1. *Buy Items Already Pre-Portioned*
   More and more food service operations are buying and using pre-portioned items. Meat is one item classification where this is especially true. You can buy steaks pre-cut to size, hamburger patties pre-formed, cheese pre-sliced, and so on. This assures uniform portion size to every guest. The advantages with this method are that your portioning has already been done for you and you know your exact portion cost.

2. *Buy Items in Bulk and Portion Them Yourself Ahead of Serving Time*
   Many food service operations buy items—some meat items, for example—that have not already been pre-portioned. They do their own precise portioning.

Here is one rather small example of how individual pre-portioning can work for you. (Apply the idea wherever you can). Assume that you sell corned beef sandwiches. First you decide how many ounces of corned beef you will put I in each sandwich. Should you use 2 ounces, 3 ounces, or more? Decide definitely before you ever make the first corned beef sandwich. The amount of corned beef you put into each sandwich will definitely affect the price you should charge for each sandwich. (So will the type of bread you use and whatever else you use to finish and garnish the sandwich.) Let us assume that you will sell a lot of corned beef sandwiches at lunch every day. In many food operations corned beef is just sliced and given to the sandwich maker, who grabs handfuls of corned beef and slaps it between two slices of bread during busy lunch periods. If this is what happens in your operation, you do not know how much corned beef is put into each sandwich. Sandwich makers probably will not have time to weigh every portion of corned beef during the lunch hour. They are almost sure to be too busy. (You hope so, anyway.) The sandwich makers try to portion by judging the amount by eye and by feel. But this certainly is not exact portioning. Amounts actually used will vary, and your costs will vary, too.

Do the following instead. During pre-preparation and setup time, have your kitchen personnel weigh each portion of corned beef on a portion scale, making up individual portions according to the weight you have decided you want in each sandwich. After the corned beef has been weighed, each portion should be separated by hamburger patty papers. Have stacks of weighed individual portions – one portion for each sandwich – ready to go before lunch cover the entire pan with a plastic sheet to keep the corned beef from drying out in the refrigerator. When the lunch rush comes, sandwich makers grab: patty paper with pre-portioned corned beef, put the meet between two slices (bread) and finish the sandwich. This method controls the amount of corned beef used in each sandwich. It is faster, too. If you do not pre-portion and your sandwich makers grab corned beef by the handful, they will probably to consciously or unconsciously to do some judging of amounts on their own they go but their well-intentioned efforts will probably just slow them down and decrease their efficiency during peak busy periods. Also-imagine what happens to your costs if you happen to have a sandwich maker with really hands! Imagine how displeased your guests will be if your sandwich maker really small hands!

You do not just pre-portion corned beef, of course. You do the same pre-weighing and individual pre-portioning with all the cold sandwich meats you can (ham, roast beef, turkey). Your own portion control and pre-portioning system is most vital to you if you buy items that do not come already portioned. Then be sure to weigh or measure and make up individual portions ahead of time where feasible.

We have just given one example for meat. Use the same idea everywhere you cannot just for meats.

3. *Portion Items at the Last Minute as You Serve Them*
   Teach your employees how to use portion control. Suppose you want a 3-ounce portion of peas. This may mean something very clear to you, but it may not mean a thing to your employees if they do not know how big or small a 3-ounce portion of peas really is. Weigh out a 3-ounce portion of peas and show it to your employees so that they know how much it is before they start dishing up portions. During busy times, employees cannot stop and weigh each 3-ounce

portion of peas, but if they have a mental picture of how large a portion 3-ounces is, they can come closer to serving that amount.

Use the same idea for other vegetables and items you want served. Make up samples so that employees know what size portions they should be serving. Have employees use all the measuring devices you can think of—cups, ladles, scoops. Have them judge by eye how much of the dish used should be filled by the portion size wanted.

Some operations get an instant colour camera and take photographs of various items on their menus, such as a shrimp salad plate, a fruit plate, a roast beef dinner. The pictures are posted near the appropriate stations and used as guides by employees so that they know what their finished product should look like in general appearance and quantities of items. It is still very true that a picture is worth a thousand words. Pictures can help give employees ideas about appropriate portion sizes.

For meat items, keep a portion scale at the carving station so that meat portions can easily be weighed as they are sliced. It may not be feasible to weigh every portion of meat, but a spot check of every third portion or so will help keep the carvers accurate in their portioning. For meat, you should:

1. Slice it.
2. Weigh it.
3. Serve it.

It would be ideal if you could weigh each portion. For example, consider the standing rib roast. If your meat carver slices a portion too thick, the guest who eats the oversized portion pays the regular price. This guest is pleased. The meat carver may try to make up for the extra thick cut by cutting the next one too thin, and the guest who gets the skimpy portion also pays the regular price. This guest is not pleased. Portions should be the same size and price for all guests (children, women, men) unless guests specifically request small or large cuts and pay accordingly. Many operations list different-sized portions of items at different prices on their menus. This is the *only* case where different portion sizes are acceptable to your guests.

Use portion control wherever you can. Meat is a high-cost item, so be particularly sure that you pre-portion it wherever possible.

Establish portion sizes and show employees what you want ahead of time. Use a size ladle for soups, sauces, and so on—one ladle equals the portion you want. Use sized icecream scoops for icecream (number 20, 16, 12, depending on the size portion you want). Scoops can also be used for meatballs and croquettes. They help you pre-portion and they help you speed up production. Determine how many portions you want from a pie—six, seven, eight. Determine all these things ahead of time. Make charts of portion sizes and post them at appropriate stations so that employees can see them, know them, and follow them.

Portion control should be an integral part of food production. You are making sure that you are not serving too little and upsetting your guests or too much and upsetting your costs.

PLANNING FOR PRODUCTION

In pre-control and pre-costing the menu, we discussed forecasting for production. Here is where you use that forecast in your daily food production planning. Food production supervisors should use the forecast when they tell cooks what amounts of items to prepare.

Many items are prepared to order in food service operations today, so you probably should not have as many problems with leftovers as food service operations had in the past. Today, most luncheon menus offer many sandwiches and the ingredients for these can usually be used tomorrow if you don't, use them today. But even in the case of comparatively simple sandwich production, if you forecast and estimate the quantities you will need in advance, it can help you avoid problems.

For example, if homemade soup is on the menu, you or your kitchen supervisor should decide—basing the decision on your forecast—how much soup to prepare. Do not leave it up to your cooks to make whatever amount of soup they think you will need. Do estimate sales and see that the kitchen staff makes the amount you have estimated you will need. You may be one of the unfortunates who has cooks who make 3 gallons of soup because when they reach up to the rack to get soup pots they happen to grab the 3-gallon pots instead of a different size. Yes, that sounds nutty. It is. But it happen your entire food production operation can evolve out of an astounding, variety of assorted nuttinesses you will never know a thing about if you not take charge. See to it that your total food production evolves from reasons you decide on. Keep on checking up and keep on enforcing your decisions. You and your supervisors should be aware of what is going on in departments.

All production should be geared according to the sales you have estimated. Steaks should be cooked to order. But how many steaks should be pulled from the freezer? With good refrigeration, a thawed steak can be held for several days. But in a lot of food operations, stew (or a fancy name for stew) appears for sale unplanned in order to use up steak meat before it goes bad—simply because someone pulled too many steaks from the freezer without planning ahead or using a valid forecast of sales.

Each department head in the kitchen should have some say in preparing work schedules for his or her own department. Work with your head pantry person, your head fry cook, your head roast cook. Help each figure out a schedule that is workable and satisfactory for her or his own staff—all depending again on how big or small your operation is.

Use a Production Schedule Sheet

The process of preparing a work schedule sheet forces your supervisors to think ahead of time about the work that needs to be done in their departments. Ideally, your production work schedule should be made out the day before the items are to be produced to facilitate delivery of items from the storeroom and to simplify the day's production. As employees report for work, all the items they will need that day should have been brought to their work stations by storeroom clerks. Ideally, they can start right in on production because they know what to prepare, how to prepare it, and how much to prepare. They will know what to make and how much to prepare because the food production schedule sheets for the day should already have been posted in the kitchen by the kitchen supervisor. If the items they are to prepare call for standardized recipes (and most items should), copies of the standardized recipes they will need should also have been posted.

Many food service operations (particularly institutional food service operations, such as hospitals or college food services) find it a good idea to prepare production work schedules a week ahead of time. They buy very large quantities of certain items and use the production work schedules as guides in purchasing these items.

Food production schedule sheets can be very complex or quite simple. Make food according to your needs, but be sure you do the following three things:

1. Make them up ahead of time.
2. Always put them in writing.
3. Write them so they are easy to read and easy to understand.

Employees should be able to read posted production schedules immediately when they come to work. They should know right away what foods they should prepare and be able to go right ahead and prepare them without confusion or questions.

How to Prepare a Food Production Schedule Sheet in Portions

The key to food production control planning and organization is the food production schedule sheet (also called a cook's worksheet). This chart includes only entrees, so this chart would be used only by a department that prepares entrees. You would need a chart every day for all other production departments in the kitchen. Salad, vegetables, desserts—depending on the size and complexity of your operation. These charts should be prepared by the kitchen supervisor for each day. You may want to add additional columns for directions for your employees, such as how much meat to thaw, which standardized recipe to follow, and so on.

Table 4.1 is an example of a food production schedule sheet in portions. This sample chart lists entries which are on the menu for the day. It gives a breakdown of entries and quantities to be prepared.

1. ***Column 1: Item***
   These entree items are taken directly from your menu for the day. In this entree chart, menu' includes items which are pre-portioned (except for the prime rib) and are ready to be cooked to order.

2. ***Column 2: Forecast in Portions***
   This column tells the entree cooks how many portions of

each item they should prepare.

3. ***Column 3: Original Amount to Prepare in Portions***
This column tells cooks how many portions to make. In the chart, this column tells them to roast 45 pounds of prime rib and marinate 15 portions of beef brochettes. It also tells them the number of portions of all other entree items to have ready to cook to order. The person in charge of the kitchen contributes the numbers in Column 3, and they may differ from the numbers in Column 2.

Table 4.1

Meal: Dinner **Date:** ________ **Day:** ________

Item	*Forecast in Portions*	*Original amt. to Prepare in Portions*	*Additional Amount Prepared*	*Total pre-Paration in Portions*	*Sales*	*Left Over*
1	2	3	4	5	6	7
Stuffed Breast of Chicken	21	20	3	23	23	0
New York Strip	56	50	14	64	64	0
Flounder	10	6	2	8	8	0
Prime Rib	51	3 Roasts of 45 lbs. Total	-	45	45	0
Chopped Steak	25	25	10	35	33	2
Trout	20	15	4	19	19	0
Beef Brochettes	11	Marinated 15	-	15	13	2
Stuffed Shrimp	31	40	-	40	36	4
Total	**225**				**241**	

4. ***Column 4: Additional Amount Prepared***
This column shows how many extra portions were prepared beyond those originally prepared (Column 3).

5. ***Column 5: Total Preparation in Portions***
This column lists the number of portions cooked or cocked to order. It is the total of Columns 3 and 4. (*Note:* The number of chopped steak sold is more than the 25 forecasted, 35 are prepared, 33 are sold, 2 are left over. Chopped steaks are

cooked to order, so the 2 uncooked can be used the next day).

6. ***Column 6: Sales***
   This shows how many portions you sold. Fill in this column after the meal period has ended.

7. ***Column 7: Left Over***
   This column is used to list any items left over. This shows you how accurately you forecasted and how well you were able to adjust your forecast in terms of actual production as the meal period went along. Cooked-to-order items left over should be used the next day. Forty-five portions of prime rib were prepared but the restaurant probably ran out since the total number of guests served was more than the total number of guests forecasted. Prime rib is the only item on this menu not cooked to order. It is the one you most need to forecast quite accurately.

FOOD PRODUCTION TIPS

Garnish

After the food has been prepared, it is, as we have said, important to serve it hot if it should be hot or cold if it should be cold. It should be attractive in every way. Aim to make it the best food your total operation can produce. Be sure food is appropriately and properly garnished. Garnish can be the plus that makes an average dish more attractive, and it is important that food be attractively presented. People do "eat with their eyes."

There are other garnishes besides parsley. Use them. For example, use spiced crabapples, different kinds of pickles (not just pickle chips), a vegetable relish, fresh fruits, and so on. Use imagination and create unique, tasty, different types of garnishes. The cost of the garnish can be more than offset by good revenue. If you present an item attractively, it may be reasonable for you to charge a higher price.

Serve Promptly

After the food has been prepared, it should be held correctly and served as soon as possible. Prompt service is important. Make sure your waiters and waitresses get the food as soon as they can after it your waiters and waitresses get the food as soon as they can after it is ready and take it to your; guests as fast as possible. Many food service operations have installed infrared spotlight "holding areas" to keep food hot in case the service personnel are delayed in the dining room and cannot get the food quickly when it is ready. Some operations have installed bell systems, light systems, or pocket buzzers to notify service personnel that their orders are ready.

Avoid Squabbles

If you can, minimize contact between service persons and kitchen staff by having:

1. A point-of-sale computer, so that orders go electronically directly to the kitchen.
2. Waiters and waitresses put orders on a spindle in the kitchen so that no one has to talk.
3. One calm and pleasant person act as a go-between (kitchen expediter) between waiters and waitresses and kitchen staff.

To help with all possible areas of misunderstanding, have:

1. Lines of authority and responsibility clear to all (post them).
2. All job descriptions clear and known to all (post them).
3. Good training.
4. Meetings with your entire staff or with individuals or small groups to discuss problems constructively and try to remedy them before they escalate.
5. All your other management control techniques in good working order.

It is extremely important that you achieve good coordination and cooperation among your entire staff and between your production personnel (cooks) and your service personnel (waitresses and waiters in particular). All of these jobs exist only to serve the needs of your customers. This fundamental fact is often forgotten. If you permit squabbles to go on between cooks and service persons (or among any employees), it can do a great deal of damage to your whole establishment. It is part of your job to help personnel work together as an efficient team. It is upto you to convince bickering employees that they must help each other. If you cannot and they will not, it is upto you to create a harmonious crew by rescheduling or replacing employees so they will work together successfully.

Service people do get mad at grumpy customers. Cooks to get hot, tired, and disgusted. When furious waiters or waitresses dash to the kitchen and demand special orders of meticulously prepared fried eggs from hot, tired, disgusted cooks for the satisfaction of cranky guests, it is usually upto you, the furious, hot, tired, disgusted, cranky manager to soothe everyone involved. Do everything in your power ahead of time to avoid the reasons for explosions by anyone.

Special Requests

There is one fairly common occurrence that can create dissension among your staff. It is when guests order items that are not on the menu or ask to have something prepared differently from the way it is listed on the menu. Pre-planning can help you here. You should realize ahead of time that your staff will get outlandish requests for food. Guests will order unusual foods cooked in peculiar ways. You and your staff should know these things will happen and be ready to handle them. Working with your staff, establish guidelines ahead of time concerning what types of requests will be refused and what types will be fulfilled. Set up clear policies on these matters and make sure your entire staff knows them. Make your policies feasible for your staff to follow and as satisfactory for your guests as you can. If unusual requests can be handled without disrupting total service, they should usually be fulfilled. Give satisfactory service and make special allowances in your procedures to please individual guests to as great an extent as you possibly can. But make these decisions ahead of time and make, them jointly with your staff so they know what will or will not be expected of them.

Once in a great while you may get an extremely inconvenient request from a guest which you should fulfill, although it is not feasible and it does interrupt production. The following true story illustrates this. In a large nightclub many years ago, a nationally known newspaper columnist ordered ham and eggs and fried potatoes for dinner. Ham and eggs and fried potatoes were not on the menu. The nightclub was right in the midst of one of its most frantically busy nights of the whole year. But the order was filled. The columnist was pleased and appreciated the special service. He was so pleased, in fact, that he mentioned the incident and the name of the nightclub in his column. The nightclub received some totally unexpected and very nice publicity. The reward for performing beyond the normal bounds of duty was repaid 1,000 per cent in this particular case. Usually, there will be no reward except one ordinary customer who got what he or she wanted. But do use discretion. Special cases should get special reactions. All customers (not just famous ones) should receive the very best service you can muster and there may be rare and special occasions when you should be prepared to do the impossible—and not just for "important" guests.

BEVERAGE PRODUCTION CONTROL

A customer ordering a drink often has a preconceived idea of how the drink will taste, based on past experience. The customer orders a daiquiri, for example. Because he or she has enjoyed the taste sensations experienced in the past from the subtle blending of lime juice, sugar and rum by skillful bartenders. A customer, who is served a cocktail that does not meet expectations, may be dissatisfied and may complain or simply not return. Therefore, it is important that any establishment offering drinks recognize and accept certain standards of customer expectation and drink preparation, and establish procedures to ensure that these standards will be met. Control must be established over quantities of ingredients used in preparation, as well as over the proportions of each in a drink. In addition, drink sizes must be standardized. When standards of ingredients, portions, and drink sizes are set, the customer has reasonable assurance that the drink will meet expectations each time it is ordered. When these standards are set and enforced by management, they can be made to hold true even in the face of a high rate of employee turnover.

By establishing and maintaining these standards, management also provides a means for controlling costs. When drinks are prepared by formula with specific quantities of specific ingredients. and served in predetermined portion sizes, each daiquiri prepared by the bartender on duty should cost the same as every other daiquiri. Because the selling price is fixed, the cost-to-sales ratio for daiquiris should be the same for each daiquiri prepared. If all other drinks also are prepared according to standards appropriate for those drinks, the cost-to-sales ratio for other drinks should also be stable. When this is true, the cost-to-sales ratio for the overall operation should be stabilized. provided that the sales mix does not vary greatly. Simply stated, it becomes possible to develop a standard cost percentage for operation to which the actual cost percentage can be compared. This will be discussed in more detail in the next chapter.

Quantity Control

One of the first steps in establishing control over production is to standardize the quantities of the most costly ingredients used: the alcoholic beverages. The amounts used by the bartender must be controlled. This involves predetermining the quantities to be used, and providing a means of measuring those quantities.

In most beverage operations, the majority of drinks prepared involve combining one kind of liquor with a mixer—Scotch and soda, gin and tonic. Rye and gingerale rum and Coke are all examples of this type of drink. Management must determine the quantity of the expensive ingredient: the liquor. The amount varies from bar to bar, from three-quarters of an ounce in some places, to as much as two ounces in others. This amount is set in advance by management and should be thought of as the amount of management is willing to give in return for the selling price of the drink. Once the amount is settled, management must provide the bartender with the means for measuring this quantity each time a drink is prepared. There are several methods for measuring quantities. The simplest and most widely used requires that the bartender physically measure the quantities poured. There are two commonly used measuring devices: shot glasses and jiggers.

The Shot Glass

In some places, the bartender is provided with small glasses that are used for measuring. There are two kids: plain and lined.

Plain shot glasses hold a predetermined quantity when filled to the brim. These are available in a number of sizes, from fractions of an ounce to several ounces. At a given bar, all should be of the same size. In many places where these are used, the bartender is told to fill the shot glass and pour the exact measure into the drink. In others the bartender is provided with shot glasses that hold slightly less than management is willing to give (three-quarters of an ounce, for example, if one ounce is the agreed or measure), and the bartender is instructed to pour the three-quarters of an ounce into the drink, and then to pour an additional small amount directly from the bottle to the glass in view of the customer. There is a psychological advantage to this method customers think they are getting more than they are entitled to.

A lined shot glass is similar to a plain one, but it has a line etched in it somewhere below the brim. In some places, the standard of fill is to the line, which is in full view of both the customer and the bartender. In others, shot glasses are used that have deceptive lines so that when the bartender fills to the line on the inside of the glass, it appears to the customer to go above the line on the outside. This is an optical illusion, but it gives the customer a sense of getting something for nothing. Another variation on the lined glass approach involves using glasses that hold the standard measure where filled to the brim, but have lines etched somewhere below the brim. These are used for the same psychological reasons.

The Jigger

The jigger is a stainless steel measuring device designed with an accurate scale of half and quarter ounces, and is a necessity for the accurate measuring that ensures perfect cocktails. It can be used for measuring straight shots as well but is more useful for pre-paring cocktails calling for varying quantities of ingredients. For these drinks, shot glasses are inappropriate for measuring. Some cocktails call for such varied measures as half an ounce of one ingredient, three-quarters of an ounce of another, and one and one-half ounces of a third. In order to measure exact quantities of each ingredient it is necessary to use the calibrated jigger.

There is another way to provide control over the quantity of liquor used in preparing drinks. It involves using one of an assortment of devices that can be fitted on the top of a bottle, which permit the pouring of only a predetermined amount. There are a number of different types but all operate on the principle of controlling the quantity poured each time the bottle is used. In an establishment where one ounce was the standard measure, the bottles could be fitted with devices that would dispense just one ounce. Each time the bartender tipped the bottle to pour, exactly one ounce would be dispensed. The psychological effect of these pouring devices is widely disputed. Some feel that the customer is given the illusion of the bartender pouring freely; others argue that the customer can feel resentful of management that neither trusts the bartender nor will permit the dispensing of an extra drop to the customer. Still others feel that such attachments are useful at a service bar, which customers never see, but should never be used in a front bar, where the customer watches the bartender mix the drink.

In recent years, several companies have developed and successfully marketed various automated devices for dispensing predetermined measures of liquor. These range from comparatively simple systems for controlling only the pouring brands to highly he elaborate control systems that not only control ounces but also mix drinks at the push of a button. These complex systems, costing thousands of rupees, are usually connected to a cash register in such a way that the sales is recorded on a guest check as the drink is prepared. In addition, meters record the quantities used and permit elaborate inventory control procedures. Many believe that these systems should be used in service bars, but never at front bars except in cases where repeat customers are the exception rather than the rule, as in the case of an airport bar.

Free Pour

Another common system for controlling quantity is really a no system. Where this is the practice, bartenders are permitted to "free pour". In effect, management relies on the experienced bartender to gauge the quantities poured by eye.

Although it is possible for an experienced bartender to do this with great accuracy, the procedure clearly reduces the degree of control exercised by management over the bar operation. In addition, in situations where rapid employee turnover is the rule, management is likely to find that it has no control at all over operations. In any bar operation, free pouring is likely to be abused by all but the most dedicated employees, leaving the door wide open for bartenders to operate more for their own advantage than for the general good of the business. However, many owners who permit free pouring seek to offset its disadvantages by adjusting selling prices upward to ensure the desired level of profit.

Glassware

In addition to controlling the quantity of liquor used in the preparation of each drink, it is desirable to control the overall size of the drinks. This is comparatively simple to do by standardizing the glassware used for service. It is the responsibility of management to predetermine the size of each drink to be served and to provide the bartender with appropriate glassware for the service.

Beverage glassware is available in a wide variety of shapes and sizes. Therefore, it is possible for management to furnish the bar with particular glassware for use in serving particular drinks. Stemmed cocktail glasses, holding 2.5 ounces may be used for all cocktails in a particular bar, for example. Because it is clearly impossible to fill the glass beyond the brim, it is impossible to serve a portion size greater than 2.5 ounce, without changing glasses or giving the customer a "dividend." By furnishing the bar with 2.5 ounce cocktail glassware, directing that all cocktails will be served in these glasses, and declaring that no dividend will be given to customer, management can effectively control the portion size. In many fine hotels and restaurants, the 2.5 ounce cocktail glass is considered too small. Management is willing to give a more generous portion for the posted selling price. In such cases, bartenders use so-called lined cocktail glasses—those holding 4.5 ounces, with a line etched around the glass indicating a three ounce measure.

In order to establish effective portion control, then, it is important to purchase glassware in appropriate sizes. Management must determine the kinds of glassware that will be needed (based on present or anticipated clientele and their preferences), then determine portion sizes. Glassware must be purchased based on these portion sizes determined by management. and bartenders must be instructed what glasses are to be used for serving particular drinks. While the neighbourhood bar may be able to get with just four or five types of glasses of as many sizes, the fine restaurant cannot. Neither can the hotel, these may require as many as twenty-five to thirty different types and sizes of glassware for beverage service. Typically, a fine metropolitan hotel or restaurant would require a supply of glassware similar to that listed in Table 4.2.

Thus, management standardizes portion sizes by purchasing particular glassware for particular purposes, and by carefully instructing bar personnel in its use.

While the standardization of portion sizes helps to control beverage costs, that alone is not enough. It is useful to stipulate that a gin and tonic will be served in an eight-ounce glass, yet this alone does not tell bar personnel what part of the standard portion should be gin, and what part should be mixer. This is an important consideration in cost control for, after all, the cost of gin is greater

Table 4.2: Standard Glassware Restaurant

Item	*Size (in ounce)*	*Par Stock at Bar*
Jigger	3	6
Jigger	1.5	12
Cordial	2	12
Cocktail	3.5	24
Cocktail	4.5	24
Champagne	4.5	24
Sour	5.25	24
Rocks	5.5	48
Brandy	5.5	12
Wine	8.5	24
Wine	6.5	24
Hi-ball	8	48
Pilsner	10	24

per ounce than the cost of mixer, and the relative amounts of each used in making the drink will affect the cost. The following two examples will show clearly the difference in the cost of ingredients effected by changing proportions.

Cost of Gin: Rs. 6/oz	Cost of Mixer: Rs. 0.80/oz.
Gin & Tonic "A"	Gin & Tonic "B"
Gin-2 oz. = 12	Gin-1 oz. = 6
Mixer-6 oz. = 4.8	Mixer-7 oz. = 5.6
16.8	11.6

In both cases, the result is eight ounces of gin and tonic. However, by varying the proportion, the costs differ considerably. If this particular drink is offered at a posted selling price of Rs. 80, there will be considerable difference between the cost-to-sales ratios as well.

Cost 16.8/Sale 80 = Cost % 21.0 Cost 11.60/ Sale 80 = Cost % 14.5

STANDARD RECIPES

Clearly, if costs are to be controlled, the same control must be established over the proportions of ingredients that go into each drink. In other words, standard recipes must be established so that bar personnel will know how much of each ingredient to use to produce a certain drink.

Generally speaking, there are two kinds of drinks prepared and served by a bartender that require the use of liquor: straight shots with mixers, such as the gin and tonic discussed above, and mixed drinks or cocktails. Many of which involve a number of ingredients that must be combined in a certain way for the drink to be right.

In the case of the former, the standard drink is controlled by providing the bartender with appropriate glassware of predetermined size as well as a jigger or other device for measuring the liquor content. The standard drink size is measured, poured over ice in the right glass, and then filled with the mixer. In effect, this constitutes the standard recipe. Each time a customer orders a Scotch and soda, the bartender will place a certain number of ice cubes in the right sized glass, measure in the standard quantity of the pouring brand of Scotch, and fill the glass nearly to the brim with soda. Every Scotch and soda prepared in this way will be the same. The customer's second drink will be the same as the first, and on returning to the bar in two weeks, he or she will be reasonably sure of receiving the same drink for the same price, barring changes in management policy. This is a major factor in establishing customer satisfaction and developing repetitive business.

Accomplishing the same end in the case of cocktails is somewhat more complicated. In most cases, there are two or more recipes for making any cocktail, the results of which are somewhat different. For example, two different mixing guides might list the following ingredients under recipes for the Manhattan cocktail:

A	B
2-1/4 *oz.* Blended Rye Whiskey	1-1/2 *oz.* Blended Rye Whiskey
3/4 *oz.* Sweet Vermouth	¾ *oz.* Sweet Vermouth
Dash bitters	Dash bitters

While the mixing of the ingredients in the prescribed way will produce a Manhattan cocktail in each case, there are substantial differences between them. In the first case, the ratio of whiskey to Vermouth is 3 to 1; in the second, it is 2 to 1. In addition, the first recipe makes a drink that is three-quarters of an ounce larger than the second. Finally, the first costs more to make because it contains an additional three-quarters of an ounce of blended rye whiskey.

It is apparent that management must decide which of several recipes will be the standard used to prepare the Manhattan. Similar decisions must be made for all cocktails to be prepared. While the most frequent approach is simply to adopt one of the standard recipe guides for use at the bar, it is by no means uncommon, particularly in chain operations, to find that a special recipe book is prepared for use in the establishment. In every case, the standard recipe would include not only the measures of alcoholic beverages to be used in preparation but the quantities of all other ingredients including the garnish, if any, as well as mixing instructions, and serving instructions.

In some cases, pictures of the drinks are provided to ensure uniformity, particularly in the face of high rates of employee turnover. Table 4.3 gives example of typical standard recipes for Manhattan and the Brandy Alexander, two common cocktail.

Table 4.3: Manhattan

2-1/2 ounces blended rye whiskey

3/4 ounce Sweet Vermouth

Dash of bitters

4 ice cubes

Stem cherry

Combine the whiskey, vermouth and ice cubes in a mixing glass and stir well.

Strain into a 4-ounce stem cocktail glass. Garnish with the cherry.

Brandy Alexander

3/4 ounce brandy

3/4 ounce Creme de Cacao

3/4 ounce heavy cream

3 ice cubes

Another important point to remember is that the book of standard recipes provides the bartender with instructions for preparing the unusual cocktails that are requested only on rare occasions. Although a number of bartenders are able to mix virtually any drink requested, there are many who have few occasions to mix a Taxco Fizz, an Opal, or an Earthquake. The presence of a standard recipe guide at the bar.

Combine all ingredients in a cocktail shaker and shake vigorously. Strain into a 4-ounce cocktail glass. has helped on many occasions to ensure the satisfaction of some one. Although standard bar recipes are a necessity from the point of view of someone interested in control, there are many bartenders and some managers who view them with disdain. In some places, therefore, they are a controversial subject.

It is theoretically possible to establish a standard recipe for each and every drink served by any bar, indicating the size of the drink and the quantities of each ingredient. As a practical matter, it is not possible to enforce standard recipes in all instances at all bars. One illustration of the problem should suffice.

Most people are familiar with the martini, a cocktail made of gin, dry vermouth, stirred with ice, strained into a cocktail glass, and served garnished with an olive. Many people order martinis every day. In some parts of the country it is surprising to find so little agreement of the proportions of gin and vermouth that should go into a "good" martini. For some, the best mixture for a three-ounce martini is two ounces of gin to one of vermouth; for others. It is three ounces of gin to one drop of vermouth. And there are an infinite number of variations. Because the bar business seeks to satisfy customer taste, it is very difficult to set up an inflexible standard recipe for the martini for a particular bar. One single standard recipe might satisfy some customers, and make others very unhappy. In many instances bartenders must be permitted a certain amount of freedom to alter standard recipes, not at their own whims, but at the request of customers. In such cases, the standard recipe should be a kind of average of all the martinis mixed in a certain bar over a period of time.

When standard recipes are established and standard portion sizes have been set, it becomes possible to calculate the standard cost of any drink.

STRAIGHT DRINKS

The cost of straight drinks served with or without mixers can be determined by first dividing the standard portion size in ounces into the number of ounces in the bottle to find the number of standard drinks contained in each bottle. This is then divided into the cost of the bottle to find the standard cost of the drink. For example, the standard portion size for the pouring brand of Scotch in a certain bar is 1.5 ounces. The bar uses quart bottles of Scotch, dividing the 1.5 ounce standard drink into the 32 ounces contained in each quart, one determines that each quart contains 21.3 drinks.

32oz/1.5 oz = 21.3 drinks.

Because there is a certain amount of spillage and evaporation in all bar operations, hopefully a minimum amount, this can be rounded off to an average of twenty-one drinks per bottle. If the purchase price of the bottle is Rs. 194 , then each of the twenty-one drinks it contains has a standard cost of Rs. 194 divided by twenty-one drinks, or Rs. 9.2.

Rs. 194/21 drinks = 9.2 per drink.

The same bar would normally offer a number of call brands of Scotch as well, and by employing the same technique it would be possible to determine the standard cost of the standard drink of each. In the case of a premium Scotch costing Rs. 338 per quart yielding twenty-one drinks, the standard cost of each drink is obviously some what higher:

Rs. 338/21 drinks = Rs. 16 = Rs. 16 per drink.

An alterative procedure for finding the standard cost per drink involves dividing the cost of the bottle by the number of ounces it contains to find the cost per ounce, then multiplying the ounce cost by the standard drink size. For example, if the pouring brand of gin costs Rs. 153.6 per quart, each ounce would cost Rs. 4.8.

Rs. 153.6/32 oz. = Rs. 4.8 per ounce

This ounce cost, multiplied by the standard 1.5 ounce drink size for gin in this particular bar, shows a standard cost for the standard measure of Rs. 7.20.

1.5-ounce standard size × Rs. 4.8 per ounce = Rs. 7.2 per drink.

Some who employ this method might prefer to divide the bottle size in ounces, but by one ounce less. This has the effect of allowing for the usual evaporation and spillage.

The use of one method rather than another is purely a matter of the personal preferences of those who perform the calculations. Once these calculations have been performed, the usual practice is to record the results on a form similar to that illustrated in Table 4.4. These are updated from time-to-time, whenever dealers' prices change. In this way, up-to-date cost figures are always available to management to use in several ways. One use for the figures is in calculating the cost of mixed drinks and cocktails.

Table 4.4

Bottle Code	*Item*	*Bottle Size (oz)*	*Bottle Cost*	*Ounce Cost*	*Drink Size (oz)*	*Drink Cost*
201	Old Bagpipe	32	192.0	6.0	1.5	9.2
206	Highland Hiatus	32	338.0	10.4	1.5	16.0
302	Guttersnipe Gin	32	153.6	4.8	1.5	7.2

Mixed Drinks and Cocktails

It is particularly important to determine the standard cost of a drink made by standard recipe in the case of cocktails and other mixed drinks. These drinks typically involve several ingredients and often require the use of two or more alcoholic beverages in preparation. Consequently, mixed drinks are usually more expensive to make than are straight drinks. Knowledge of the cost per drink is important in making intelligent pricing decisions.

In order to determine the standard cost of cocktails and other mixed drinks and to maintain record of the information, it is useful to obtain a supply of Recipe Detail and Cost forms similar to those illustrated in Table 4.5 and 4.6. Both are in fairly common use and can be made up either by a printer or by a secretary who has access to a duplicating machine.

The first step in determining the standard cost of the drink is to record on the form all the information from the bartenders' recipe guide for each drink. It is essential that all ingredients used by the bartender in preparing the drink are taken into account in determining cost. The cost of any of these drinks should and does include the cost of all the various non-alcoholic ingredients that may be used.

Table 4.5: Standard Recipe—Detail and Cost

Item Martini	*Bar Recipe* # 55	
Selling Price	Rs. 60	
Cost	Rs. 20.4	
Cost Percentage	20.7%	
Ingredients	*Quantity*	*Cost*
Guttersnipe gin	2 oz.	9.6
Dry vermouth	1/2 oz.	2.0
Martini olive		0.8
Total	2-½ oz.	Rs. 12.4

Procedure

Pour gin and vermouth into glass mixer, add cracked ice and stir gently, pour into 3-oz. cocktail glass, add olive and serve. Glassware: 3 oz. Cocktail juices, eggs and heavy cream are but a few of the other ingredients that must be taken into consideration. In addition, various garnishes for the drinks must be included where appropriate. These might include such varied items as olives stem cherries, cocktail onions; and slices of various fruits. The cost of all of these must be added to the cost of the basic alcoholic ingredients in order to arrive at the true cost of the drink.

It should be noted that both the forms given have space left near the bottom for including the standard preparation procedure and the standard glassware. When this information is recorded from the bartenders' guide, management is provided with a complete set of the standard recipes, in a loose-leaf book, or in a card file for ready reference.

Once the basic information has been recorded from the standard recipe, it is necessary to find the cost of each ingredient, both alcoholic and non-alcoholic. The location of this information will vary considerably from place to place. It is particularly helpful here to have the information in a form such as in Table 4.4. In some large establishments the beverage controller will have the cost of beverages in perpetual inventory records, or in an up-to-date price book.

In some smaller operations, it may be necessary to refer back to invoices, receiving sheets or inventory books. In the case of non-beverage items, such as the food items transferred from the kitchen, it may be necessary to refer to the relevant transfer memos. In other cases, it might be the appropriate practice to ask the steward for the most recent purchase prices for each item. Here too, the procedure will vary considerably from place to place. In general, the exact procedure followed is of no particular importance, so long as it results in ascertaining the correct cost figures for each item in the recipe.

The techniques for recording the data are different forms illustrated. In the first instance it is necessary to calculate the cost of quantity used before recording any cost information on the form. In the example given, the cost of two ounces of gin is recorded as Rs. 9.60. This is determining by referring back to the chart in Table 4.4, which indicates that one ounce of pouring brand costs Rs. 4.80. This multiplied by the two ounces in the recipe gives the cost figure to records.

If a firm similar to the second example is used, it would be necessary as the first step to record the size and cost of bottle of the pouring brand. In the example shown the 32 ounces bottle of gin is recorded as costing Rs. 153.60. The next step is to divide the number of ounces in to the cost of bottle, and to multiply the result by the number of ounces of gin in the recipe. This is exactly the same kind of calculating that one would have already performed in compiling the figures illustrated in Table 4.4.

The only real advantage of the form shown in second example is that to provide a space for recalculation of drink costs as the cost of ingredient change.

When this form is adopted, it may thus be used for a relatively longer period of time before it becomes necessary to rewrite the cost records.

Once the costs of all ingredients have been determined, the figures are totalled and the result is the standard cost for preparing the drink according to the standard recipe.

This cost is recorded at the top on the line provided, and divided by the selling price to determine the cost-to-sales ratio for the drink. This is recorded as the cost percentage for that particular drink. If selling prices have not yet been determined the cost per drink should certainly be one of the chief considerations in arriving at a reasonable figure. Even in those cases where selling prices have been set before costs were calculated, all the selling prices should be reviewed in the light of the newly developed cost figures.

Table 4.6: Standard Recipe: Detail and Cost

Item : Maurice Cocktail
Bar Recipe : 77

	Date 9/11	*Date*	*Date*
Selling Price	Rs. 60.00		
Cost	10.40		
Cost %	17.3%		
	Bottle Data		
Ingredient Cost	*Date 9/11*	*Date*	*Date*
Guttersnipe Gin	Rs. 153.60		
	Drink Data		
Ingredient Cost	*Date 9/11*	*Date*	*Date*
Juice of ¼ orange	1.20		
½ oz. sweet vermouth	2.00		
½ oz. dry vermouth	2.00		
1 oz. gin	4.80		
Dash Bitters	0.40		
Total	Rs. 10.40		

Procedure: Combine all ingredients in glass shaker. Add cracked ice and stir. Strain in to 4 0z. cocktail glass.

Standard glassware: 4 oz. Cocktail

STANDARD SELLING PRICE

Once standard costs for standard drinks are known and listed, it is normally desirable to establish a similar list of selling prices. One obvious reason for doing this is to enable management to post selling prices at the bar or to list them in a menu, depending on the type of establishment. It is generally good practice to maintain a complete list of these standard selling prices in the beverage controller's office.

The techniques for maintaining such lists of standard selling prices are many and varied. As in so many other cases, the simplest is often the best; and for that reason it is recommended that selling prices for cocktails and mixed drinks be maintained on the recipe detail and cost cards, and the prices for straight drinks be kept on an expanded version of, the list first shown in Table 4.4 now show in its expanded form in Table 4.7.

Table 4.7

Bottle Code	*Item Size*	*Bottle Cost*	*Bottle Cost/oz*	*Ounce Size*	*Drink Cost*	*Drink S.P.*
200	Qt.	214.0	6.68	1.5 oz.	10.00	60
202	Qt.	324.0	10.12	1.5 oz.	15.20	80
203	Qt.	325.6	10.16	1.5 oz.	15.20	80
206	Qt.	334.0	10.40	1.5 oz.	15.60	80
207	Qt.	364.0	11.48	1.5 oz.	17.20	80
210	Qt.	356.0	11.12	1.5 oz.	16.80	80
212	Qt.	484.0	15.12	1.5 oz.	22.80	100
213	Qt.	568.0	17.64	1.5 oz.	26.40	100

It is absolutely essential in any bar operation that the selling prices be standardized for each drink sold, for straight drinks as well as for cocktails and other mixed drinks.

When selling prices are standardized, customers can be properly charged for the drink they order, and the prices will not vary from day-to-day. The possibilities for customer satisfaction are increased, for the customer who has been charged Rs. 50 for a particular drink on Tuesday has reasonable assurance that an identical charge will be made for the same amount for the same drink on Wednesday.

In some places, the list of standardized drink prices is made available to customers, by posting it on signs over the bar or by printing it in a menu. This posting of standard selling prices has the additional effect of eliminating many possible arguments over drink prices.

Perhaps the most important purpose behind the standardization of selling prices is the maintenance of a planned cost-to-sales ratio for each drink sold. The drink costing Rs. 12 when prepared according to standard formula, which sells for Rs. 60, has a cost-to-sales ratio of 12 to Rs. 60 more commonly expressed as 20 per cent. The sale of each such drink results in the addition of Rs. 60 to daily sales figures and Rs. 12 to daily cost figures, the net effect being a gross profit on the sale of Rs. 48. In the case of this particular drink, this is the desired, preplanned effect of each sale. The net effect is not a matter of the whim of the bartender; it is planned by management. Ingredients and consequently costs are planned. With this in mind, selling prices are set and have a predetermined relationship to the costs. In addition, each sale has a predetermined impact on the overall gross profit of the operation. In effect, the profit on each sale is planned when both cost and selling prices are set by management. Thus, it becomes possible to plan and maintain profit levels.

One important part of the control procedure is the regular measuring of the effects of operation to see if events are conforming to plans. There are many ways of measuring results, varying considerably from place to place. The differences in techniques arise chiefly from differences, in the size and scope of operations, as well as from some differences in management philosophy. Regardless of differences, the techniques for measuring operations fall into three principal categories, one based on cost percentages, a second on ounce consumption, and a third on potential sales value *versus* actual sales.

5
CONTROLLING FOOD AND BEVERAGE COST

FOOD CONTROLLING: THE ESSENTIAL OF CONTROL SYSTEMS

Calculation of Food Cost

The main emphasis here is on one area of cost control—food. By food we mean all food items plus all non-alcoholic beverage items.

"Food cost" (which usually means the same thing as "cost of food sold") means all the money you spent to prepare the meals you served. Food cost includes only food and non-alcoholic beverage items. It does not include anything else—not labour and not overhead and not profit.

"Food cost per cent" is the percentage of your sales revenue you spent for food, a food cost formula is a method you use to find your food cost and your food cost per cent. You need this information to help you plan and control business.

If your food cost per cent is too high, you take immediate steps to correct it. You can do the following:

1. Increase efficiency of operation by applying and tightening all controls (purchasing, receiving, storing, production, cash and sales controls, so on).
2. Put in a small price increase or maybe more for some items. A price increase can be comparatively small in money (you raise hamburgers from Rs. 30 to Rs. 40 a piece, Rs. 10 more)

but big in percentage (that Rs. 10 is a 33 per cent rise from your hamburger's previous 30 rupee price).

3. Change the same prices but cut your quantity or portion size so that your cost go down (try not to do this.)

USE A FOOD COST FORMULA

Two food cost formulas are described in this chapter. Either one will shot how your food cost and food cost per cent are going from day-to-day during the month. Use whichever formula suits you and your food operation best, modify one of these formulas, or make a combination of both formulas to suit your own needs. (If you have a computer it can work on your food cost formula.) But definitely do use a food cost formula to keep track of your food cannot control your food cost or food cost per cent if you have no idea what they are. And you certainly cannot control them during the month's food cost or food cost per cent when food cost while a month is still in progress, so you can act during that month to control your food cost and change it if you need to.

Food Cost Formula 1
(Purchases Formula)

How to Use Formula 1

This is the easiest food cost formula to use. It can be used by food service. It needs a more sophisticated system or do not have the time or vote to a more complicated system. Formula 1 is not as thorough or as accurate as Formula 2 (discussed later in the chapter), but it can be is certainly better than nothing.

There is only one equation in Formula 1. It is:

All Food Purchases divided by *Food Sales* multiplied BY 100 (to convert to a percentage) equals *Food Cost Percent per Ruppee Sale.*

The easiest way to use this formula is to prepare a chart on column paper (or put it in your computer) as shown in Chart 5.1 and do the steps described below. The following wing comments on each column tell you how to fill it all in, day-by-day and column by column, as you go through a month. Check the following in each column with Chart 5.1 as you read. This may look at it really is not. (This is also true of Chart 5.2 discussed later in this chapter.)

Column 1: Date

Always start a new chart the first of each month, so your Date column starts with 1.

Column 2: Day

In the Day column, put whatever day the first of the month happens to fall on (S for Saturday, W for Wednesday and so on). In our sample , you are starting on March 1, a Monday. COLUMNS 3, 4 AND 5 ARE "TODAY' FIGURES–JUST DAILY, DAY-BY-DAY– NOT INCREASING, NOT ACCUMULATING AS YOU GO.

Column 3: Today Food Purchases

To get this figure, you add together all your invoices for all the food you receive each day. In Chart 5.1, on Monday, March 1, your invoices total Rs. 29,766.80.

Column 4: Today Food Sales

This figure represents your total food sales for Monday , March 1. Get this figure from Monday's cash register tape . In our chart the figure is Rs. 6,670. Get your closing cash register tape figure every day and put it in this column.

Column 5: Today Food Cost Per cent

To get this figure, divide Column 3 today food purchase by Column 4 today food sale. For example, to get this figure for Monday, March 1, you divide the Column 3. Today food purchase Date 1 figure Rs. 29,766.80 by Column 4. Today food sales Date 1 figure Rs. 66,590.00. You get 0.4070. Multiply 0.4470 by 100 to convert to a percentage and you get 44.70 per cent. Monday's food cost percent is 44.70 per cent. *Columns 6,7 and 8 are "To-Date" Figures. These Columns do incre Ase and do Accumulate for the Month as you go along.*

Column 6: To-Date Food Purchases

Just for the first day of the month, your Column 6 To-Date Food purchase figure Date 1 is the same as your Column 3 Today Food purchase Date 1 figure–Rs. 29,766.80. After the first day of the month, you start adding.

To get your Column 6 To-Date Food Purchases Date 2 figure for Tuesday, March 2, add your Column 3 Today Food Purchases Date 1 (Monday) figure Rs. 29,766.80 and your Column 3 Today Food Purchases Date 2, Tuesday) figure Rs. 32,859.60. You get Rs. 62,626.40. This Rs. 62,626.40 is your Column 6 To-Date Food Purchases Date 2 (Tuesday) figure.

To get your Column 6 To-Date Food Purchases Date 3 figure, you add your Column 3 Today Food Purchases Date 3 figure Rs. 44,499.60 and Column 6 To-Date Food Purchases Date 2 figure Rs. 62,626.40. You get Rs. 1,07,126. This Rs. 1,07,126 is your Column 6 To-Date Food Purchases Date 3 figure.

Follow this procedure everyday for the rest of the month. For Thursday, March 4, your Column 6 To-Date Food Purchases figure is 14,37,160.00 (the total of Column 3 for Monday, Tuesday, Wednesday, and Thursday). Keep going this same way until the end of the month. Your total for the Month figures at the bottom line of the chart should be identical in Columns 3 and 6. You spent Rs. 10,83,809.20 for food in March.

Column 7: To-Date Food Sales

Use the same method for Column 7 as you did for Column 6. Just for the first day of the month, your Column 7 To-Date Food Sales figure is the same as your Column 4 Today Food Sales figure Rs. 66,590.00. After the first day of the month, you start adding.

To get your Column 7 To-Date Food Sales figure for Date 2 (Tuesday), add your Column 4 Today Food Sales Date 1 (Monday), figure Rs. 66,590.00 and your Column 4 Today Food Sales Date 2 (Tuesday) figure Rs. 68,928. You get Rs. 1,35,518. This Rs. 1,35,518 is your Column 7 To-Date Food Sales Date 2 (Tuesday) figure.

To get your Column 7 To-Date Food Sales Date 3 figure (Wednesday), you add your Column 4 Today Food Sales Date 3 figure Rs. 84,678.00 and your Column 7 To-Date Food Sales Date 2 figure Rs. 1,35,518. You get Rs. 2,20,196. This Rs. 2,20,196 is your Column 7 To-Date Food Sales Date 3 (Wednesday) figure.

Follow this procedure daily for the rest of the month. Your Column 7 To-Date Food Sales Date 4 (Thursday) figure is Rs. 2,91,352.00.

Column 4 for Monday, Tuesday, Wednesday and Thursday. Keep going this same way until the end of the month. The Total for Month figures at the bottom line of the chart should be identical in Columns 4 and 7. Your food sales were Rs. 2,80,3906 in March.

Column 8: To-Date Food Cost Per cent

Just for the first day of the month, your Column 8 To-Date Food Cost per cent Date 1 figure is the same as your Column 5 Today Food Cost per cent Date 1 figure. After the first day, it gets cumulative. This is the column you watch like a hawk.

To get your Column 8 To-Date Food Cost per cent Date 2 figure, you divide Column 6 To-Date Food Purchases Date 2 figure Rs. 62,626.40 Column 7 To-Date Food Sales Date 2 figure Rs. 1,35,518. You get .4621 Multiply this .4621 by 100 to convert to a per cent. You get 46.21 per cent. Your Column 8 To-Date Food Cost per cent Date 2 figure is 46.21 per cent. To get your Column 8 To-Date Food Cost per cent Date 3 figure, you divide your Column 6 To-Date Food Purchases Date 3 figure Rs. 1,07,126 by your Column 7 To-Date Food Sales Date 3 figure Rs. 2,20,196. You get .4865. Multiply this .4865 by 100 to convert to a per cent. You get 48.65 per cent. Your Column 8 To-Date Food Cost per cent Date 3 figure is 48.65 per cent. Keep going this same way until the end of the month. The Total for month figure the bottom line of Table 5.1 for Column 8 To-Date Food Cost per cent is also 38.65 per cent. The totals should be identical in Columns 5 and 8. This 38.65 per cent is your food cost percent for March.

The bottom figures in Column 5 Today Food Cost per cent Column 8 To-Date Food Cost per cent are not totals. You get the bottom figure 38.65 per cent in Column 5 by dividing Column 3 Total for Month Today Food Purchases figure Rs. 10,83,809.20 by Column 4 Total for Month Today Food Sales Rs. 28,03,906.00.

You get the Column 8 bottom figure 38.65 per cent by just brings down your last figure for the month in this Column. Column 8 is the result of your cumulative figure for the month . The figures in Column 6, 7 and 8 for Wednesday, March 31, are the cumulative figures in Columns 6, 7 and 8 for Wednesday, March 31, are the same as totals for month figure in Column 3, 4 and 5.

Chart–5.1

Purchases Formula (Food Cost Formula 1)

Date	*Day*	*Today Food Purchases*	*Today Food Sale*	*Today Food Cost Per Cent*	*To-Date Food Purchases*	*To-Date Food Sale*	*To-Date Food Cost Per Cent*
1	2	3	4	5	6	7	8
1.	M	29766.80	66590.00	44.70	27966.80	66590.00	44.70
2.	T	32859.60	68928.00	47.67	62626.40	135518.00	46.21
3.	W	44499.60	84678.00	52.55	107126.00	220196.00	48.65
4.	TH	36845.60	71156.00	51.78	143971.60	291352.00	49.42
5.	F	71520.80	113722.00	62.89	215492.40	405074.00	53.20
6.	S	8349.60	122714.00	6.80	223842.00	527788.00	42.41
7.	S	00.00	80452.00	00.00	223842.00	608240.00	36.80
8.	M	38815.60	68974.00	56.28	262657.60	677214.00	38.79
9.	T	35350.80	72450.00	48.79	298008.40	749664.00	39.75
10.	W	38187.20	91668.00	41.66	336195.60	841332.00	39.96
11.	TH	36778.80	66990.00	54.90	372974.40	908322.00	41.06
12.	F	63738.00	121914.00	52.98	436712.40	1030236.00	42.39
13.	S	10810.80	130240.00	8.30	447523.20	1160476.00	38.56
14.	S	00.00	78140.00	00.00	447523.20	1238886.00	36.12
15.	M	37252.80	70256.00	53.02	484776.00	1309142.00	37.03
16.	T	44832.40	71300.00	62.88	529608.40	1380442.00	38.37
17.	W	53505.20	91902.00	58.22	583113.60	1472344.00	39.60
18.	TH	46808.40	62516.00	74.87	629922.00	1534860.00	41.04
19.	F	68289.20	125898.00	54.24	698211.20	1660758.00	42.04
20.	S	7467.20	139932.00	5.34	705678.40	1800690.00	39.19
21.	S	00.00	79798.00	00.00	705678.40	1880488.00	37.53
22.	M	36941.60	77406.00	47.72	742620.00	1957894.00	37.93
23.	T	44038.40	70938.00	62.08	786658.40	20720.80	38.77
24.	W	53821.20	99266.00	54.22	840479.60	2128098.00	39.49

(Contd.)

1	2	3	4	5	6	7	8
25.	TH	42722.40	69354.00	61.60	883202.00	2197452.00	40.19
26.	F	78568.80	129576.00	60.64	961770.80	2327028.00	41.33
27.	S	8289.60	135162.00	6.13	970060.40	2462190.00	39.40
28.	S	00.00	88134.00	00.00	970060.40	2550324.00	38.04
29.	M	37828.40	76568.00	49.40	1007888.80	2626892.00	38.37
30.	T	39912.40	73990.00	53.94	104780.20	27000882.00	38.79
31.	W	36008.00	103024.00	34.95	1083809.20	2803906.00	38.65
		1083809.20	2803906.00	38.65	1083809.20	2803906.00	38.65

Advantages in Food Cost Formula 1

What are the advantages of using Formula 1? What can it tell you?

1. Formula 1 is simple and easy to do.
2. Formula 1 gives you a general indication of the trend your food cost is taking for the month. About 10 days after the beginning of each month is an important time for your food cost control programme because that is when cumulative figures begin to mean something concrete to you.

Look at Chart 5.1, Column 8, Date 10, Wednesday, March 10. Your To-Date Food Cost per cent is 39.96 per cent. Let us say you want a food cost per cent of 39 per cent for the month of March. It is only the 10th of the month, so you have 21 days left in March to reduce your food cost per cent for the month. Look at the very bottom line of Column 8—Total for the month. Your cumulative To-Date Food Cost per cent for the month of March winds up at 38.65 per cent. This is 1.31 per cent lower than the cumulative To-Date Food Cost per cent of 39.96 per cent you had on Wednesday, March 10, 1.31 per cent may sound small, but it can represent a lot of revenue. In our example, 1.31per cent multiplied by Column 7 To-Date Sales Total for Month Rs. 28,03,906.00 equals Rs. 36,731.20—quite a few revenue.

The point is, if you do not like your Column 8 figure after the first week or 10 days of a month, do something about it. You know where you stand and you still have time during the month to take action that will fix your cumulative food cost per cent so you will like the figure that counts—the figure at the bottom of Column 8 in your chart, which is your food cost per cent for the month—at the end of the month.

The first 10 days of every month indicate the trend your food cost is taking for the month. If it is high, reduce your purchases. Try to buy less. The 10th day of the month is important when it comes to perishable food, too. By the 10th you should have used up any perishable food you bought on the first of the month. If you have not, it is probably spoiled. Despite freezing and special spoilage-retarding chemical additives, foods still spoil. By about the 10th, if you have thrown out perishables you bought the first week, your food cost percent will be high because these foods are not inventory (they went out in the garbage) and you have no revenue for them.

3. Another advantage of Formula 1 is that after the first 10 days of the month, each daily input of purchases and sales does not drastically change your to-date cost per cent, as daily input of purchases and sales are apt to do in the first two or three days of the month. As the month progresses, each input of daily food purchases figure. Each input into Column 6 To-Date Food Purchases has a smaller impact on Column 6 as the month goes along.

As a month progresses, any one day's accumulated purchases constitutes a smaller percentage of the total purchases for the month. So, as the end of the month gets closer, the food cost figure you get from Formula 1 will come closer to your actual food cost. To illustrate this point, look at Chart 5.1. Look at Column 8 To-Date Food Cost per cent Date 4 (Thursday, March 4) figure. The figure is 49.42 per cent. For the next day, the Column 8 Date 5 (Friday, March 5) figure is 53.20 per cent. There is a difference of 3.88 per cent between these two figures. Now look at the Column 8 To-Date Food Cost per cent Date 30 (Tuesday, March 30) figure. Your cumulative food cost percent so far for March is 38.79 per cent. Look at the Column 8 figure for the next day, March 31. The figure is 38.65 per cent. There is only 0.14 per cent difference between these two figures.

Not that every Sunday there is a large drop in the Column 8 To-Date Food Cost per cent cumulative figure. The food service operation open on Sundays and food is sold, but nothing is purchased.

As you go along in the month, closer to the end of it, your cumulative To-Date Food Cost per cent figure in Column 8 settles into a pattern of figures that vary less from each other day-to-day and that are closer, what your actual food cost per cent for the month is going to be.

After you have kept your chart for the first 10 days of a month, you can begin to see the pattern in your purchasing and sales and food cost per cent. It is still early in the month and you have time left to take corrective action if your food cost per cent for the first 10 days is too high. If you are over the food cost you want, look in your storeroom. Estimate whether your inventory has increased. If it looks to you as if it has increased, you are probably okay. If it looks as if it has decreased, have probably used food from inventory instead of purchasing food all your food cost at the end of the month will probably be higher than Formula 1 indicates. "Looks" seems flimsy. It is-until you develop ability in judging your inventory. This takes a little time but your judgment can eventually become fairly accurate.

You can control your food cost per cent with Formula 1 only if you purchase for immediate use. Purchase carefully so that you use food without increasing decreasing your inventory. Some days you will increase your inventory; some days you will take food out and decrease it. But on the average, inventory should be stable. You want it to be, for example, Rs. 2,40,000 on the first of the month and Rs. 2,40,000 on the 31st of the month. In between, it will fluctuate.

Disadvantages in Food Cost Formula 1

Formula 1 has Some Disadvantages, Too

Your Column 5 Today Food Cost per cent figure is not apt to be very accurate. Formula 1 is a simple formula. It does not allow for inventory fluctuation from the end of one month to the end of the next month, and therefore Column 5 will be only as accurate as the accuracy with which you manage your inventory. Formula 1 assumes that all purchases will be charged and used immediately - but in most establishments that is not really what happens. On some days, you buy more than you use up that day. The excess goes into your inventory. On other days, you use more than you buy that day, so you take food out of inventory. This makes Column 5 higher if you increase your inventory and lower if you decrease your inventory.

To illustrate this, look at Chart 5.1, Column 3 Today Food Purchases for all the Sundays-March 7, 14,21 and 28. The figure is always zero. No items were counted as purchased on any Sunday because you did not get any deliveries of food on Sundays. But (in our chart) you were open for business on Sundays, so you took food out of inventory and used it on Sundays. In Column 5, all Sundays are zero because you did not buy anything, and you cannot divide a sales figure into zero.

For each Sunday, the Column 6 To-Date Food Purchases figure is the same figure as the figure entered for each Saturday right above it. Purchases are the same on Saturday and Sunday each week. Sales are not, however. You do sell food on Sundays. Sales figures in Column 7 To-Date Food Sales are not the same Saturday and Sunday every week.

The fact that you do not receive food on Sunday but you do use food from the storeroom decreases your Column 8 To-Date Food Cost per cent figure for each Sunday. You do use food out of inventory, and this definitely lowers your cumulative To-Date Food Cost per cent for Sundays.

Formula 1 does not include the cost of feeding employees or the cost of transfers of items to or from the bar. Formula 2 includes both. (These two factors are the main reasons for the difference between the cumulative Column 8 To-Date Food Cost per cent for March in Chart 5.1 for Formula 1 and the cumulative Column 17 To-Date Food Cost per cent for March in Chart 5.2 for Formula 2).

The key to success with Formula 1 food cost control system work is inventory management. With experience you should be able to develop some accuracy in judging inventory fluctuations. If your food cost is higher for the first 10 days, but you see that you have a lot of food in the storeroom, your accumulated food cost percent should go down later in the month because you should not have to buy much food.

The actual physical inventory figure at the end of the month should not be very different from your actual physical inventory figure at the beginning of the month. (The ending inventory figure for one month is the opening inventory figure for the next month.)

One thing you can do to control inventory fluctuation is to try to limit what you buy toward the end of the month. You will have to buy some items at the end of the month. Maybe you will have to buy extra items for a banquet you will serve at the beginning of the following month. You will get the banquet revenue next month. Next month your To-Date Food Cost per cent should be lower because you have already bought some of the banquet food and should have fewer banquet purchases next month. This should reduce your food purchases for next month and give you a lower food cost per cent next month.

If you get—and keep on getting—a lot of inventory fluctuation from month to month, the Food Cost Formula 1 system is not working well for you. Your inventory will fluctuate up or down on a day-to-day basis. But you want your inventory to be very similar in actual revenue from one month end to the next month end. If your closing inventory February 28 was Rs. 2,40,000 for example, you want your closing inventory on March 31 as close to Rs. 2,40,000, you can get it. After you have used this system for a while, you will probably be able to eliminate or at least reduce some of the inventory fluctuation. Do not give up on Formula 1 too quickly. It will generally serve you better as you more adept at making it work for you.

Inventory can and will fluctuate some, but this does not have to have drastic an effect on the to-date cumulative food cost per cent you get Formula 1. Even when your inventory does fluctuate, Formula 1 can still give you an indication of the trend your food cost per cent is taking. Say, example, that your food service operation has average monthly sales Rs. 2,40,0000. You spend an average of Rs. 9,12,000 a month for food purchases. You maintain an average food inventory of Rs. 2,40,0000. Suppose that your inventory varies down Rs. 24,000 or up Rs. 24,000 from this Rs. 2,40,000 figure. Down Rs. 24,000 means a food cost of Rs. 8,88,000 and a food cost per cent of 37 per cent. Stationary at Rs. 9,12,000 means food cost of Rs. 9,12,000 and a food cost per cent of 38 per cent. Up Rs. 24,000 means a food cost of Rs. 9,36,000 and a food cost per cent of 39 per cent.

With Formula 1, you calculate your corresponding changes in food cost per cent. With Rs. 24000 inventory fluctuation up or down from average, you have still stayed relatively close – 1 per cent up or down – to the food cost per cent for food purchases of Rs. 9,12,000. Your food has fluctuated up or down 10 per cent. Even with inventory fluctuation, Formula 1 does tell you the trend of your food cost percentage.

Food Cost Formula 1 is not as accurate as Formula 2, but it is certainly better than nothing and it can give you some helpful information. Nothing is helpful, however, if you do not act on information. Take action to correct a food cost that is not what you want it to be.

If you take pains, Formula 1 can work quite well for you, although the food cost per cent it gives you will usually be higher than your actual food cost percent. This is because Formula 1 does not consider cost of employees' meals, transfers to and from the bar, or inventory fluctuation.

If you use Food Cost Formula 1, you can help to see to it that you do come close to your actual food cost per cent by:

1. Watching your purchases throughout the month and reducing purchases where you can if food cost per cent gets too high.
2. Attempting to minimize inventory fluctuations.

Formula 1 can tell you the trend your food cost is taking. It can give you a pretty good indication of what your actual month's food cost will turn out to be before you deduct for employees' meals and thus lower your food cost.

How Food Cost per cent Figure is Obtained for statement of Income Your Food Cost per cent is the figure that is put on your statement of income for the month. It is calculated as follows (only for use with Formula 1):

1. RUPEES VALUE OF OPENING PHYSICAL FOOD INVENTORY (this figure was your closing total food inventory figure last month) plus TOTAL RUPEES VALUE OF FOOD PUR–CHASES FOR THE MONTH (add up all invoices for month or get figure from your general accounting records where you have records of all food purchases for month) equals TOTAL FOOD AVAILABLE.

Chart 5.2
Purchases Formula (Food Cost Formula 2)

1	2	3	4	5	6	7	8	9
Dt.	*Day*	*Opening Food Storeroom Inventory Beginning of Day*	*Storeroom Purchases*	*Total Food Available Storeroom*	*Food Requisitions*	*Direct Purchases*	*Transfers to Kitchen*	*Cost of Food Used*
1.	M	26984960	23947.20	293796.80	20414.00	5819.60	136.40	26370.00
2.	T	273382.80	27781.60	301164.40	24313.60	5078.00	98.80	29490.40
3.	W	276850.80	40622.00	317472.80	30304.00	3877.60	00.00	34181.60
4.	Th	287168.80	34444.00	321612.80	26254.40	2401.60	00.00	28650.40
5.	F	295358.40	64935.00	360294.00	33269.60	6585.20	216.40	44071.20
6.	S	327024.40	6498.88	333523.20	42050.80	1850.80	116.00	44017.60
7.	S	291472.40	00.00	291472.40	30954.00	00.00	00.00	30954.00
8.	M	260518.40	33573.60	294092.00	21680.40	5242.00	319.20	27241.60
9.	T	272411.60	29343.20	301754.80	24226.40	6007.60	50.00	30284.00
10.	W	277528.40	33430.80	310959.20	30008.40	4756.40	00.00	34764.80
11.	Th	280950.80	34154.80	315103.60	23711.20	2626.00	00.00	26337.20
12.	F	291392.40	56533.60	347926.00	37608.40	7204.40	231.40	45044.40
13.	S	310317.60	8626.00	318943.60	4511.00	2180.80	47.20	47348.00
14.	S	273827.60	00.00	273827.60	31275.20	00.00	00.00	31275.20
15.	M	242552.40	31536.40	274088.80	21789.60	5716.40	136.80	27642.80
16.	T	252299.20	3951.20	291950.40	25964.40	5181.20	00.00	31145.60
17.	W	265986.00	47956.00	313942.00	34107.20	5549.20	118.40	39774.80
18.	Th	279834.80	42968.00	322802.80	20308.80	3840.40	00.00	24149.20
19.	F	302494.00	61632.80	364126.80	40170.00	6656.40	58.00	46884.40
20.	S	323956.80	5485.60	329442.40	51626.00	1981.60	296.00	53903.60
21.	S	277816.40	00.00	277816.40	31323.60	00.00	00.00	31323.60
22.	M	246492.80	30620.00	277112.40	25605.60	6321.60	00.00	31927.20
23.	T	251507.20	39669.20	291176.40	24928.00	4369.20	206.00	29503.20
24.	W	266248.40	47303.60	313552.00	29211.20	6517.60	00.00	35728.80
25.	Th	284340.80	39394.80	323735.60	23599.60	3327.60	00.00	26927.20
26.	F	300136.00	70703.20	370839.20	40974.80	7865.60	280.40	49120.80
27.	S	329864.40	6495.60	336360.00	50192.40	1794.00	74.80	52061.20
28.	S	286167.60	00.00	286167.60	36576.00	00.00	00.00	36576.00
29.	M	249591.60	32561.20	282152.80	24785.20	5267.20	90.00	30142.40
30.	T	257367.60	34008.00	291375.60	21794.40	5904.40	00.00	27698.80
31.	W	269581.20	30852.80	300434.00	34865.20	5155.20	48.00	40068.40
Ap. 1	Th	265568.80	–	–	–	–	–	–
To Total Month		265568.80	11,54,727.60		959008.40	129081.60	2524.00	

Proof of Inventory

Opening Inventory	269849.60
Storeroom Purchase	954727.60
Total	**1224577.20**
Requisitions	959008.40
Closing Inventory	265568.80

10 *Employees Meals*	11 *Transfers from Kitchen to Bar*	12 *Today Cost of Food Sold*	13 *Today Food Sales*	14 *Today Food Cost Per cent per Rupee Sale*	15 *To-Date Cost of Food Sold*	16 *To-Date Food Sales*	17 *To-Date Food Cost per cent Per Rupee Sale*
2200.00	409.60	23760.40	66590.00	1427.20	23760.40	66590.00	1427.20
2160.00	513.20	26817.20	68928.00	1556.40	4977.60	135518.00	1492.80
2240.00	221.60	31680.00	84678.00	1496.40	82257.60	220196.00	1494.40
2380.00	270.40	26005.60	71156.00	1462.00	108263.20	291352.00	1486.40
2580.00	406.00	37085.20	113720.00	1304.40	145348.40	405074.00	1435.20
2680.00	507.20	40830.40	122714.00	1330.80	186178.80	527778.80	1411.20
2300.00	00.00	28654.00	804552.00	1424.80	214832.80	628240.00	1412.80
2160.00	456.80	24624.80	68974.00	142800.00	2394576.00	677214.00	1414.40
2240.00	424.40	27619.60	72450.00	1524.80	267077.20	74966.40	1425.20
2400.00	336.60	32028.80	91668.00	1397.60	299106.00	841332.00	1422.00
2320.00	258.40	23758.80	66990.00	1418.80	322864.80	908322.00	1422.00
2560.00	447.20	42037.20	121914.00	137920.00	364902.00	1030236.00	1416.80
2520.00	566.00	44247.60	130240.00	1358.80	409149.60	1160476.00	141040
2200.00	00.00	29075.20	78410.00	1483.20	438224.80	1238886.00	1410.80
2080.00	404.00	25158.80	70256.00	1432.40	463383.60	1309142.00	1416.00
2240.00	442.00	28463.60	71300.00	1596.80	491847.20	1380442.00	1425.20
2440.00	299.60	37035.20	91902.00	1612.00	528882.40	1472344.00	1436.80
2200.00	257.60	21691.60	62516.00	1388.00	550574.00	1534860.00	1434.80
2640.00	658.40	43586.00	125898.00	13848.00	594160.00	1660758.00	1431.20
2720.00	558.00	50625.60	139932.00	1447.20	644785.60	1800690.00	1432.40
2040.00	00.00	29283.60	79798.00	1468.00	674069.20	1880488.00	1434.00
2040.00	324.00	29563.20	77406.00	1424.00	703632.40	1957894.00	1437.00
2160.00	398.40	26944.80	70938.00	1519.00	730577.20	2028832.00	1440.40
2440.00	332.40	32956.40	99266.00	1328.00	763533.60	2128098.00	1435.20
2320.00	261.60	24345.60	69354.00	1404.00	787879.20	2197452.00	1434.40
2640.00	524.00	45956.80	129576.00	1418.80	833836.00	2327028.00	1433.20
2880.00	574.40	48606.80	135162.00	1438.04	882442.80	2462190.00	1433.60
2640.00	00.00	33936.00	88134.00	1540.00	916378.80	2550324.00	1437.20
2080.00	358.00	27704.40	76568.00	1447.20	944083.20	2626892.00	1437.60
2160.00	457.60	25081.20	73990.00	1359.20	969164.40	2700882.00	1433.60
2440.00	336.00	37292.40	103024.00	1448.00	1006457.00	2803906.00	1436.00
–	–	–	–	–	–	–	–
73100.00	11056.20	1006456.00	2803906.00	1436.00	1006456.00	2803906.00	1430.00

Proof of Cost

Opening Inventory	269849.60	Transfer to Bar	11057.20
Storeroom Purchase	958727.60	Employees Meals	73100.00
Direct Purchases	129081.60	Closing Inventory	265568.80
Transfer to Kitchen	2524.00	Cost of Food Sold	102456.80
Total	**1356182.80**		

2. TOTAL FOOD AVAILABLE minus RUPEES VALUE CLOSING PHYSICAL FOOD INVENTORY and minus RUPEES VÁLUE EMPLOYEES' MEALS (if you feed your employees free meals equals COST OF FOOD SOLD.
3. COST OF FOOD SOLD divided by TOTAL FOOD SALES FOR MONTH (add every day's closing cash register tapes for month or get from your general accounting record) multiplied by 100 (to convert to a percentage) equals FOOD COST PER CENT FOR MONTH AS IT APPEARS ON YOUR STATEMENT OF INCOME.
4. FOOD COST FORMULA 2 (Chart 5.2).

How to Use Formula 2

Formula 2 is more complex than Formula 1. It takes more time, but it more accurate.

There are five equations in Formula 2. They are:

1. OPENING FOOD STOREROOM INVENTORY plus STOREROOM PURCHASES equals TOTAL FOOD AVAILABLE STOREROOM.
2. TOTAL FOOD AVAILABLE STOREROOM minus FOOD REQUISITIONS equals CLOSING FOOD STOREROOM INVENTORY. (This second equation can also be written: TOTAL FOOD AVAILABLE STOREROOM minus CLOSING FOOD STORE. ROOM INVENTORY equals FOOD REQUISITIONS).
3. FOOD REQUISITIONS plus DIRECT PURCHASES plus TRANSFERS TO KITCHEN equals COST OF FOOD USED.
4. COST OF FOOD USED minus EMPLOYEES' MEALS minus TRANSFERS TO BAR equals COST OF FOOD SOLD.
5. COST OF FOOD SOLD divided by FOOD SALES multiplied by 100 (to convert to a percentage) equals FOOD COST PER CENT PER RUPEES SALE.
   Start a new chart the first day of each month.

The easiest way to use this formula is to prepare a chart on column (or put it in your computer) as shown in Chart 5.2 and do the following steps:

1. Column 1: Date—You always start a new chart the first of each month, so your date column always starts with 1.

2. Column 2: Day—In the Day column, put whatever day the first of the month, happens to fall on. (S if Saturday, W if Wednesday, and so on). In our sample Chart 5.2, we say you are starting on March 1 and say it is a Monday.

COLUMNS 3 THROUGH 14 ARE TODAY FIGURES—JUST DAILY, DAY-BY-DAY—NOT INCREASING, NOT ACCUMULATING AS YOU GO.

Column 3: Opening Food Storeroom Inventory Beginning of Day

This figure is the total rupee value amount of all food in your food storeroom on the first day of the month-Monday, March 1 in our chart. You get this figure from your closing physical food storeroom inventory for the last day of the preceding month. Or you could take the bottom figure in Column 3 from your February chart if you did not take a physical inventory at the end of February.

In Chart 5.2, on Monday, March 1, your Column 3 Opening Food Storeroom Inventory Beginning of Day figure is Rs. 2,69,849.60. Get this figure from your closing physical storeroom inventory you took the last day of last month. On Monday, March 1, you start the day with Rs. 2,69,849.60 worth of food in your storeroom. Column 3 always has one figure more than it has days in the month. That is because you are using Column 3 to record both opening and closing inventories for the month.

Your closing inventory figure for Monday, March 1, is your Column 3 Opening Food Inventory Storeroom Beginning of Day figure for Tuesday, March 2. Closing Inventory for Date 1 is Rs. 2,73,382.80 (see *(a)* and *(b)* below). Put this in Column 3 Date 2 because closing inventory for Date 1 is Opening Food Storeroom Inventory Beginning of Day for Date 2.

To get Date 2 for Column 3, do the following steps:

(a) Add Column 4 Storeroom Purchases Date 1 Rs. 2,39,47.20 and Column 3 Opening Food Storeroom Inventory Beginning of Day Date 1 Rs. 2,69,849.60. You get Rs. 2,93,796.80. This Rs. 2,93,796.80 is your Column 5 Total Food Available Storeroom Date 1 figure.

(b) Subtract Column 6 Food Requisitions Date 1 Rs. 2,04,14.00 from Column 5 Total Food Available Storeroom Date 1 Rs.

2,93,796.80. You get Rs. 2,73,382.80. This Rs. 2,73,382.80 is your Column 3 Opening Food Storeroom Inventory Beginning of Day Date 2 figure.

Column 4: Storeroom Purchases

On Monday, March 1, you received Storeroom Purchases of Rs. 2,39,47.20 worth of food. You get the figure for Column 4 Storeroom Purchases by adding the rupee value of all food invoices for the food you put in the food storeroom each day. This figure is all food items that will go into the storeroom. When they leave the storeroom, requisitions will be written for the items and they will go into food production. The food should not leave the storeroom unless it is requisitioned in writing.

Put as many purchase items into this Column 4 Storeroom Purchases category as you can instead of into the Column 7 Direct Purchases category which are not requisitioned. Storeroom Purchases items are issued only by written requisition, and when you have written requisitions you can get a more accurate food cost with Formula 2.

Column 5: Total Food Available Storeroom

To get this figure for Monday, March 1, Rs. 23,947.20. You get Rs. 2,95,116.80 This Rs. 2,93,796.80 is your Column 5 Total Food Available Storeroom figure for Monday, March 1.This figure is the rupee amount of your total inventory plus items you received and put into the storeroom that day.This is the value of food you had to start with Monday morning March 1 plus what you received Monday—the total value of food available to you on Monday, March 1.

Column 6: Food Requisitions

You get this figure by adding up all your food requisition slips for Monday, March 1. For Monday, March 1, the figure on Chart 5.2 is Rs. 20,414.00. Add up all your food requisitions for the day to get your total ruppee cost of all food items removed from your storeroom that day.

Rs. 20,414.00 worth of food was removed from your storeroom on Monday, March 1. Requisitions were written for all this food. All this food went to food production in the kitchen.

Column 7: Direct Purchases

In Chart 5.2 for Monday, March 1, the figure is Rs. 5,819.60. On Monday, March 1, day, March 1, you received Direct Purchases of Rs. 5,819.60 worth of food. This food goes right to production. It never goes to the storeroom at all. There are no requisitions.

Examples of these types of items could be bread, milk, icecream. pies, pastries—items that should be used that day. These items generally have to be called Direct Purchases. They must go right to the kitchen and cannot sit on a shelf in the storeroom. But do not classify any food as Direct Purchases unless you have to—the fewer the better. Put everything that can reasonably go to the storeroom in the Column 4 Storeroom Purchases category instead, so you do use requisitions and will have more accurate records for your food cost.

Column 8: Transfers to Kitchen

Transfers to kitchen are items you use in the kitchen in food production. But you do not requisition them from the food storeroom. They are not direct purchases, either. These are items you transfer to your kitchen from another department in your operation, usually the bar. The chef (or anyone you authorize in the kitchen) makes written requisitions for items the kitchen wants from the bar and gives them to the bar in exchange for the items. Whoever makes up this Formula 2 chart get the information from the bar and puts the ruppee amount of transfers to kitchen for the day in this column.

Examples of transfers to kitchen would be beer requisitioned from the bar and used in the kitchen for cooking, and so on. These are bar beverage items. But they are used in the kitchens ingredients in food . Charge their cost to food cost, not bar or beverage department cost. (And do not forget—if your cook drinks some of this beer or wine, it is part of your food cost for the day).

Column 9: Cost of Food Used

To get this figure, you add Column 6 Food Requisitions, Column 7 direct Purchases and Column 8 Transfers to Kitchen. Put the total in Column 9. It is the total rupees value of food available each day.

In Chart 5.2, Column 9 Date 1 is Rs. 26,370. You get this by adding Column 6 Food Requisitions Date 1 Rs. 20,414.00 and Column

7 Direct Purchases Date 1 Rs. 5,819.60 and Column 8 Transfers to Kitchen Date 1, Rs. 136.40.

To get Column 9 figure for Date 2, add Column 6 Date 2, Column 7 Date 2, and Column 8 Date 2. Keep doing this the same way the rest of the month.

Column 10: Employees' Meals

You deduct for employees' meals because if you give food to your employees free (or at discount price), it costs you money to feed employees. (There are several different ways you can get this figure.)

In the food service industry, you generally feed the employees who on duty in the food service department. If food service employees put in eight-hour shift in a food service operation, they may get one meal, may be more. If you buy food that you give free to your employees, it is ; for you, and you must recognize it and deduct it from the cost of food used. This amount is recorded as an expense in your accounting records. The rupees value for employees' meals for each day is recorded in Column 10.

Column 11: Transfers from Kitchen to Bar

This column includes items you transfer from the food department to the beverage department. The bar can requisition things like cream, milk, eggs, oranges, lemons, limes, cherries, or olives from the kitchen sent to the bar, and used in drinks. Do not charge these to food cost. Charge them item to the bar.

Bartenders write requisitions for food items they need and give them to the kitchen personnel—probably cooks, or anyone you designated. Cooks keep these requisitions until you (or whoever is keeping the Formula chart) get them from up for the day, and put the figure in this column.

Some operation ignore transfers to kitchen because they do not think there is enough money involved to bother with making the calculations and putting them in the chart. It is upto you to decide if you think it is worthwhile for you or not. You should whoever be aware that food items from the kitchen used in drink preparation cannot be sold as food, and beverage items used in the kitchen cannot sold as bar items, so there will be an effect on bar and kitchen cost if there are transfers. How big the effect will be will depend on how much transferring goes on and how much the items cost.

Column 12: Today Cost of Food Sold

To get this figure, you add Column 10 Employees' Meals Date 1 Rs. 2,200.00 and Column 11 Transfers from Kitchen to Bar Date 1 Rs. 409.6. You get Rs. 2,609.60. Subtract this Rs. 2609.60 from Column 9 Cost of Food Used Date 1 Rs. 26,370. You get Rs. 23760.40. This Rs. 23,760.40 is your Column 12 Today Cost Food Sold Date 1 figure. Follow this same procedure through the rest of the month.

Note that there are only two deductions you make from Cost of Food Used to get your Column 12 Today Cost of Food Sold. They are Employees' Meals (Column 10) and Transfers from Kitchen to Bar (Column 11). You subtract these two costs (if they occur) from Column 9 Cost Food Used to get rupee value for Column 12 Today Cost of Food Sold. Any mistakes in direct purchases, requisitioning, overproduction, discarded food, and the like should be (and by this method will be) charged into the cost of food sold for the day they happen.

Column 13: Today Food Sales

The Date 1 figure in this column is the total food sales for Monday March 1. You get this figure from your cash register tape for Monday. Chart 5.2 you had Rs. 66,590 in food sales on Monday, March 1. Get the closing figure from your cash register tape each day for this column.

Column 14: Today Food Cost per cent per Rupee Sale

You get this figure by doing the following: Divide Column 12 Today Cost of Food Sold Date 1 Rs. 23760.40 by Column 13 Today Food Sales 1 Rs. 6659J. You get .3568. Multiply by 100 to convert to a percentage. You get 35.68 per cent. Your Column 14 Today Food Cost per cent per rupee Date 1 is 35.68 per cent.

Follow this procedure for the rest of the month.

COLUMNS 15, 16 AND 17 ARE "TO-DATE" FIGURES. THESE COLUMNS DO INCREASE AND DO ACCUMULATE FOR THE MONTH AS YOU GO ALONG.

Column 15: To: Date Cost of Food Sold

For Date 1, column 15 is the same as Column 12 Today Cost of Food Sold Date 1 Rs. 23,760.40. To get Column 15 Date 2 , add Column 15 To-Date Cost of Food Sold Date 1 Rs. 23,760.40 and Column12 Today cost of food Sold Date 2 Rs. 50,577.60. This gives you 15 to date cost of food sold date 2 Rs. 50, 577.60. To get Column 15 date 3, at Column 15 to date cost of food sold date 2 Rs. 50, 777.60 and Column 12 Today Cost of Food Sold Date 3 Rs. 31,680.00. This gives you Column 15 To-Date Cost of Food Sold Date 3 Rs. 82,257.60.

Follow this procedure for the rest of the month.

Column 16: To-Date Food Sales

For Date 1, Column 16 is the same as Column 13 Today Food Sales Date 1 Rs. 66,590. To get Column 16 Date 2, add Column 16 To-Date Food Sales Date 1 Rs. 66,590 and Column 13 Today Food Sales Date 2 Rs. 68,928. This gives you Column 16 Date 2 Rs. 1,35,518. To get Column 16 Date 3, add Column 16 To-Date Food Sales Date 2 Rs. 1,35,518 and Column 13 Today Food Sales Date 3 Rs. 84, 678 This gives you Column 16 Date 3 Rs. 2,20,196.00.

Follow this procedure for the rest of the month.

Column 17: To-Date Food Cost per cent per Rupee Sale

To get this figure, divide Column 15 To-Date Cost of Food Sold Date 1 Rs. 23,760.40 by Column 16 To-Date Food Sales Date 1 Rs. 66,590.00. You get .3568. Multiply by 100 to convert to a percentage. You get 35.68 per cent. Your Column 17 To-Date Food Cost per cent per rupee Sale for Date 1 is 35.68 per cent.

Follow this same procedure for the rest of the month.

Note: When you compute Column 17 To-Date Food Cost per cent per rupee Sale, always divide Column 15 To-Date Cost of Food Sold by Column 16 To-Date Food Sales. Never try to average your cumulative food cost per cent. It will not be accurate.

The figures you put in Column 17 To-Date Food Cost per cent per Dollar Sale each day are the figures you go through the entire routine to get. Every day, all month, you watch Column 17 like a hawk. You take action if you need to in order to get the daily, and thus ultimately the monthly, food cost per cent you want.

"Food cost per cent" is just a guide for you. It can be a very good tool to use, but it is just a tool. Treat it that way. "Food cost percentage" is just words unless you understand and use the facts the words symbolize. Your goal is not "food cost per cent." Your goal is net profit in rupee. Controlling your food cost per cent as you go can help you achieve that goal.

Advantages in Food Cost Formulation 2

What are the advantages of Food Cost Formula 2?

1. Formula 2 is more accurate than Formula 1 Because Formula 2:

   (a) Includes changes in inventory in storeroom.

   (b) Includes transfers to and from kitchen and to and from bar.

   (c) Deducts for cost of employees' meal.

2. Formula 2 makes it possible for you to calculate what you closing storeroom inventory should be. (Formula 1 does not).

Disadvantages in Food Cost Formula 2

This formula also has disadvantages:

1. Formula 2 is more work than formula 1 because with Formula 2:

   (a) You must write down all requisitions make extensions on requisitions. "Extensions" means you multiply the cost of each item by the number of amount of that item. (One pound of butter costs Rs. 60.00, five pounds costs Rs. 300.00-300 is the extension.)

   (b) You must write down and make extensions on all transfers from kitchen to bar and from bar to kitchen.

   (c) You must compute the cost of feeding all your employees everyday (but you should this last one any way.

2. Formula 2 does recognize food storeroom inventory, but it does not consider total inventory because it does not consider goods in process in the kitchen. (Formula 1 does not recognize any inventory.

The Key to Success with Formula 2

The key to having Formula 2 work right for you is to keep accurate records. Some food service operations find Food Cost Formula 2 unsatisfactory because they fail to do this Formula 2 will not work well if you cannot or will not keep accurate records and make accurate extension for requisitions. It does take time and effort to see that all items are written on requisitions and that proper price extensions are made on all requisitions.

Many operations also fail to keep track of requisitions to and from the bar and to and from the kitchen. They think that the rupee amounts involved are so small that they are unimportant and that ignoring transfers will not have any significant effect on their cost formula. Other operations do keep track of all requisitions to and from the bar and kitchen. For them, there is enough money involved to make it significant. That is a decision you have to make based on the cost of doing the work and on the amounts of money involved. Whatever you decide, do recognize that when beverage items from the bar are used in the kitchen in food preparation, it is a food cost, and when food items from the kitchen are used in the bar, it is a bar cost. Be aware of how much transferring goes on and decide whether you really need to keep records on these transfers or not. If there is enough money involved, it can affect the accuracy of Formula 2.

The same holds true for other situations where there are transfers to and from other departments besides kitchen and bar. Maybe you have more than one kitchen and have transfers between them. Or maybe you have an employee cafeteria and transfers items to it from the main kitchen. In hospitals, there may be special diet kitchen that transfers items back and forth between the main kitchen. It is upto you to decide how detailed your records should be and how closely you need to be able to predict the results. Some food service operations do not keep track of transfers to and from the kitchen, but they do keep track of food requisitions from the storeroom directly to other departments besides the kitchen. For example the bar may requisitions items directly from the food storeroom. In the chart the opration would recognize this by an additional column "requisitions from storeroom to bar". This would be used in computing opening food storeroom inventory beginning of day, but bar requisitions would not be included when the operations computes today and to-date food cost and food cost per cent.

How Food Cost per cent Figure is Obtained For Statement of Income?

At the end of the month the food cost per cent you get from Formula 2 should be very close to the food cost per cent on your statement of income. To get the food cost per cent figure for the statement of income, Do the following (for use only with formula 2) :

1. Opening total physical food inventory in rupees (this figure is your closing physical inventory figure from the preceding month) plus total food purchases in rupee (take Chart 5.2 Column 4 storeroom purchases total for month figure plus Column 7 direct purchases total for month figure, or if you don't use the chart, add up all food purchases invoices for month or get from your general accounting records where you records all food purchases) plus the transfer to kitchen (add up all requisitions for items sent from bar to kitchen Column 8 transfer to kitchen) equals total food available in the establishment.
2. TOTAL FOOD AVAILABLE IN THE ESTABLISMENT minus RUPEE VALUE FOR TRANSFERS FROM KITCHEN TO BAR (Column 11 transfers from kitchen to bar, or if you donot use the chart, add requisitions of all items sent from kitchen to bar) minus RUPEE VALUE EMPLOYEES' MEALS and TOTAL CLOSING PHYSICAL FOOD INVENTORY IN RUPEES (take physical inventory—this figure will be your opening inventory figure next month) equals COST OF FOOD SOLD AS IT SHOULD APPEAR ON YOUR STATEMENT OF INCOME. (This cost of food sold figure is the one that appears on your statement of income).
3. COST OF FOOD SOLD divided by FOOD SALES (Total Column 13 Today Food Sales or add all closing cash register tapes or get from general accounting records where you have recorded all food sales) multiplied by 100 (to convert to a percentage) equals ACTUAL FOOD COST PER CENT PER RUPEE SALE.

Differences between Formula 2 Inventory Figure I and Physical Inventory Figure on Statement of Income Both opening and closing inventories for physical inventory figures on the statement of income are composed of two parts:

1. Inventory food in storeroom.
2. Inventory food in process.

1. *Inventory Food in Storeroom*

Formula 1 takes no account of inventories at all. Food Cost Formula 2 does take opening and closing inventory of storeroom into consideration. But it does not take opening and closing inventory of food in process into consideration. Fluctuation between opening and closing inventory food in process will cause the variation between the Food Cost Formula 2 figure and the cost of food sold figure on the statement of income.

At the end of the month, compare the inventory you get from Food Cost Formula 2 for the storeroom with the physical inventory figure for the storeroom you get by counting everything in your storeroom.

The formula you use for calculating the rupee value of your food storeroom inventory:

OPENING FOOD STOREROOM INVENTORY plus FOOD STOREROOM PURCHASES minus FOOD REQUISITION should equal CLOSING FOOD STOREROOM INVENTORY.

This helps you compare the result of your months works and test the accuracy of your procedures for checking food in and out of the storeroom. For example in Chart 5.2, on Monday, March 1, you had a Column 3 Opening Food Storeroom Inventory Beginning of Day figure of Rs. 2,69,849.60. To this you add column 4 Storeroom Purchases Total for the Month figure Rs. 9,54,72760. This gives you a Food Available Storeroom Total for Month figure of Rs. 12,24,577.20 (this figure is not on Chart 5.2). From this you subtract Column 6 food requisitions Total for Month figure Rs. 9,59,008.40. You get Column 3 Opening Food Storeroom Inventory Beginning of Day bottom figure in Column 3 (Thursday, April 1) Rs. 2,65,568.80 (same as "Closing Inventory" figure under "Proof of inventory" at bottom of chart).

In Chart 5.2, Rs. 2,65,568.80 (bottom figure in Column 3) is your calculated figure for your closing food storeroom inventory. Rs. 2,65,568.80 is the figure your actual physical food storeroom inventory and extensions should give you, too.

The first few times you use Formula 2, the physical food storeroom inventory figure you get will probably be less than your calculated inventory value. Why? The explanation is simple. Somebody took items from the storeroom without filling out requisitions. Now the question is What happened to items? Did someone use them in food production without handing in a requisition? Were the items stolen? Take action to stop the theft or the lack of requisitioning causing the unaccounted-for disappearance of food from your storeroom.

Some very slight discrepancy between calculated inventory and physical inventory is almost sure to occur due to the necessary rounding off of rupee in requisitioning items and valuing inventory. This is a small matter, and there is no way to avoid it. The usual way to round off figures is to round down one the figure is less than one-half rupee and round up one rupee if it is exactly one-half rupee or more than one-half rupee.

As a guideline, the value of the inventory you get by your calculated method should not vary by more than 1 per cent of total rupee value of inventory from the value of inventory when you make physical count and do extensions and multiply the individual items by their own cost. If there is more than a 15 variation, Formula 2 is not working as well as it should. On a Rs. 2,00,000.00 inventory, a 15 variation would be Rs. 2,000.00; on a Rs. 2,40,000.00, it would be Rs. 2,400.00 and so on. One per cent is not very large variation but you should not get more than that.

2. *Inventory Food in Process*

The food cost per cent you get from Food Cost Formula 2 should vary less than 1 per cent from the actual food cost per cent on your statement of income. As we said, there will be some variation between Formula 2 food cost percentage and statement of income food cost per cent because Formula 2 does not count food in process in the kitchen and the statement of income does.

There will be some food in the kitchen at the beginning of the month when opening physical inventory is taken, and there will be some food in the kitchen at the end of the month when closing physical inventory is taken. This food is counted in a statement of income but is not counted in Formula 2.

There will always be some food in the kitchen in varying stages of production—a half-gallon of mayonnaise, some portions of cold roast beef for sandwiches, a partially used bottle of chicken base, and so on. Under normal conditions, however, the overall amounts of these items—considering them over a period of time—will probably be relatively constant. When you actually do take your physical inventory, you will have to make estimates concerning the items in this food-in-process category in the kitchen. The half-gallon of mayonnaise is probably a little more or a little less than precisely a half gallon, but you can write down the amount as a half gallon. Maybe you should actually weigh or count some of the more expensive items and compute a fairly accurate value for them.

After you have tried to count, measure, and evaluate everything in the entire kitchen, you just about have to lump remaining odds and ends together and assign them as close a cash value as you can. This is a standard, normal practice and there is nothing wrong with it. These should be calculated estimates. You cannot be totally accurate, but try to be consistent. Your estimates of cash value may be a bit off, but if you are consistently off by about the amount, it will not really distort your food cost.

When you have counted some of the expensive items in the kitchen and added your "lump sum" for the rest, you have your "food in process in kitchen" figure. Add this total rupee value to your rupee value of store inventory figure. This gives you total rupee value of total food inventory.

Methods Food-Cost Control

When partially and fully processed products were introduced into the food service industry, changes should have been made in purchasing, accounting-and control systems. The old rules and techniques applied by most operators, purchasing agents, and chefs were no longer valid.

Yet personnel in the field continued to use archaic mathematical formulas and computations to determine food-cost data. Although improved information could be obtained today from computers, the use of computers in food service control still is minimal. So the daily food-cost percentages, the quantities to buy, and the determination of which products to buy are still largely performed on a rule-of-thumb basis that permits the operator to "guesstimate," ideally within 5 per cent of actual needs.

But profits today are normally averaging only 5 per cent. Thus using this rule-of-thumb basis, the operator may be working with a loss even before beginning to process food service products. Unless closer attention is paid to food purchasing and control systems and better techniques are applied, the entire food service industry may be jeopardized.

The primary calculations with which every purchasing agent, chef, or food service supervisor is daily confronted are the same. The calculations are repetitive, involving both fixed and variable data. The variables usually are changes in wholesale prices and in the number of persons to be served.

THE BASIC FORMULAS

This chapter is concerned with the basic formulas needed for reaching correct answers and decisions. It also represents easy way to make calculations once the variables are none.

Terminology

As purchased (AP) weight: Amount purchased, including bones, fat , unusable trim, outerlayers, excess moisture, and so on.

As served (AS) weight: The actual net amount that must be obtained after processing has been performed. As-served (AS) price: The actual food cost per pound or per portion after all processing has been performed and no further loss will occur due to shrinkage or cooking.

Equivalent product **(EP):** An alternate market form in which a comparable product may be purchased. (*Note:* This term formerly was used to define edible product or edible portion but had the same meaning as as-served). Equivalent product information is necessary both in regard to weight and price. Various calculations must be performed to determine equivalent weights required or Equivalent rupee values for products.

Portion size: Normally in ounces, the amount served to each individual; any unit of measure may be used (cups, grams and so on).

Waste: The amount of unusable food that is lost due to processing, cooking, portioning. To determine the waste percentage, the weight of the total loss is divided by the AP weight of the product.

Waste or weight of loss + AP weight = waste percentage

Yield: The amount of usable product remaining after all processing, cooking, portioning is done. The figure is the reciprocal of the waste percentage (waste yield % = 100%). The yield percentage can be obtained independently by dividing the AP weight into the net weight of the final usable product. The net usable weight is also called the yield:

Yield + AP weight = yield percentage

Problems in Food-Cost Control

Daily Problems: Although all food supervisors are confronted with innumerable other decisions on a daily basis, there are three basic problems related to cost, solved every day:

1. The amount to buy, based on predictable counts (paid lunches, bed counts, minimum guarantee on parties, or forecasts).
2. The portions cost .
3. Which product to buy based on lowest market price.

Amount to buy: For every function served, every guest in a restaurant, or every menu item served, some determination must be made about the quantity of every specific items that must be purchased.

Table 5.1 : How Much to Buy—Old Method

Number of person x Portion size = AS Weight in Ounces
AS Weight Oz. ÷ 16 = AS Weight in pounds
AS Weight ÷ Yield % AP Weight
Example 100 Portion Size 4 oz.—Yield 50%
100 × 4 =400 ÷ 16= 25 lbs.
25 lbs. ÷ .50 = 50 lbs. AP Weight

Information as to the predicted number of persons to be served is sometimes obtained from the sales department or from forecasts made by managerial personnel. In turn, the portion size for each item must be combined with the expected number of persons. An adjustment must be made for the losses in cooking and processing. Finally, a fudge factor must be added or subtracted, due to the efficiency or inefficiency of either the kitchen or other departments. These calculations yield an amount that—it is hoped—is within tolerable limits (See Table 5.1).

Portion cost: A determination of the actual portion cost for every menu item must be made. Although this may be done only at infrequent intervals, the fluctuating market costs of the raw products that the industry uses frequently require updating of menu prices. All too often this updating information is omitted because the food and beverage controller is not readily able to calculate these costs. Yet the information needed to perform these tasks efficiently can be available within moments once the initial data are calculated.

Most-economical purchase: To complicate matters still further, there may have been changes in the market prices of these items during the interim. Certain products may have gone up in price, others may have gone down, and some products may no longer be available. These complicating factors are often made by personnel charged with purchasing is to utilize the waste per cent figure rather than the yield per cent. In doing so, the AS Weight is utilized as follows:

Table 5.2 : Portion Cost-Old Method

Amount Purchased × Price = Total Cost
Total Cost ÷ Portions Served = Portion Cost
Example: Yield 50% - Price Rs. 40 lb.
50 Ibs. × Rs. 40 = Rs. 2000
Rs. 2,000 ÷ 100 portions = Rs. 20 Portion Cost

AS Wt. = 25 lbs. AS Wt. + (Waste % x AS Wt) = A.P. Wt.
For example: 25 Ibs. + (.50 x 25) = 37.5 Ibs. AS Wt. (Incorrect figure)

This basic mathematical error presumes that if 25 lbs. are required and it is known that there is a 50 per cent loss, then by multiplying AS Weight by the waste % and adding these figures. The AP Weight is obtained: 25 +25(.50) = 37 1/2lbs. AP Weight. After utilizing this technique several times and not having enough to serve the purchasing agent of chef adds a fudge factor to allow for "inefficiency" and eventually ends up by guessing at how much to buy.

Ignored for several reasons. By changing products, the easy routine and computations with which the controller or purchasing agent is familiar will have to be adjusted or changed. Also, how exactly does one compare the price of beef chunk with that of round? The yield are different product may be different, and even the quantity may vary. But for many menu items, these can be used interchangeably. Thus, the buyer can compare beef ribs at different stages of processing and select which product to buy based on lowest portion cost. In fact decisions such as this must be made almost every day by purchasing agents (see later in this chapter for a discussion of the labour costs factor).

For example, even in selecting hamburger, should one purchase regular ground beef at Rs. 39.60 per pound or extra lean ground beef at Rs. 63.60 per pound? If these items meat loaf, for which the net amount of the cooked product is the primary factor, then determining the true cost can save hundreds of rupees even for a small operation.

Each week, due to fluctuations in predicted sales or as new functions are booked, the same type of information is thus pumped into the system. The numbers game calculations are again performed, and once again an answer is obtained.

Variable and fixed data. The variable and fixed data with which we must operate are outlined next.

Variable

1. Market price of raw goods.
2. Number of persons expected.

Fixed

1. Portion sizes.
2. Yield percentages of products utilized.

Why a Simplified Systems Needed

For the three primary problems that confront the foodservice supervisor, two factors change on a day-to-day basis and two remain unchanged for extended periods of time, as has been discussed. With this in mind, let us now examine present practices and compare them with the simplified system.

Under the system presently being utilized by many operators, the food buyer determines the amount of purchase by the procedure illustrated next. If for example, 100 people are to be served and the item being served is corned beef in 4-ounce portions, the buyer would be multiply 4 ounces by 100 to get 400 ounces. Next, the buyer would divided by 16 to convert to pounds, arriving at 25 pounds. Then, allowing the fact that much of the corned beef is waste (presuming about 50%), he or she would divide the yield percentage into the original figure and arrive at final total—50 pounds. Every time the number of persons to be served changes, the buyer performs the same calculations and wastes the same amount of time in determining the correct amount.

To determine portion costs, the buyer has any number of systems that may be used. The simplest one takes the total purchase price for any item and divides it by the number or persons that can be served. The resulting answer is the portion cost. The actual true cost is usually available only after the function, since the actual amount served cannot be determined until that time.

To determine which of the following two products to buy, the same type of calculation must be performed for each product. Every time the market price changes, the buyer must recalculate the costs by going through the same steps. Figure 4.5 is the comparison of the cost of corned beef round (Item 2) and corned brisket of beef (Item 1). At what market price these two products are of equal value in relationship to each other is difficult to determine. Normally, as the market price of each changes, the purchasing agent recalculates both sets of figures to determine which then has the lowest portion cost.

In summary, under the methods generally used, each time the buyer purchases a varying amount of merchandise, he or she must go through all the steps shown in Table 5.3. Or, if this takes too much time, a guess is made, and the excess amount is fed to the staff or a run-out occurs.

Portion costs are determined at infrequent intervals and are calculated normally after the food has already been served, far too late for money-saving decisions. Finally, due to the complexity of the mathematics, the selection of which item to:

Table 5.3 : Comparison of Best by Old Method

Item 1	*Item 2*
Price Rs. 140 lb. Yield 50%	Price Rs. 188 lb. Yield 75%
Total Amount Required *50 lbs. AP Weight* *(previously determined)*	*Total Amount Required* *25 lbs. AS Weight* *(known)*
50 × Rs. 140 = Rs. 7,000	*Step 1* 25 lbs. ÷ 75% = 33 lbs. AP Weight Rs. 7000 ÷ 100 portions = Rs. 70 portion cost
	Step 2 33 × Rs. 188 = Rs. 6,204
	Step 3 Rs. 6,204 ÷ 100 = Rs. 62 portion cost

Buy is too often based not on lowest cost but rather on the purchasing agent's friendliness with the purveyor, familiarity with the product, or half a dozen other reasons, none of which answers the major primary question: which is the most economical buy?

How the Simplified System Works?

The simplified system enables the food service operator to utilize a basic mathematical formula to calculate the solutions to all three of the primarily problems in cost control: (1) amount to buy; (2) portion costs; and (3) most-economical product, presuming the same quality. The formula can remain the same in operations for extended periods of time and the constant figures can be utilized for indefinite periods.

Simplified Mathematical Formula

New terms
Portion divider (PD)
Portion factor (PF)

Information given or available AP price (varying market prices) Portion size yield percentage.

Information Desired

1. Portion factor – calculated only once
2. Portion divider – calculated only once

3. Amount to buy
4. Portion cost
5. Most economical purchase

Two new terms are introduced at this point. *Portion divider* is a mathematical constant that can be used for indefinite periods. For those who have access to computers, the constant can be fed into the computer, and desired information can be obtained with it.

The second, *portion factor,* is not really a new term. All food operators use it but perhaps call it by another name. It is the actual number of portions served per unit of purchase for any given product. The portion factor may differ for each menu item, but normally it does not change. In the United States the portion size is usually listed in ounces and the unit of purchase is given in pounds. However, in Europe and other parts of the world, portion sizes are normally measured in grams, and the unit of purchase is kilograms. Portions may be measured in cups, milliliters, scoops, or any other unit of measurement. Concurrently, if an item is purchased in gallons, individual number 10 cans, by the case, by count (shrimp or oysters), or by the bushel, the basic formula will automatically convert into the appropriate portion factor. For example, if the portion is by the piece (6) and there are 400 pieces purchased (400 oysters per bushel), then the portion factor is calculated as:

$$400 \div 6 = 66.67 \text{ PF}$$

If an item is purchased in grams, the computation with a 300-grams portion is:

$$1000 \div \text{portion in grams} = \text{PF}$$

or

$$1000 \div 300 = 3.33$$

Information available to the buyer that also seldom changes is the *portion size yield percentage* for any product. Yield-percentage information may be available to the controller or buyer from data supplied by various associations and purveyors. Preferably, however, it should be obtained by performing yield tests in the establishment. Figures available to the buyer that do change frequently are the *market the forecast of sales.*

In order to set up a simplified system, several calculations must be performed initially. Once these are done, these figures will remain the same. For every menu item, a portion factor and portion divider must be ascertained. Once these are established, the system is ready for operation, so that the buyer or controller can quickly perform his or her duties.

Portion Factor

To determine the portion factor, simply divide the portion size of the menu item into 16 (ounces per pound); the result is the portion factor. (See Table 5.4). Note that several different portion factors for the same kind of products may be used in the establishment. A 12-ounce strip steak and a 14-ounce strip steak may be served in the hotel in different dining rooms. Each menu item has its own portion factor.

Portion Divider

To ascertain the portion divider for each menu item, multiply the portion factor by the yield percentage of the product used. The answer is the portion divider (See Table 5.5).

When different products are used for one menu item, each product has a different portion divider. In the example shown in Table 5.5, the portion divider is calculated for 4-ounce portions. In Item 1, when this product (corned brisket of beef) used with a normal yield of 50 per cent, the portion divider is 2. If corned rounds are used and a 75 per cent yield is obtainable, the portion divider for the rounds is 3. (Although other products may be used for this menu item, such as prepared or cooked meats, only these two examples are demonstrated in the following calculations). All future calculations concerning this menu item are now simple to do.

Table 5.4 : Determining Portion Factor

Unit of Purchase ÷ Portion Size = PF	
Example:	Calculated only once. 16 ÷ 4 oz. = 4

Portion Divider

To ascertain the portion divider for each menu item. multiply the portion factor by the yield % of the product used. The answer is the portion divider.

Table 5.5 : Determining Portion Divider

	Yield % × FP = PD
	Item 1 - Corned Brisket
Example	.50 × 4 = 2.0
	Item 2-Corned Round
	.75 × 4 = 3.0

Amount to Buy

Using the new method, the expected number of covers, or persons, is simply divided by the portion divider, and the answer is the amount that must be purchased (See Table 5.6.) Note that the answer is the true AP weight. Allowance need not be made or shrinkage or losses. Other daily information can also be obtained by utilizing the portion divider.

Portiȍn Costs

Determining portion costs, even with fluctuating prices, is an easy process. Simply divide the portion divider into the current market price. The resulting answer is the new portion cost for the menu item. If rounds are selling at Rs. 192, divide Rs. 192 by the portion divider for that product, which in this case is 3. The new portion cost is Rs. 64.

In the examples shown in Table 5.7, the portion cost for Item 1 is Rs. 70 and for Item 2, Rs. 62. In systems now commonly used for obtaining this information, the calculations would be more difficult and probably less accurate.

Table 5.6 : Determining Amount to Buy

No. of people ÷ PD = AP Weight
Item 1
100 ÷ 2.0 = 50 Ibs. Item 2
100 ÷ 3.0 = 33.3 Ibs.

Table 5.7 : Determining Portion Cost

AP Price ÷ PD = PC
Item 1
Rs. 140 ÷ 2.0 = Rs. 70
Item 2
Rs. 188 ÷ 3.0 = Rs. 62.4

The Best Buy

The market price of one item in relation to a similar product often increases or decreases. At some stage of this fluctuation, it may become desirable for the purchasing agent to switch from one product to another to save money. Using the portion divider, this point of change can readily be determined by the process shown Table 5.8.

The price of Item 1 in Table 5.8 is Rs. 140 per pound. The portion cost is obtained by dividing the portion divider (2) into this purchase price. To determine at price to switch products, the portion cost for the product presently being used (Item 1) is multiplied by the portion divider of the other product (Item 2). The resulting answer is the price at which both products are of equal value. If the purchase of Item 2 is below that value, then it is a better buy. When the price of Item 2 is higher than the equivalent value, Item 1 is a better buy.

The simplified system presented in this chapter can easily be utilized in any operation having a computer. More importantly, for the majority of operators without computers, vital day-to-day information can be obtained by utilizing the portion divider. Exact quantities to purchase can quickly be calculated with only one mathematical computation simply by dividing the portion divider into the expected number of persons (See Figure 5.6). New portion costs can be obtained even with fluctuating prices, again by the simple process of dividing the portion divider into the new market price of the item, (See Table 5.7.) Finally, the point at which the purchasing. It should switch from one product to the next can quickly be obtained by merely tip lying the portion cost of any item by the portion divider of the alternate (See Figure 5.8).

Table 5.8 : Determining Product to Buy, Based on Fluctuating Market Prices

Item I

AP Price + PD = PC Rs. 140 + 2 = 51.75

Item 2

PC Item 1 × PD Item 2 = Equal Market Price

Rs. 70 × 3 = Rs. 210

The simplified system may be utilized in all types of food service operations, including hospitals and schools, whether profit-orientaed or not. It may be utilized by wholesalers and purveyors. It may be used for purchasing and comparing convenience products. It may also be adapted to obtain other data on modified, depending on the products that are purchased. It is not only method that can be used. In the long run, however, it is the simplest.

Establishing a Simplified Programme

1. Determine portion sizes for each menu item.
2. Determine yield percentages for each product that may be used for any menu item.
3. Determine the portion dividers for all possible products that may be purchased for each menu item.
4. The system is now ready. If a computer is available, formulas may be programmed into computer. If not, either a desk calculator or tables may be used, so that information is immediately obtainable.

Example: Hot corned beef sandwich, portion size 4 ounces.

Products that may be purchased:

1. Raw corned rounds of beef	75% yield
2. Raw corned briskets of beef	50% yield
3. Cooked corned rounds of beef	95% yield
4. Cooked corned briskets of beef	90% yield

Portion Factor = 4

Portion divider:

1. Raw rounds of beef	$.75 \times 4 = 3.0$
2. Raw briskets of beef	$.50 \times 4 = 2.0$
3. Cooked rounds of beef	$.95 \times 4 = 3.8$
4. Cooked briskets of beef	$.90 \times 4 = 3.6$

The programme is now ready to be fed into a computer, or a simple chart may be made up with the information obtained. As market prices change or the number of covers to be served changes, the new information (variable) is fed into a computer, or a simple computation is made by using a desk calculator, slide rule, or even pencil and paper. Table 5.9 illustrates the portion factor of the most common portion sizes. The portion factor in this table may be multiplied by the yield percentage of a product to obtain the portion divider for the product.

Table 5.9 : Portion Factors For Common Portion Sizes

Portion Size	*Portion Factor*	*Portion Size*	*Portion Factor*
1 oz	16.00	5 oz	3.20
1 ½ oz	10.67	6 oz	2.67
2 oz	8.00	7 oz	2.29
2 ½ oz	6.40	8 oz	2.00
3 oz	5.33	10 oz	1.60
3 oz	4.57	12 oz	1.33
4 oz	4.00	16 oz	1.00

First determination which product is most economical to purchase:

1. Raw rounds at Rs. 180/lb ÷ 3 = Rs. 60
2. Raw briskets at Rs. 140/lb ÷ 2 = Rs. 70
3. Cooked rounds at Rs. 240/lb ÷ 3.8 = Rs. 63.16
4. Cooked briskets at Rs. 228/lb ÷ 3.6 = Rs. 63.33

Raw rounds appear to be most economical, but an additional cost should be added to labour and utility costs incurred when cooking the meat. Initially, the lowest portion cost can be the determining factor. If prices fluctuate at a later time, the switch point method may be used (see Table 5.6).

If management decides to purchase cooked briskets, then the final step is to divide the portion divider (PD) of the briskets (3.6) into the expected number of persons to determine the amount to purchase:

700 persons ÷ 3.6 = 195 lb AP weight

The as Served Prime Cost System (ASPC)

Although the use of the portion divider simplifies the task of determining food cost, the work of the food and beverage controller is only partially completed. Food cost food-cost percentages are only one portion of the two major factors contributing to cost for any operation. The second major contributing cost factor is labor, specifically, preparation for labour.

It is no longer satisfactory to evaluate the performance of the purchasing agent, chef, or controller on the basis of food cost or food-cost percentages. Products can be purchased today that are ready-to-serve or partially processed or in the raw, unprocessed stage. If the food is purchased unprocessed, then it is obvious that the food cost by itself is lowest, but then the in-house processing must be performed (which is now charged to labour). It is the value of this labour plus the food cost that should be considered when evaluating the real final cost to the establishment. The two costs together are called prime cost.

PAs have always been directed to "obtain the best quality for a specific purpose at the lowest possible."

PURCHASING STRATEGY: AS SERVED PRIME COST SYSTEM

A more realistic objective for the manager is to maximize profits, and for the PA the real goal is purchase products at the lowest possible total cost not the lowest price. To assist in obtaining both these goals it is necessary to combine the major contributing costs, namely, food and labour, into One Unit, which is defined as *prime cost*.

The first signs of developing the concept of combining these costs was in the mid-1970s, when several authors and authorities defined the new term for the combined food and labour cost in menu items.The term *prime cost* was used by Kaiser and Kallio (1974), although they may not have been the originators of the term.

Subsequent texts (including this author's) (1976). Do not continue with the concept and current articles have added little to the advancement of the theory.

Although the concept of prime cost has been discussed for some time, little attention has been paid to developing solutions or techniques that apply prime costs in purchasing strategies. Patterson (1976) in his article, "How prime costtion can maximize profits," does elaborate on the topic of prime costs but confines his material to the effects on menu pricing strategies. Much work is still required to fully develop the theory of prime costing particularly in devising purchasing strategies for operators, but first an understanding of the basic theory is needed as will be demonstrated by the as-served prime cost system (ASPC). The ASPC evaluates the two major cost contributing factors, labour and food, which must be including in establishing overall costs for any menu item. With proper implementation ASPC will permit the PA to readily identify the food products with the lowest total cost. At the same time it demonstrates to the food and beverage manager the real cost of processing foods in-house and in turn, points out the value of purchasing partially prepared products even though they may initially appear to cost more.

To understand the objectives and methods, however, it is first necessary to clearly define the trade terminology as presently used and in some cases to redefine words when the meaning is either unclear or too broad.

Definitions

AP- as purchased: Refers to the market from of a product when purchased and prior to any processing in-house. Most items usually may be purchased in several market forms.

AP price: The cost of the item when obtained from the purveyor.

EP: Normally in trade terminology the definition was either *edible portion* or *edible product*. This term was used interchangeably with *as served*. A better definition and one which is not presently clearly defined by any authority is to use this term to mean *equivalent product*.

EP or equivalent product: Any alternate market form in which a comparable product may be purchased. A typical example of an item where several equivalent products are available is for the menu item strip steak. Meat for this menu item may normally be purchased:

(*a*) Bone-in whole strip lion.
(*b*) Boneless strip lion.
(*c*) Boneless portion cut strip steaks.

The challenge for the PA and food beverage manager where (a), (b) or (c) are available the finished menu item at the lowest total cost. AS—as served: The final form or weight in end which a product is normally evaluated it may be cooked or uncooked depending upon the menu item. For example; boneless strip steak would be uncooked, whereas the shrimp in this study were cooked in their final form.

AS labour cost: The total labour cost for preparing a particular product including adjustments for yield and productivity.

Note: This does not include additional labour costs incurred for final preparation and service of a specific menu item (dish-up or waiter/ess service).

AS prime cost (ASPC): All food and labour costs incurred to bring a product to a stage just prior to final preparation and service.

Yield: The amount of a product remaining after all losses have been considered. Losses may include trimming, boning, butchering, cooking, service, spoilage and so on. Normally expressed as a percentage based on a formula:

Final weight/Original weight = yield percentage.

Wage rate: The cost of labour including fringe benefit such a social security, meals, vacations workmen's compensation, etc.

Productivity (%): The amount of time a worker actually spends on producing products or performing the job. Rest breaks, meal periods, clean-up time, walking and the like are not considered productivity time. If a worker is paid for an 8-hour shift but is allowed two 15-minute breaks, is reduced by 1/8. The productivity percentage is 87.5% 7 hours time/8 hour shift= 87.5%.

To illustrate ASPC and understand the technique, a test study was made utilizing a common menu item, shrimp cock tail. Shrimp can be purchased in various market forms, all of which up as a peeled, cooked, deveined shrimp (P and D or P&D). Regardless of whether processed in house or off the premises, the cooking technique is basically the same (boiling) and yield would be uncooked, whereas the shrimp in this relatively constant.

Study were cooked in their final form. AP labour cost: labour cost for processing a per product. This cost must then be adjusted to de-allow for yield and productivity.

Raw as Labour Cost: An Intermediate Labour Cost

Shrimp were available either raw, in the shell at Rs. 287.60 per pound-(green headless) size 26-30 pound or the same size cooked, peeled and veined shrimp were available for Rs. 359.60 per pound. (Note that the quality of the latter product used in this study was considered to be inferior to the raw product.) To determine the

ASPC of the finished product the following factors must be considered:

1. Food cost.
2. Labour cost including fringe benefits.
3. Yield percentages.
4. Worker productivity.

Tables 5.10 and 5.11 illustrate the yield percentage obtainable from raw, in the shell shrimp, and the

Table 5.10 : Typical Yield Percentage Obtainable from Raw in the Shell Shrimp, If Utilized for Shrimp Cocktail

Formula: Final Weight/Original weight = Yield Percentage

Form	*Weight*	*Formula*	*Yield (%)*
Raw	10 lb		
Peeled & deveined	8.6 lb	8.6/10=	86
Cooked P & D	6.3 lb	6.3/10=	63

If calculated from P&D to cooked P&D = 73% (6.3 ÷ 8.6)

Ten pounds of raw shrimp were peeled and deveined (P & D) resulting in a yield of 8.6 lb (uncooked). An additional 2.3 lb were lost in cooking, for a final yield weight of 6.3 lb equivalent prices that would have to be paid to the purveyor (excluding labour, etc.) should the product be purchased in a processed form.

Table 5.11 : Technique and Equivalent Prices that Would have to be Paid to Purveyor (excluding Labour etc. should be Product be Purchased in a Processed Form

$$\text{Fomula } \frac{\text{AP Price}}{\text{Yield}} = \text{Equivalent Price}$$

Price Raw	*Price P&D*	*Price Cooked*
Rs. 287.60	Rs. 334.40	11.41
	(Rs. 287.60/86%)	(Rs. 287.60/63%)

This is obvious as much as the purveyor originally had 10 pounds of shrimp priced at Rs. 287.60 or Rs. 2,876 worth of shrimp.

If, however, the purveyor sold raw P&D shrimp, only 8.6 pounds would be available at Rs. 234.40 per Although it at first appears that the labour costs pound = Rs. 2,876, or 6.3 pounds of cooked P&D

shrimp at 11.41 = Rs. 2,876. [If the EP uncooked P&D were purchased, the number per pound would be 32.5 (280 ÷ 8.6) or if purchased cooked, P&D 44 per pound (280 ÷ 6.3)].

There then must be an additional charge for labour if processed by the purveyor since the workers would have had to perform the tasks of peeling, deveining and cooking the product.

To determine actual labour cost, the 10 pounds of shrimp were processed from raw to the final cooked P & D stage. Table 4.14 illustrates the time study that was made.

A base wage rate of Rs. 240.00 per hour (Rs. 4.00 per minute) was utilized (average base wage for pantry chef, 2008 wage rate in Delhi). Since fringe benefits must also be included (minimum of 22%) an additional Rs. 52.8 per hour must be added Rs. 80 cent per minute. [Friedman (1979) states that a 40 per cent figure should be used.] The AP labour cost per pound is shown next:

Formala:

Labour cost = <u>time x (wage rate + fringe benefits)</u>
= 26 min × Rs. 48.8 cents/min /10 lb
= Rs. 126.80/10 Ib shrimp
= 1268
= 2168 Rs. lb.

Although it at first appears that the labour costs shrimp is 1268 rupees per pound, two additional factors must be considered. First, if the operator were to purchase the shrimp in a processed form, he or she would be buying only 6.3 pounds of shrimp! (Table 5.12). The purveyor would be able to allocate his labour costs only to the total cost of the 6.3 pounds. Thus an operator also must allocate costs based on the weight of the finished product.

Table 5.12 : Time Study

Peeling and deveining by	sample 10 lb
Machine and hand	size-26-30
P & D	shrimp raw lb 16 min
Cutting (splitting in machine)	4 min
Cooking-draining-cooling- cleaning	6 min
Total time	26 min

To define the terms more accurately, the Rs. 126.80 is the labour cost as purchased (AP) per pound. The new labour cost for the finished product (raw AS labour cost) is:

AP labour/yield (%)= raw AS labour cost

or

Rs. 12.68/.63= Rs. 20 lb

By utilizing a machine an average time of 14 shrimp/min was obtained. This is very efficient (280 shrimp/20 min) for just peeling and developing would have to be allocated to the net weight received by the buyer or: Rs. 126.8/6.3 lb = Rs. 20 per pound.

This is the same basic concept as shown before, where the purveyor had to receive Rs. 2,876 for the shrimp regardless of the market from.

The Rs. 20 per pound is however, preliminary figure since time study measured only the actual productive time of the worker. A second corrective adjustment must now be made to account for worker productivity. Non-productive task such as thawing of shrimp, transporting of product, cleaning up, walking, break time, and meal time most also be considered. If the product was purchased finished from the purveyor, this time would have been accounted for by the purveyor in the sales price, and an operator must perform the same calculation. An establishment to accurately measure productivity would need to calculate the total productivity for each work everyday and allocate a labour cost dollar value to each product. A simpler method for estimating is to utilize standards already established for the industry. Kotschevar (1966) estimated food worker productivity at 45 per cent but in his latest work (1974) has revised the figure to 47 per cent.

The final adjustment thus becomes:

Raw AS labour cost per pound/productivity (%) = AS labour cost per pound Rs. 20/47% = Rs. 42.40 AS labour cost per pound. The prime cost per pound of shrimp used for shrimp cocktrail would then be:

AS food cost/lb 456.40
AS labour cost/lb 42.40
AS prime cost/lb Rs. 498.80

If the PA purchased the product in this form (precooked, peeled and deveined), a purveyor Would have to charge Rs. 498.80 pound excluding any additional profit and presuming the same wage rate and fringe benefits were paid to workers.

Veined and cooked shrimp could be revaluated by new price by the cost factor. For Example, green shrimp new price × cost factor = AS peeled deveined cooked shrimp. Green price Rs. 379.6 × 69.20 Rs. 656.40. It the price of cooked peeled and deveined Shrimp were raised (or reduced) a comparable calculation would be performed: Cooked peeled and deveined price/Cost factor = equivalent green price. For many products the evidence is not as apparent as in the preceding situation. In most cases.

Not also that if the product was purchased in this form the entire cost under present accounting systems would be allocated to food cost rather than a portion (about 9%) being allocated to labour cost.

Food 456.40/498.80 = 91 per cent food cost (%)
Labour 42.40/498.80= 9 per cent labour cost (%)

Normally a purveyor specializing in one line of products (fish or meat) will achieve a higher percentage of productivity just by processing larger quantities. For example, a fish purveyor might process 2000 pounds of fish a day and only need cleanup at the close of the day. A restaurant might need to process only 200 pounds of fish. Cleaning would be necessary after processing the fish, and this non-productive time may cost exactly the same as for the fish purveyor. Whereas the purveyor would allocate the cost to 2000 pounds of fish, the restaurateur would only be able to charge it to the 200 pounds of fish that were processed in-house. For the purveyor the entire plant may be designed for the processing of fish, whereas the restaurateur may process meats, produce, and so on. Additional non-productive time for such activities as setting up and for rearranging equipment flow will result in higher labour costs and thus lower worker productivity percentages.

If indeed, the quality of the cooked and peeled shrimp (those priced at Rs. 359.60 per pound) were acceptable, it is clear that they would be a much better buy. For most PAs, however, it would be necessary to go into long explanations to management as to why they did not purchase the lowest priced product (Rs. 287.60 versus Rs. 359.60 per pound). Presuming yields and labour costs remain constant, a cost factor could be utilized if purveyor's prices fluctuate Based on the study, the cost factor would be 69.20: 498.80/287.6 = 69.20.

If green shrimp prices were to be raised by any amount, the new equivalent price for peeled, de-just the food cost of the products at various stages of multiplying the processing are considered without including the AS labour cost, which adds substantially to the prime cost of product. It is thus clear that with the continuing development and use of processed and convenience foods, the challenge to the PA to purchase products at the lowest possible total cost is more demanding than even before. A complete understanding of the complexities of the problem, the factors involved and the inter relationship of yields, labour cost and productivity is mandatory.

It is also evident that further work is required so that some industry standards may be developed which could universally be applied by operators.

BEVERAGE CONTROL

In the area of beverage control, one of your main jobs is it control your beverage cost. beverage cost may be high due to poor practices by your bartender—overpouring, for example, mistakes in any steps between buying beverage and selling it can cause high beverage cost and reduce your profit, poor methods, errors, or lack of good controls in purchasing, receiving, storing, issuing, preparing, pricing, collecting money, and analyzing sales can cost you money. You can be cutting your own profits if you fail to apply standard control procedures—and a very important one among these procedures is your system to control theft.

Some operators are satisfied with the profits they get from their beverage operation and some are not most all of them could get better profits if they improved their complete beverage operation control system.

Divide the Work

Most bartenders are honest. If bartenders do try to steal, it is upto you (management) to prevent them from succeeding. It is your fault if bartenders have the opportunity to steal and are not detected if they try it.

It is your job to divide work and responsibility in all phases of food and beverage control so that opportunity for stealing is at least reduced or—ideally—eliminated. It is particularly important for you to divide work and responsibility in the area of liquor control. If you put one bartender in charge of purchasing, receiving, storing, issuing to the bar, mixing drinks, collecting money for drinks, and recording sales—in complete charge of your total beverage operation-you are making stealing extremely tempting and easy for a bartender who is less than totally honest. Try not to put one person in complete charge of your total beverage function. If you do, you have no right to be surprised if you do not get the profits you want from your bar.

Apply checks and balances to your beverage system and pinpoint responsibility. The work of purchasing, receiving, storing, and issuing beverages should be kept completely separate from the work of mixing drinks and collecting cash. The more you can divide the beverage operation into small jobs handled by different people, the better your chance for controls will be. Usually, however, it is difficult to do this. For most operations the volume of business is too small to cover labour costs that would be involved in having several different employees handle separate, divided tasks in the whole beverage procedure. Most businesses have to run on a system of having the bartenders mix the drinks and also collect the money for them. This is normal practice, but it makes it very difficult to put in complete beverage controls and eliminate stealing, temptation is built in.

It is more difficult for a bartender to steal from a beverage operation if the work is divided. Even in small operations, the bartender should not have complete control. There is usually a manager and a bartender, and the manager can at least issue the liquor to the bar.

Ideally, you want to pinpoint responsibility at each level, have one person receive beverage and another person issue it if you can. It is ideal if you can have just the bartender, no one else, mix drinks, and just the cashier, no one else, collect money for the drinks. Unfortunately, staffing arrangements like this are not possible in most bars because they cannot afford it.

Most bartenders are honest, but from a management standpoint, controls should be established anyway. if the bartender is honest, all is well. if the bartender is not honest, controls can help cause this fact to show up in increased costs and make it much easier for you to uncover dishonesty.

Try to divide work so that more than one person is involved. If a bartender has complete charge and steals, he or she has only himself or herself to worry about, but if other employees handle other areas of work, the bartender will have to have the help of the other person or persons in order to steal, and this does a lot to reduce the temptation. It is collusion if more than one person is involved in theft, and it makes theft more complicated to perform, harder to hide and riskier.

Many employees figure that if a bartender wants the employee to help steal, the bartender is crooked, cannot be trusted as a partner, and would probably blow the whistle on the employee if caught. Most employees would not take the risk, this is why it is so important to establish controls and set things up so that the only way an employee can steal is if there is collusion. It should be pointed out, however, that where collusion does exist, you are apt to be taken for a lot more than you probably would be if only one person is stealing—mainly because the stolen money has to be split more ways, so they will take more.

The number of people who actually steal is small. unfortunately, they have given a rather bad reputation in general to all who handle liquor. You need to protect the innocent and detect and dismiss the guilty. Whether you can or cannot split beverage jobs among several people, there are other beverage controls that you can and should use.

Liquor Control

Liquor control is similar to food control. Many of the routines and methods discussed in previous chapters on food control apply to liquor control. In the following chapters on beverage control we emphasize some of the differences.

Beverage control is easier to maintain and simpler than food control, but beverage control has to be tighter than food control and it has to be more strictly enforced because:

1. It is easier for beverage employees to steal money than it is for food employees to steal money.
2. Liquor is more tempting to many employees than food.
3. Liquor is more expensive than most food items.

Beverage control is simpler than food control because you are dealing with a much smaller number of items. Even if you have quoted a large variety of beverage items in inventory, it is still small compared to the vary large number of items involved in a food operation.

Another reason why beverage control is simpler than food control is because beverages always come to you in standard-sized bottles and containers. Most establishments use liters, 1.75 liters, and so on. Beer is purchased in bottles, or by quarter-barrel or half-barrel. It is simpler to keep track of bottles or half-barrels as they move from storage through a beverage department than it is to keep track of 10 kg of flour,15 kg of sugar, 30 kg of stew meat. Food items may be purchased and stored in standard sizes of 50 or 100 kg bags for flour, sugar, and so on, but you do not use them in this form. The small operator usually takes broken amounts (less than a 100 kg bag) from the storeroom, so theft is simpler and less noticeable for these items than it would be for beverage.

Beverage control needs to be tighter than food control because it is not generally a great temptation to steal 10 kg of flour. It can be a great temptation to steal a bottle of liqur, however—especially if employees feel they can get away with it.

Employee Theft

There is peculiar thing to consider about beverage theft control. Some employees do not think it is really stealing to take a drink of whiskey from their employer without paying for it. They can convince themselves that there is so much liquor at the bar that a shot or two—or a bottle or two-will not be missed. some employees who will steal your liquor if they can would not steal your money even if it would be rather easy to do it. Somehow they see a difference.

A true story illustrates this, a manager wanted to test this theory that employees are more likely to take liquor than money. He left a Rs. 200 bill and a bottle of whiskey in plain sight of all employees, in a very short time the whiskey was gone but the money was still there. Later the money disappeared, too. An employee had taken the bottle of whiskey, later the same fellow had come back and taken the money. He was reluctant to steal the money, but he could not find a way to steal more whiskey, so he took the money so he took the money so he could go buy some.

Some employees seem to think it is all right to take your liquor. Some really do not seem to feel it is stealing, most will not take money, or if they do they will be much more hesitant about it. That is one reason why you have to devise thorough and strict beverage control procedures.

Unfortunately, no beverage control system is perfect, but you have got to keep beverage theft to a minimum. Try to convince all employees of the importance of working toward the common goal of making money for the whole establishment and making money for themselves legitimately in the process. See that your employees—especially your beverage employees-make good money for their work.

There is a notion that liquor "evaporates". If you are in an extremely dry amount disappears from opened bottles, it could have evaporated. If more than a little "evaporates", it did not evaporate. It was probably stolen or wasted by overpouring or careless handling. When a bottle is opened, topped with a pour spout, and left sitting on a shelf for a long time, a little of it could evaporate, but liquor in unopened bottles with unbroken seals does not evaporate, and neither do glass bottles. If your liquor seems to disappear into the air, 99.9 per cent of the time it is not evaporating. It is vanishing because of bad beverage controls. Install tight beverage controls to stop it. If entire unopened bottles disappear, you certainly cannot blame "evaporation". Blame yourself for bad controls.

Standand Drink List

If there are problems in your beverage operation, do not simply condemn your bartenders and blame all bar problems on them. Work with your bartenders.

Many bars carry a much larger inventory than they need to. Do not tie up money unnecessarily in inventory. A good way to analyze your inventory is to sit down with your head bartender and develop a list of probably about 25 mixed drinks-the ones most requested in your beverage operation. (It does not have to be precisely 25, or course-more or less depending on your operation). In the United States, bloody mary and margarita may head the list. After that the list will very depending on what part of the country you're in, although drinks such as martini, manhattans, whiskey sour, Tom Collins, or old-fashioned arc apt to be included in your list.

You will probably find that more than 90 per cent of your mixed drink orders come from the list you have made. The remaining 10 per cent of sales will consist of a variety of drinks. But you will know what most of your mixed drink orders will be. After you have prepared the list, you and your head bartender should develop a standard recipe for each one of these mixed drinks. Write each recipe down in a card file or notebook and have this available for all bartenders. Make sure that all bartenders use these, each recipe should clearly specify the exact amount of each ingredient to be used.

If you do not have standardized recipes, bartenders will make drinks according to their own whims or the way they learned to make them at the last place they worked. If you ask five martini drinkers how to make a martini, you will probably get five different martini recipes. There is even one old recipe (which would not go over well today) that calls for a proportion of three parts gin to one part vermouth. Today most people would consider this too much vermouth, Have your own regular recipe for martinis (and everything else).

The standard for a martini today is probably eight parts gin to one part vermouth. When customers ask for martinis, some of them would prefer it if your bartender would lightly spray vermouth in the general direction of the gin with an atomizer, or, better yet, wave the vermouth bottle cork very briefly over the gin. A lot of customers who order "dry!" martinis really want straight gin.

Decisions need to make about how you will prepare all your mixed drinks, when and how you will change your recipes, and what prices you will charge. For example, in a brandy alexander or a grasshopper, the standard recipe calls for light whipping cream, but today very few establishments use real cream in either of these mixed drinks. Most use half-and-half. If your is the unique establishment that does use light whipping cream in these drinks, though, you should come out with a better product than half-and-half would give you and you should charge more. Whipping cream incorporates air better than half-and-half and you might get more overrun (larger volume) because of the air. May be you could use less whipping cream than half-and-half. It may still cost you more to use whipping cream than it would cost you to use half-and-half, but if the end product is better, your customers may not object to paying a bit more. Unfortunately, many beverage operations say they use real whipping cream and charge a whipping cream price but use half-and-half.

This is just one example of the type of thing you should know about, think about and make decisions about. Set your prices so you get the profit you want. You and your bartender have to work out decisions for all drinks and set selling prices that are fair to you and your customers. Go through every item that goes into every drink on your list of 25 (or however many) standard drinks. You will have to make decisions that will affect your costs. Consider every detail before you establish your selling price.

Other Drinks

There is still the problem of the remaining drinks not on your most requested list of 25 or so. Make sure your bartenders have a book — or several books-available to them at the bar on how to prepare varieties of drinks, including rare and unusual ones. Some beverage companies put out books on how to mix good drinks. Their recipe book will tell you to use their own brands, but you can substitute other brands if you whish. Check with beverage companies about getting copies. You can get other books on drinks from book stores and industry publishers. Recipes in these can serve you as guides to your bartenders for making drinks not included in your own standardized list of drink recipes.

Of course, an excellent source of information on how to prepare a particular new or unusual drinks may be guests who order it. If they just arrived from a different area where a new or different drink is a favourite, they will probably be glad to explain to the bartender how to make it. They will usually also be quite willing to pay a good price to get this special drink. Special order drinks should not be bargains, but they should not be exorbitant, either. If special new drinks really catch on and become popular with your guests, develop standardized recipes for them and add them to your other standardized recipes.

We suggested at the outset that you establish a list of about 25 drinks. Revise this list periodically as you need to and add popular new drinks to this list of recipes. With time, you may wind up with a list of 50 or more standardized drink recipes, and that is okay. This will help train future bartenders and help control overall beverage costs.

Specify Brands

Work with your bartenders. Establish what ingredients they should use. You should probably also list specific brands by name. Decide what brands you will use for bar whiskey, bar gin, bar scotch, and so on. A brand used as "bar" whiskey in one beverage operation may be used as "call" whiskey in another. The "bar" whiskey (or "bar" gin, or "bar" anything) is a brand you can get for less cost than some other brands. It is the brand you use if no brand is specified by the guest. When customers ask for whiskey, gin scotch (anything) without naming a specific brand name, they get your bar brand. It can be a brand that is not especially well known, but it should be of good quality. To many people, the term "bar" whiskey (gin, scotch, etc.), means cheap and inferior. Do not use really inferior quality liquors for your bar brands. Bar brands should be comparatively inexpensive for you to buy but should be of good quality.

"Call" whiskey (or "call" gin, "call" scotch, etc.) is whiskey that guests ask for by brand name. Normally, you will sell call liquors at a higher price than bar liquors. If guests just say, "Give me a whiskey and water", give them your bar whiskey at your set, standard price, but if they say, "Give me brand X whiskey and water," give them brand X whiskey and water. They should pay a reasonably higher price for this than they would if they had just ordered whiskey without naming a brand. You are justified in charging more for call whiskey because it costs you more than your relatively less expensive bar whiskey, and you are providing a service by giving guests brands they specifically request.

Make good decisions about your choices of liquors and beverage recipes. Serve a product which is of a quality that is suitable for your type of beverage operation. Use good quality bar whiskey, bar gin, bar scotch, and so on. You will use these in mixed drinks when guests do not specify brand names. They should be good drinks and they should bring you a good profit.

Use a Shot Glass

We have discussed your list of 25 standard, most common drinks. you work out exact proportions for these. But there are a lot of other details you will have to work out, too. For example, when someone orders whiskey and water, what size shot glass will you use? One and a fourth ounce? one and a half ounce? Decide on a specific size of shot glass (or other measuring device) and insist that it is used at all times. Many bartenders claim they can pour accurately without measuring, and perhaps they can, but there is danger of overpouring or underpouring unless they use an exact measurement every time.

In a bar operation there will be many details to consider. Rules and routines must be established and followed. Your bartenders should not set these policies and make these decisions. You, the manager, working with the bartenders, should. Set bar operation procedures ahead of time, then make sure they are followed.

THE BAR CONTRIBUTES TO THE PROFITABILITY OF THE TOTAL BUSINESS

The fact that you have liquor for sale does not mean you will automatically make a profit. There is profit to be made in operating a bar, but you have to set a correct price for each drink. In the first place, you have to collect properly for each drink, and you have to have volume. Many people entering the food and beverage industry have the idea that their bar is sure to make plenty of money, so their food can be sold at breakeven of loss. Wrong. Both beverage and food must contribute to the food and beverage operation.

An average food and beverage establishment will normally take in about Rs. 40 in beverage sales for every Rs. 160 it gets in food sales. This average is somewhat slanted by the fact that some operations sell only food and no beverage and some sell mostly beverage and very little food. Beverage laws of most states require beverage establishments to sell food. Some beverage operators who do not want to get into much food service solve this by selling their food for very high prices. They intentionally overprice their food so they will not get many orders for it.

But an average food and beverage operation that wants to sell as much of both food and beverage as possible should try for a reasonable balance of food and beverage sales.

How Costs are Computed

One reason a bar can look like it is making a lot of money even if it really is not is the way bar costs are computed. In most food and beverage operations, the bar is charged only for:

1. Material cost—can run anywhere from 20 to 30 per cent of the sales rupee.
2. Direct payroll—includes the salaries and wages of bartenders and cocktail waiters and waitresses and can run from 12 to 20 per cent of the sales rupee.
3. Direct bar overhead—includes glassware, cocktail napkins, giveaway items, and so forth, and can run from 5 to 15 per cent of the sales rupee.

A typical bar might, for example, have beverage cost 20 per cent, direct payroll cost 15 per cent and direct overhead cost 10 per cent. If you look at it this way, the bar makes a 55 per cent profit. But the items just mentioned are direct charges only. Heat, light, and proportionate rent and taxes (among other things) are not charged to the bar. These expenses should be charged against combined food and beverage sales. they should not be charged just to the food department or just to the bar department. Do not arbitrarily try to allocate these expenses as a proportionate amount to either department. Charge direct costs affecting the food department to the food department. Charge combined total indirect charges against combined food and beverage sales.

If all costs for heat, light, rent, and so on are charged just to food and none of it to bar, it looks at first glance like the bar has a 55 per cent net profit. But it really does not. Actually, it has a 55 per cent operating profit, which is not net profit. The bar contributes to the total profitability of the entire food and beverage operation. The bar helps you sell food. food helps you sell beverage. Both should contribute to your profitability.

The cost of service personnel is one to examine closely, for instance. Many beverage operations do not have separate cocktail service personnel. They use the regular food service personnel to serve drinks to guests in the dining room. This cost is usually just charged against total combined food and beverage sales, and it should be. This is recommended accounting procedure and it is fine-but it may make the bar's departmental profit look better than it really is. The bar's direct costs (such as cost of beverage sold, direct labor, and direct overhead) should be charged to the bar and computed and compared against beverage sales. If special cocktail waiters or waitresses are used, their wages should be charged directly to the bar operation. This will help define a norm for the bar to use in setting its standards. The bar operation should compare itself to its own norm. all direct bar costs should be charged to the bar so you have the actual facts on the bar profit, not just part of the picture.

The bar should be expected to contribute substantially to the overall profitability of the business and it should be analyzed realistically according to its real expenses and its real profits.

Costing and Pricing Drinks

Work out potential costs for liquor. You can apply the concepts we discussed for potential food cost to potential beverage cost, Say you buy a liter of whiskey to sell in your operation. You pay Rs. 400.00 for it, you estimate that you expect to get 25 one-and-one drinks from it. Divide Rs. 400.00 (total whiskey cost to you) by 25 (number of drinks). This tells you that the whiskey costs you Rs. 16.00 per drink.

Next you figure out the average cost to you for mix and all other ingredients (garnish, soda, ice) per drink. These additional items (not including the main ingredient, which is whiskey) are called "surrounding costs." Suppose you find the average you spend for surrounding costs is Rs. 2.00 per drink. Add the 2 rupee to the 16 rupee and you get your total average beverage cost per drink-18 rupee per drink.

It is probably better to find an average figure for your surrounding costs. Some guests will order whiskey and soda (soda is surrounding cost), some will order whiskey and water (no surrounding cost for water). So whiskey and water will not cost you exactly the same amount of money as whiskey and soda do. Normally, however, you will sell both drinks for the same price. You figure the average cost per drink including averaged surrounding cost.

To get the selling price, you decide what beverage cost percent you want a 20 per cent beverage cost percent. You divide 20 per cent into 100 per cent. Your markup percent is 500 per cent. You multiply the 18 rupee average cost per drink we just discussed by the 500 per cent markup. You get a selling price of Rs. 90 per drink.

Not all beverage items (or food items either) are prices by the same standard markup. You should probably use lower than 500% for others. Suppose, for example, you compute the cost and markup for a brandy Alexander. According to your calculation you should sell it for Rs. 100. Many operations might price a brandy Alexander at Rs. 110. They add 25 cent as a nuisance value cost because there is extra work involved in clearing the mixer after a cream drink is prepared. When special extra in time and work as involved in a particular item, allow for them in your pricing. Adjust prices individually when you need to, so you will get the beverage cost want.

Many operators group their beverage prices into 4 to 6 major categories (Rs. 80, Rs. 90, Rs. 104, Rs. 110 etc). Some operations but their bar drinks in one price category, call drinks in another, special drinks in another, and so on, in order to try to achieve their overall desired beverage cost per cent.

Working with your bartender , decide (ahead of time) what you will do about pricing drinks that are not on your stander drink list. For instance, you could set guidelines for pricing – bartenders should change a specific amount per ounce for cordial, for whiskey, for gin, for vermouth – plus a set amount per drink for surrounding cost. Bartenders should have recipe sources plus pricing guidelines for drink not on your stander list.

Price should be in line with your other prices. Drinks not on your drink list should be profitable for you. It may take extra time for your bartender to make them (they should have to look at the recipe, get special ingredients). Keep price reasonable for you and your guests. Guest should be usually primarily concerned withering what they want. The 10 rupees or more for special drink, may not mean very much to your guests, but 10 rupees (or whatever amount) extra for many special drinks you serve can mean a lot to you. It could mean better profitable for your total food and beverage operation.

DISPENSING MACHINES

There are many types of liquor dispensing machine in the market. They range from very simple to very sophisticated. In many, you set the machine's controls on the amount you want, invert the bottle into machine, and the machine will measure and dispense the portions you have set on the machine. Some will keep count of how many drinks they measure out.

Advancement of Dispensing Machines

The following are advantages with most dispensing machines:

1. Drink size is per-set.
2. Drink to automatically measured, so there is no overpouring or underpouring.
3. Yield per bottle is consistently better because the bottle drained completely into the dispenser.
4. Each portion is precisely and accurately measured.
5. Besides dispensing liquor, some machines can meter each drink. They can count and keep visible records This helps to take inventory.
6. Machine can be specially useful for mixing martinis, manhattans, or the like, where the precise amounts of vermouth and gin or vermouth and whiskey are measured into standard drink.
7. Properly set-up some machines can do the entire drink making job faster than a bartender can.
8. There is no spilling.
9. If machines meter drinks, it cut theft. Bartender cannot alter the number sold. The bartender should have money in cash register for each drink meter by machine.
10. Some machines are so sophisticated that they can measure, dispense, count the drinks, print the guests check and maintain a perpetual inventory.
11. Machines never drink on the job, steal , or give drinks to their pals.

Disadvantages of Dispensing Machines

There are some disadvantage with dispensing machines:

1. *Expense:* A major disadvantage of beverage dispensing machine in the cost of buying them. Decide whether you should or shouldn't get a beverage dispensing machine on the basis of what it can and cannot do for you. Can you

offset the cost of buying or leasing a dispensing machine by tighter control, higher yield per bottle, better revenue? Is it worth the price? Normally you should have high volume to justify buying (or leasing) and installing some of the more expensive, sophisticated types of dispensing equipment. Equipment for automatically measuring and/or dispensing beverage as improved considerably. You can get very simple device that you attach with the bottle to measure the exact shot. You can get many types of devices ranging all the way upto very sophisticated machines that measure the drink and record it on guest check and in a memory bank. Operation which have high volume, transient clientele and transient employee (racetrack bar, for example) might give very serious consideration to installing sophisticated measuring and dispensing machine.

2. *Unpopularity in some operation:* A luxurious private club with about, for example, 400 members might do better no getting complicated equipment the atmosphere and requirement of a private club are very different from those of restock bar. Members of private club might prefer to have their own bartender for the comradery and individual personal service that a bartender in a small club can provide. There have been instances where private clubs members have thoroughly disliked automated drink dispensers and have rejected them where they have been tried. The management of private club should bow to members' preferences in a matter like this.

Investigate Equipment Available

Many food and beverage operations have installed various kind of automatic beverage measuring and dispensing equipment, and many extremely satisfied with them. The range available equipment is changing constantly. If you are contemplating installing equipment, check the market carefully. Find out what is available , what it costs and whether you can justify the expense or not. The equipment has improved mechanically and in term of design. A lot of the new equipment look better these days and can be bought in size, shape, colour, and design to fit in with the total décor of different kinds of establishments.

The equipment also works better. Operators who put in dispensing systems some years ago sometimes fund that the equipment was slow, which caused real problem during rush period. Some also fund that they needed more than one unit. The equipment they had was inadequate and slow, so they did not use it and went back to hand pouring. When they needed their systems the most during busy times—They did not use them because they were to slow. As a result, the equipment available today is fast, efficient, and more attractive than it was several years ago.

Automatic beverage dispensing equipment today usually comes with a total programme of beverage control. The equipment company usually provides forms they have devised that help you take inventory and compute your bar cost. A standardized programme used with machines can help you get the beverage cost you want.

Evaluate the pros and cons of installing dispensing machines as you would evaluate advantages and disadvantages of purchasing any new equipment. Analyze what an automatic beverage machine can and cannot do to help you run your operation more efficiently and help you to get the profit you want. As a guideline, the cost of installing and maintaining the beverage equipment should be returned to you through increased efficiency, lower labour cost for your volume of business, and a reduced beverage cost per cent. The saving should be converted to dollar amounts and these savings should pay, over a period of time, for the cost of installing the equipment. They should increase your profits.

OPERATING YARDSTICKS/PROFIT PLANNING

We said that one of the main reasons food service operations fail is the fact that managers do not understand accounting records. You, as a manager, should understand basic accounting. Accounting is a vital tool of management.

Accounting Records

In the food and beverage industry, you use accounting records mainly to:

1. Keep track of assets, liabilities, and capital accounts. (Capital means owner's investment in the business—the same thing as owner's equity) These three are called "balance sheet accounts."
2. Keep track of income and expense accounts. These two are called "statement of income accounts."

Balance Sheet

A balance sheet is a statement of the financial condition of a business at a specific instant in time. The balance sheet is dated the last day of a month or *y* of a year.

Statement of Income Chart

The statement of income shows income and expenses of a business over a period of time. A statement of income would be headed "For the month ending (date)" or "For the year ending (date)." Our sample statement of income (Chart) is headed "For the year ending December 31, 2007, which means that this statement shows all sales and expenses during the year 200____through the close of business on December 31 of that year.

Assets	
Current Assets	
Cash	Rs. 13,60,000
Account Receivable	10,40,000
Inventory	8,80,000
Prepaid Expenses	3,20,000
Total Current Assets	Rs. 36,00,000
Fixed Assets	
Land	Rs. 16,00,000
Building	92,00,000
Furniture and Fixtures	56,00,000
Total Fixed Assets	1,64,00,000
Total Assets	Rs. 2,00,00,000
Liabilities and Capital	
Current Liabilities	
Accounts Payable	Rs. 12,00,000
Taxes Payable	2,40,000
Accrued Expenses	9,60,000
Total Current Liabilities	24,00,000
First Mortgage ·	64,00,000

(Contd.)

Capital

Capital Stock	Rs. 80,00,000
Retained Earnings	3,20,00,000
Total Capital	11,20,00,000
Total Liabilities and Capital	Rs. 2,00,00,000

Chart—Restaurant balance sheet December 31, 20____

	Rs.	
Food Sales	3,20,00,000	100.00%
Cost of Food Sold	1,15,20,000	36.00
Gross Profit	2,04,80,000	64.00%
Controllable Expenses		
Payroll (Labour)	86,40,000	27.00%
Payroll Taxes and Employee Benefits*	10,00,000	3.13
Direct Operating Expenses*	14,00,000	4.37
Advertising and Promotion*	7,20,000	2.25
Utilities*	12,40,000	3.88
Administrative and General*	10,80,000	3.38
Repairs and Maintenance *	12,80,000	4.00
Total Controllable Expenses	1,53,80,000	48.00%
Profit Before Occupation Costs	47,20,000	16.00%
Occupation Costs* (includes rent, insurance, interest and real estate taxes)	8,80,000	2.75
Profit Before Depreciation	42,40,000	13.25%
Depreciation*	8,00,000	2.50
Profit Before Income Tax	34,40,000	10.75%
Income Tax*	12,00,000	3.75
Net Income to Retained Earnings	22,40,000	7.00%
Total Desired Profit:	22,40,000	7.00%
Total Labor	86,40,000	27.00
Total Overhead	96,00,000	30.00
Total Food	11,52,0000	36.00
Total	3,20,00,000	100.00%

*These are overhead.

Restaurant statement of income for the year ending December 31, 19.

Your statement of income will tell you which one of the three following situations your operation is in:

1. Your sale are greater than your expenses. You have a profit.
2. Your sales and your expenses are close to equal. You are close to break-even
3. Your expenses are greater than your sales you have a loss.

The object of this discussion is to tell you how to plan for and get a profit.

Uniform Systems of Accounts

In the food, beverage and lodging industry there are three very important books:

1. *Uniform System of Accounts for Restaurants.*
2. *Uniform System of Accounts for Hotels.*
3. *Uniform System of Accounts and Expense Dictionary for Small HoMotels, and Motor Hotels.*

These three books tell you how to classify accounts for recordkeeping purposes for the various types of operations indicated. If you are in a corresponding type of food and beverage operation, study the Uniform System of Accounts that applies to your own unit. If you happen to be in a food operation not included in the Uniform System of Accounts just listed (hospital service, for example), your food department will probably have its own system. You might suggest that your unit use the *Uniform System of Accountants for Restaurants* for your food service department if it seems feasible.

When you have learned how to use one of the Uniform System of accounts books, you will know how to classify and set up the books for your firm. Make your books conform to the appropriate system. (There is information about understanding and using the systems in *How to Use the Uniform System of Accounts for Hotels and Restaurants.)*

As a food and beverage operations manager, you should not have to how to use a lot of different accounting systems. You should learn how to use the appropriate Uniform System of Accounts well and make your own unit's books conform. If you do, you can easily compare how you are doing with industry averages (which you can get through your Trade Association). It will also make it easier for you to move from one food and beverage operation to another. Set up the books wherever you are working and make them conform to the appropriate Uniform System. You will not have to learn a new way of keeping books. If you shift from one type of operation to another (from a hotel food service to a free-standing restaurant, for example), get out the Uniform System that now applies to you, learn it, and use it.

Plan for a Profit

You need to understand these two types of financial statements balance sheet and statemen of income so that you can do profit planning. Do not just subtract expenses from sales to determine what your profit was. Instead, subtract ahead of time from expected sales the amount of money you will be able to spend for expenses and still get a profit. That is what profit planning is.

It is correct to use the following traditional accounting formula when you write up your monthly statement of income:

SALES minus ALL EXPENSES equals PROFIT.

For profit planning, however, use the following profit planning formula: ESTIMATED SALES minus DESIRED PROFIT equals.

Maximum Amount You can Spend for Expenses

Do not just hope that profit will be there when you receive your statement of income. Do not wait until the period of time has ended to find out if you have a profit. Plan ahead of time-before you go after profit and while you are going after it. Use the profit planning formula stated above (ESTIMATED SALES minus DESIRED PROFIT equals MAXIMUM AMOUNT YOU CAN SPEND FOR EXPENSES) and make it work as you go.

Procedures for Profit Planning

Table 5.13 shows a procedure in both dollars and percents for profit planning. Deduct profit first. What is left is the maximum you can spend for labour cost, overhead cost, and food cost. Then deduct labour and overhead. What is left is the maximum you can spend for food. Deduct labour and overhead before food, because labor and overhead are relatively fixed. Food cost is the only *truly* variable cost that is supposed to vary in relation to sales.

Table 5.13 : Profit Planning

Estimated Sales	Rs. 3,20,00,000	100%
minus Desired Profit	Rs. 22,40,000	7
equal Maximum Amount You Can Spend for Labour, Overhead and Food	Rs. 2,97,60,000	93%
minus Labour	86,40,000	27
equal Maximum Amount You Can Spend for Overhead and Food	Rs. 2,11,20,000	66%
minus Overhead	96,00,000	30
equals Maximum Amount You Can Spend for Food	Rs. 1,15,20,000	36%

Let's say that your total capital (owner's total investment) is Rs. 1,15,20,000 and you want to earn a 20 per cent rate of return on this total investment. You arrive at the profit rupees you want by doing the following:

1. Rs. 1,15,20,000 total capital multiplied by 20 per cent desired rate of return equals Rs. 22,40,000 desired return on investment in dollars.
2. Rs. 1,15,20,000 desired return in rupees divided by Rs. 3,20,00,000 estimated sales equals 7 per cent. This 7 per cent is your minimum profit percentage of the sale revenue

Now we will discuss and explain how and why you perform this calculation. For purposes of this discussion, let us say that you are the sole owner of a food service establishment. Consider the amount of money you have invested in your business—your total capital. ("Amount invested" means only your total capital—your capital stock and your retained earnings, not the total assets of the business).

Steps in Profit Planning

There are eight steps in profit planning:

1. Total investment
2. Desired return on investment

3. Estimate your sales for next year
4. Calculate profit per cent
5. Labor
6. Overhead
7. Food
8. Labour, overhead and food costs

1. Total Investment

First, examine your balance sheet. It is important to separate your investment (total capital) from total liabilities. Your investment is composed of original investment plus your retained earnings. "Retained earnings" means any profits you have put back into your business. The amount of your total investment will have a direct bearing on the amount of profit you should expect. The more you invest, the more profit in rupees you should get.

2. Desired Return on Investment

You know what your total investment is in rupees. Now decide what return in profit rupees you want. Most owners say, "All I can get." This is forthright but not very informative. You may be satisfied with a percentage return of 10, 15, 20 or 25. Say you have a total investment of Rs. 1,12,00,000, composed of Rs. 80,00,000 original investment and Rs. 3,20,0000 retained earnings. A 10 per cent annual return would be Rs. 11,20,000 a year profit; a 15 per cent return would be a Rs. 16,80,000 profit; a 20 per cent return would be Rs. 22,40,000 a year profit, and so on. We are talking about return on investment now, not return on sales rupees.

You arrive at a feasible amount for return on investment by considering these factors:

(a) *Returns on money:* What return would you get if you had put your money into insured savings accounts or insured certificates of deposit instead of into a food service operation? You would get the current rate of interest. You would also get no work, no worry, and no danger of losing any of your money.

(b) *Risk:* The riskier a business is, the higher the rate of return from that business should be. People who invest their money in the food service business (or any other business) should get a higher return than they would if they had put their money into savings accounts or certificates of deposit. The food service industry is a very high risk business, so investors should expect an even higher return than they would from some other types of businesses. Many people who invest in food service operations are very disappointed with their profits. In fact, many go broke. High risk in any investment heightens the expectation of and hopes for a large profit. It also increases the possibilities of failure. Risk is an important factor. In the food service business, risk is very high.

(c) *Entrepreneurship:* This means that you assume the ownership and risks of a business operation. You have taken your knowledge of the food service business (if you have any), you have sought out and hired people who (you hope) know their special functions in a food service operation, and you have placed these people in an operation that you hope will be attractive a service for the community by providing a food service operation. For this service you are justified in expecting a return.

(d) *Combination of return, risk and entrepreneurship:* Suppose you have Rs. 1,12,00,000 invested in your food service operation. As we said above, you could have invested your money in certificates of deposit, which would pay you perhaps 8 per cent interest a year, and you would get Rs. 8,96,000 return each year for your investment with no work or risk whatever. If you invest in a food service operation instead, you cannot be blamed for wanting an 8 per cent return on money, plus a 10 per cent return for risk plus a 2 per cent return for service, for a total of a 20 per cent return on your total investment. A 20 per cent return is higher than return would be for lower-risk ventures. Because of the greater risk involved, you should always get higher return in this industry. You are providing a food service unit for your community and you are risking your money. You could lose the entire Rs. 1,12,00,000. Many have lost much larger amounts of money than that in the food service business.

It is easier to evaluate return than it is to evaluate risk and entrepreneurship. How do you put a value on risk and entrepreneurship? As general guideline, 12 to 20 per cent is considered a reasonable total return your money in the food service industry. This will vary with the money market. Ask your local restaurant and/or hotel association, or check current trade publications for more information on this. Perhaps you will also have access to special studies prepared by national accounting firms for their clients. Consider the risk you take in investing your money in the food service business. What chance do you really have of succeeding? How much do you know about the food service business, its problems and intricacies? Some who invest have no food industry background what soever. Some of these people do well, some do not. Even if you do have knowledge of the industry, it is no guarantee that you will be successful. A food service operation is virtually always a high-risk venture. Unfortunately, there is no definite, perfectly accurate guideline for deciding what return you should get and for setting values on risk and entrepreneurship. Most food service owners try for a total return on investment (for risk, entrepreneurship, and interest return) of more than 15 per cent return on investment per year. Actual rate of return on investment.

(e) *Payback period:* Another way of looking at return on investment is: How long does it take it take you to recover your original investment? Many in the industry believe that if food service owner recover their original investment in five years or less, they have a good food service operation. The number of years it takes to recover the original investment is called the "payback period" if the payback period is five years, there would be an average return of 20 per cent per year; 100 per cent divided by five years would equal a 20 per cent return on investnent per year.

(f) *Actual rate of return on investment*: To compute the rate of return you actually receive, you use the following formula: NET PROFIT divided by TOTAL CAPITAL equals RATE OF RETURN ON INVESTMENT.

If you are satisfied with your current return, use your current return figure as your profit figure when you do profit planning for the future. If you are not satisfied with your current level of return, use a higher rate of return figure in your profit planning for the future.

(g) *Desired return in dollars*: Based on all the preceding

information, decide on your desired rate of return. Multiply it by your total investment. For example, we have said that you have Rs. 1,12,00,000 as your total capital in your operation, so you would say:

TOTAL CAPITAL Rs. 1,12,00,000 multiplied by your DESIRED RATE OF RETURN 20 per cent equals your DESIRED RETURN IN RUPEES 22,40,000.
You have invested Rs. 1,12,00,000 and you want at least Rs. 22,40,000 as your profit every year. (NET INCOME equals TOTAL CAPITAL multiplied by RATE OF RETJRN).

3. Estimate Your Sales for Next Year

The third step in profit planning is to estimate your sales for next year. Look at your past records. Examine past and recent trends in your sales. Consider the economy, local changes, competition, local city's growth patterns and the like. Analyze next year from every angle you can think of.

For example, if your food service operation did Rs. 3,10,00,000 in annual sales last year, and if you have some new promotion ideas for increasing sales, perhaps you will be justified in estimating next year's sales at Rs. 3,20,00,000. The key is – little on a realistic figure of what you honestly do expect next year's sales volume will be.

4. Calculate Profit Per cent

Use your desired return in rupees. You have calculated above in step g, "desired return in rupees." Divide this return in rupees figure by your estimated sales figure. This gives you the figure for the minimum profit per cent you want per sales rupee.

In our example above, you want a Rs. 22,40,000 return on investment in rupees. This means that you want Rs. 22,40,000 minimum profit each year – Rs. 22,40,000 desired minimum profit return in dollars divided by estimated sales of Rs. 3,20,00,000 results in a minimum of 7 per cent profit of the sales rupee. In this situation, sales is 100 per cent and minimum profit is 7 per cent. You can spent 93 per cent of each no more-for food, labour, and overhead combined. Individual percentages for food, labour, and overhead can go up and down and vary in relation to each other, but do not let the total of these three exceed 93 per cent or you will be cutting into your profit.

5. *Labour*

To make an estimate of what you expect your labour cost will be in the future, the first thing you do is find out how much you spent for labour costs in previous years. Decide whether you think this amount is apt to increase or decrease or stay about the same. Think ahead. Presumably you will intend to try to reduce payroll through increased efficiency. But maybe you are also contemplating raises for your employees, which could overcome reductions for more efficiency and result in an increase in your payroll costs anyway.

Suppose that your payroll last year was Rs. 80,00,000. You hope and expect to increase efficiencies and thus reduce your payroll by Rs. 1,60,000 (Rs. 80,00,000 minus Rs. 1,60,000 equals Rs. 78,40,000). But you also plan raises for your employees, especially key employees, which will increase your payroll by Rs. 8,00,000 (Rs. 78,40,000 plus Rs. 80,00,000 equals Rs. 86,40,000). So you estimate total labour cost for next year will be Rs. 86,40,000.

You started with Rs. 3,20,00,000 estimated sales. Subtract Rs. 22,40,000 for profit. This leaves Rs. 2,97,60,000 maximum available for all expenses-labour, overhead and food. Now subtract Rs. 86,40,000 labour from the Rs. 2,97,60,000. This leaves Rs. 2,11,20,000—the maximum amount you can spend for overhead and food.

The estimated labour cost is 27 per cent—Rs. 86,40,000 ESTIMATED LABOR COST divided by Rs. 3,20,00,000 ESTIMATED SALES equals 27 per cent ESTIMATED LABOUR COST.

6. *Overhead*

The sixth step in profit planning is to estimate the rupees you will spend for overhead. Examine your books from previous years. You will probably find that overhead was a fairly constant per cent of sales. If it was not and if it has been increasing, examine the areas where it has increased. Find out why overhead has increased and figure out ways that you can lower it if you possibly can. Make a realistic evaluation of each item in overhead expense. Decide whether you think each is apt to increase, decrease, or stay about the same. Consider cost of utilities. Is your rent stable? Taxes going up? Cost of cleaning supplies increasing? Can you cut the cost of cleaning supplies by changing brands or training employees how to use the supplies more economically? Look realistically at all overhead costs. Examine details. Cut where you can and realize that some costs will go up. Examine all factors as well and as thoroughly as you can.

Now you have analyzed all rupee items in the overhead category and you have estimated a total rupee amount for overhead. Subtract this rupee amount estimate for overhead from the amount available for overhead and food. This gives you the amount you can spend for food. If, for example, you decide you will probably spend about Rs. 96,00,000 for overhead, then subtract the Rs. 96,00,000 from the Rs. 2,11,20,000 available for overhead and food. This leaves Rs. 1,15,200,00, which is the maximum amount you can spend for food.

The estimated overhead cost is 30 per cent—Rs. 96,00,000 ESTIMATED OVERHEAD COST divided by Rs. 3,20,00,000 ESTIMATED SALES equals 30 per cent ESTIMATED OVERHEAD COST.

7. Food

We just concluded in the preceding step that the most you can spend for food is Rs. 1,15,20,000. The estimated food cost is 36 per cent—Rs. 1,15,20,000 ESTIMATED FOOD COST divided by Rs. 3,20,00,000 ESTIMATED SALES equals 36 per cent ESTIMATED FOOD COST.

If any expense—food, labour, or overhead-goes over your estimated percentage, you must reduce something else somewhere in food or labour or over-head, so that you do not go over 93 per cent for the three of them combined. That untouchable 7 per cent is your profit.

8. Labour, Overhead and Food Costs

Now use labor, overhead, and food cost per cents as guidelines to help see to it as you go along, day, that you will get that minimum 7 per cent profit per cent you want.

Percentage Analysis

"Tradition" has at times taught the food service industry to put too much emphasis on percentages and not enough on actual rupees. "percentage annlysis" is also called 'common size analysis'. It mean you have reduced a business to a common size—in other words, sales equal 100 per cent.

Percentage analysis can help you analyze your business. In the food service business, percentage analysis means:

1. Sales is 100 per cent.
2. Every other item is expressed as a percent of sales.
3. Sales is the denominator.
4. Expenses is the numerator.

Percentages are helpful guidelines in achieving rupees of profit. For a lot of people, it seems to be simpler to compare increases or decreases in percentages from one period to another than it is to compare increases or decreases in rupees from one period to another.

Your costs are going to fluctuate during the year (or in whatever time period your profit planning is being applied to). If labour cost is 26 per cent, food cost is 37 per cent, and overhead cost is 30 per cent (93% total), you are okay. If labour is 28 per cent, food is 36 per cent, and overhead is 29 per cent (93% total), you are okay. If one cost increase is offset by another cost decrease within the 93 per cent total of costs, okay. Individual costs will vary. But keep track of the total combined cost. You have set 7 per cent a your profit goal. So if your total combined food, labour, and overhead costs go over 93 per cent, you are going into that 7 per cent which is your only hope for profit. Act fast. Put cost reduction policies into effect. Make reasonable increases in prices. Do both. Take action. Do something to help make sure that by the end of the year (or whatever time period you are working on) you will get that 7 per cent minimum profit percent you started out to get. You cannot wait until the end of the time period to take corrective action. That's too late.

If your operation is running soundly, if your standards are where you want them, if your volume is where you want it, if your costs are currently below the levels computed and your profits are higher than you had planned (perhaps 8, 9 or 10% profit instead of the 7%

profit you had planned according to our example), it does not mean you have to increase costs and lower your profit goal. It means that you are getting more profit than you had set as your minimum profit goal. Great! In our example, 7% is the minimum profit you want. If more comes in, fine. The purpose of profit planning is to find out what your minimum profit should be and help you get that amount or more.

So far we have not discussed a salary for the owner. If you are an owner of a food service operation that is set up as a corporation and you also work as manager, you will pay yourself a salary. Deduct your salary along with the rest of the labour expenses. If you are an owner and also work as manager and do not pay yourself a salary (and you won't pay yourself a salary if your operation is set up as a partnership or a proprietorship because of tax law), you should add to your return on investment the amount you would have to pay someone else to work as manager. If you are in this situation (owner with no salary to live on), you would probably withdraw a certain amount of money from the business each month as a partial distribution of your annual profit.

PROFIT PLANNING WITH BOTH FOOD AND BEVERAGE SALES

The preceding profit planning discussions concerned food service operations that sell only food, no beverage. It is more complicated if you sell both food and beverage.

Table 5.14 Profit Planning Food and Beverage shows an establishment that sells both food and beverage. The following is a discussion of the information in Table 5.14, showing how last year's numbers are used as guidelines to establish this year's numbers.

In Table 5.14, last year's sales were Rs. 3,50,00,000. This year's sales are estimated at Rs. 3,60,00,000. Last year the per cent of profit was 9 per cent. The owner wants a 9 per cent profit again this year. Last year's figures are historical. You estimate and calculate and modify to arrive at this year's figures.

Nine per cent of Rs. 3,60,00,000 total sales is an Rs. 32,40,000 profit. Rs. 32,40,000 profit subtracted from Rs. 3,60,00,000 total sales is Rs. 3,27,60,000. Rs. 3,27,60,000 is the maximum amount you can spend for labor, overhead, and cost of goods sold. "Cost of goods sold" means cost of food sold and cost of beverage sold combined.

Last year your labour cost was Rs. 84,80,000. For this year you estimate it will be Rs. 90,00,000. Rs. 90,00,000 subtracted from Rs. 3,27,60,000 is Rs. 2,37,60,000 – the maximum amount you can spend for overhead and the total cost of goods sold combined.

You estimate that your overhead expenses will be Rs. 1,21,60,000. Rs. 1,21,60,000 subtracted from Rs. 2,37,60,000 is Rs. 1,16,00,000 the maximum you can spend for food and beverage combined (cost of goods sold).

To get your estimate of what you think your food cost and your beverage cost will be, you have to make some decisions and do some more computations. Last year your food sales were 78.86 per cent. Last year your beverage sales were 21.14 per cent. This year you estimate you will have an increase in food sale and decrease in beverage sales as per cent of total sales. You estimate that food sales will be 80 per cent of total sales and beverage sales will be 20 per cent of total sales. Eight per cent multiplies by Rs. 3,60,00,000 total sales is Rs. 2,88,00,000 food sales. Twenty per cent multiplied by Rs. 3,60,00,000 is Rs. 16,72,00,000 beverage sales.

Last year your cost of food sold was 86.06 per cent of cost of goods sold and your cost of beverage sold was 13.94 per cent of cost

Table 5.14: Profit Planning and F & B

	Last Year		*This Year*	
	Rupees	*Per Cent*	*Rupees*	*Per Cent*
Total Sales	3,50,00,000	100.00	3,60,00,000	100.00
minus Profit	31,50,000	9.00	32,40,000	9.00
equals Maximum Amount You Can Spend for Labour, Overhead and Cost of Goods sold	3,18,50,000	91.00	3,27,60,000	91.00
minus Labor	84,80,000	24.23	90,00,000	25.00
equal Maximum Amount You Can Spent for Overhead and Cost of Goods sold	2,33,70,000	66.77	2,37,60,000	66.00
minus Overhead	1,18,90,000	33.97	1,21,60,000	33.78

(Contd.)

	Last Year		*This Year*	
	Rupees	*Per Cent*	*Rupees*	*Per Cent*
equals Maximum Amount				
You Can Spend for				
Cost of Goods Sold	1,14,80,000	32.80	1,16,00,000	32.22
Food Sales	2,76,00,000	78.86	2,88,00,000	80.00
Beverage Sales	74,00,000	21.14	72,00,000	20.00
Total Sales	3,50,00,000	100.00	3,60,00,000	100.00
	% of CGS		*% of CGS*	
Cost of Food Sold	98,80,000	86.06	1,00,92,000	87.00
Cost of Beverage Sold	16,00,000	13.94	15,08,000	13.00
Cost of Goods Sold	1,14,80,000	100.00	1,16,00,000	100.00
	Food Cost%		*Food Cost %*	
Cost of Food Sold Food Sales	98,80,000= 35.80 2,76,00,000		1,00,92,000 = 35.04 2,88,00,000	
	Beverage Cost%		*Beverage Cost %*	
Cost of Beverage Sold Beverage Sales	16,00,000 = 21.62 74,00,000		15,08,000 =20.94 72,00,000	
Recap	F & B Cost		F&B Cost	
	as % of Total Sales		*as % of Total Sales*	
Cost of Food sold Total Sales	98,80,000 = 28.23 3,50,00,000		1,00,92,000 = 28.03 3,60,00,000	
Cost of Beverage sold Total Sales	16,00,000 =4.57 3,50,00,000		15,08,000 = 4.19 3,60,00,000	
Cost of Goods Sold Total Sales	1,14,80,000 = 32.80 3,50,00,000		2,90,000 = 32.22 3,60,00,000	

of good sold. You estimate that your food sales will go up as a present of total sales. So you increase cost of food sold from 86.06 per cent to 87 per cent of cost of goods sold. 87 per cent multiplied by Rs. 1,00,92,000 is 1,00,92,000—your cost of food sold for this year. You estimate that beverage sales will decrease from 13.94 per cent to 13 per cent for this year. 13 per cent multiplied by Rs. 1,00,92,000 is Rs. 15,08,000 your estimate for beverage cost for this year.

Now you have come up with rupee values for food and beverage sales and for cost of food sold and for cost of beverage sold. Divide food sales into cost of food sold and divide beverage sales into cost of beverage sold. You find that for this year you need a food cost per cent of 35.04 per cent and a beverage cost per cent of 20.94 per cent.

Toward the bottom of Table 5.14 you have a recap of the rupees value for the cost of food sold and cost of beverage sold as per cent of total sales. Your cost of food sold as a per cent of total sales is 28.03 per cent. Your cost of beverage sold as per cent of total sales is 4.19 per cent. 28.03 per cent plus 4.19 per cent is 32.22 per cent—the maximum you can spend for cost of goods sold this year.

Table 5.14 shows how you use last year's figures as guidelines for estimating and establishing your costs. (We did pretty much the same thing in Table 5.13, but that was just for food).

The important thing to remember about Tables 5.13 and 5.14 is that first, you estimate sales. Then you calculate amount of profit desired as a per cent of sales. What is left goes for expenses. Deduct profit first. Then you use your past records and make calculated estimates to forecast your expenses for labor and overhead and to arrive at the amount for cost of goods sold.

Profit Planning is a Guide

Profit planning is another tool you use to give you a better chance of actually making a profit. It has proved very effective for many who have used it correctly. It is not magic and it will not guarantee that you will get the return want, but if you use profit planning, you will have a much better chance. It is certainly a better approach than no approach, or a play-it-by-ear approach, approach in which management reacts thoughtlessly to ups and downs out a logical, complete plan. If you do use profit planning, you will know what amount of your sales rupees you can safely spend for expenses and still get profit.

6

SALES PROMOTION

Promoting Restaurants and Lounges

While word-of-mouth advertising lends exceptional credibility to a restaurant, it is usually not enough to properly promote the facility. Even if a restaurant has a popular menu, a good atmosphere, and an excellent staff, it won't be profitable if no one (or only a small group of loyal patrons) knows it's there. The restaurant must be promoted in order to attract guests and make a profit.

TYPES OF SALES PROMOTIONS

Sales promotions are useful for generating quick sales increases and can be targeted to times when business is most needed. Promotions can also be used to introduce new products or services (and stimulate trial purchases), to build excitement and entertainment for both guests and employees, and to build repeat business.

There are three basic ways to promote a hotel restaurant:

1. Personal promotions.
2. In-house promotions.
3. Outside promotions.

Personal Promotions

Personal promotions include sales calls (both telephone and in-person) and sales letter to introduce prospective guest to the restaurant. Restaurant sales calls differ very little from sales calls made for rooms or banquet business. Whether the sales call is made by the restaurant manager or a member of the food service or sales staff, it should follow the basic presentation sales call format: an opening, getting prospect involvement, the presentation, overcoming objections, and closing the sale. Restaurant representatives should thoroughly familiarize themselves with these steps before attempting to make telephone or in-person sales calls.

Sales letters are another important phase of personal promotion, and may be used either as an introductory or follow-up tool to supplement telephone or in-person sales calls. Sales letters should be tailored to individual needs-a restaurant manager should not send the same letter to a business group and a bride!

In-House Promotions

In-house promotions range from coupons and contests to drawings and special events. The types of in-house promotions a restaurant engages in depend on the size, type, and staff of the restaurant as well as its typical markets and target markets. Promotions must be with the positioning of the facility, and present a good reason for guests to patronize it. Creative promotions not only generate additional business, but also help to build guest goodwill and word-of-mouth advertising. In-house promotions that are cost-effective, build enthusiasm among the staff, and provide a benefit to guests (whether value or excitement) greatly enhance the image of the property as a friendly, comfortable place to eat and be entertained, and can help to overcome the stereotype of the boring hotel restaurant or dreary lounge. Some of the most popular in-house sales promotions include:

"Four Walls" Sales Promotion

The three major purposes of sales promotions are to: increase guest traffic, increase the frequency of guest visits, and increase the average guest check.

While there are many ways to accomplish these goals, some of the best opportunities to increase business can be generated within the restaurant's own four walls.

Stimulating Lunch Business

Lunch business can be increased by offering "express" lunches (meals guaranteed to be served within 15 minutes or the meal is free) or by offering salad bars (this option not only provides variety, but allows guests to serve themselves).

Stimulating Dinner Business

One of the most effective ways to increase dinner business is by offering "early bird specials," dinners served at a reduced rate before the regular dinner crowd arrives (usually between 4:30-5:30 P.M.). Mike Hurst's 15th Street Fisheries in Fort Lauderdale, Florida, offers a Rs. 200 discount off any entree during its "early bird" hours, attracting scores of retirees during a time that would otherwise be a slow period for the restaurant.

Special Promotions

Two other offers that generate additional traffic are birthday clubs and gift certificates. Birthday clubs usually offer the birthday guest a free item (from a dessert to a complete meal) or a meal at a reduced rate. The honoured guest rarely comes alone—he or she will usually bring along at least one other person who will dine at regular prices. Similarly, gift certificates often result in additional sales. In many cases, the recipient will spend more than the gift certificate amount-and will usually not dine alone.

Increasing Guest Visits

Two popular options for increasing guest visits are the use of punch cards and bounce-back coupons. Punch cards usually consist of 5 to 10 boxes (depending on the length of the promotion) that are punched as requirements (purchase amounts, specific items, or number of visits) are met. Bounce-back coupons, which offer additional discounts at a later time, are a good way to build business during weak periods. If Tuesday dinner business is slow, for example, a weekend guest can be given a coupon good only on Tuesday night. An interesting-and profitable-variation to the bounce back is the "split meal" offered by hotels in the theater districts of London and New York. Dinner guests are given a dessert coupon to be used following the show, stimulating additional beverage sales (coffee, tea, liquor, cordials, wines, etc.) later in the evening.

Building Name Recognition

Giving guests something to take home often stimulates repeat sales. Popular items are calendars, pads of paper, pins or buttons, pens, matchbooks, and the business card of the manager.

- Coupons.

- Premiums.
- Sweepstakes, games and contests.
- Specials or special discounts.
- Special-occasion clubs.
- Gift certificates.
- Sampling.
- Food festivals and other special events.

Coupons

Coupons are a popular way to offer a discount, introduce new items, or boost. sales of a particular item. There are many types of coupons that can be used (Figure 6.1). While all of the coupons listed in fig 6.1 can generate immediate sales, it is important to note that coupons also have disadvantage. Some food outlets have" over-couponed," continually discounting the same item leading guests to perceive the coupon price as the true value of the item so they are reluctant to purchase the item at its regular price.

To avoid misunderstandings and ill-will, coupons should always be specific – the terms of the offer and any restrictions ("not valid on weekends," etc.) should be clearly spelled out, and each coupon should include an expiration date. Guest contact employees should always be informed of any coupon offers and redemption procedures.

Premiums

Premiums are items that are either given away free or sold at cost. The most successful premium promotions involve a series of items given out OVE multiple purchases – one item at each visit. McDonald's has been highly successful with this approach, as has Choice Hotels, which in 1992 sold a new character in series of "Batman Returns" characters each week.

To be effective over the long-term, premiums must reflect the positioning the restaurant and appeal to the restaurant's target market. An upscale restaurant for example, would not want to give away cheap toys or novelties; conversely, budget family restaurant probably would not find it cost-effective to promote top-of-the-line premium.

Sweepstakes, Games and Contests

Sweepstakes, games and contests are exciting ways to generate interest and build business. Sweepstake winners are chosen at random. There are no games to play and no skill is required—guests simply register or fill out a combination coupon and entry form Games are similar to sweepstakes, but utilize game "pieces", such as match-and win game pieces or scratch cards that reveal the prize contestants have won. Contests, unlike sweepstakes and games, require the entrant to demonstrate some ski in order to win.

Sweepstakes, games and contests are even more effective if they require multiple visits. Holiday Inns, for example, offered a promotion that featured daily prizes, grand prizes and bonuses for entrants, who were given another chance to win each time they visited. This type of promotion can be easily adapted for use restaurants.

Figure 6.1: Types of Coupons

Buy-One-Get-One-Free (also known as Two-For-One)

No charge for an item or meal of the same or lesser value with the purchase of the promoted item.

Single or Multiple Item Discounts

A discount such as Rs. 40 off the purchase of two salad bars or half off one dinner.

Combination Meal at a Discount

A special price for a promoted meal (may include dessert and beverage, appetizers and so on).

Discounts on Selected Sizes, or a Large Item for the Price of a Smaller Item

Discounts on a medium-sized item, a large coffee for the price of a smaller coffee, etc.

Discounts on Specific Purchase Amounts

Can be offered as percentages (20% off all checks over Rs. 1000) or discounts (Rs. 40 off all purchases over Rs. 200).

Free Item with Purchase of Another Item

Free cup of coffee with dessert, free salad bar with dinner entree, and so on.

Time-Fused Coupons

A series of coupons that are good during specific times of a particular promotion. Perhaps a different special each week, or a different individual item offered each week during the promotion.

Bounce-Back Coupons

Coupons that are given for future purchases. These are usually handed to guests when they leave, or they may be included on place mats or affixed to or inserted into "to go" packaging. Like time-fused coupons, bounce-back coupons can be used to stimulate business during otherwise slow. In the Renaissance Center periods – bounce backs should be good only on "slow" days or be for specific items that need increased sales.

Specials or Special Discounts

One of the most popular specials is the "Early bird" dinner. This type of offer, which gives a discount to early diners, both satisfies guests who wish to dine early and builds business during what would otherwise be a slow time before regular diners arrive. Other discount options include offering discounts to seniors, students and military personnel; offering free meals to children dining with their parents; and featuring discounts on a traditionally slow night (no coupon required).

Figure 6.2 : Contests as In-House Promotions

Games, contests and sweepstakes are often used to generate interest and build business. This contest, promoted by Marriott Hotels and Resorts, gives lounge customers the chance to win roundtrip tickets for two on Continental Airlines. *(Courtesy of Marriott Hotels and Resorts)*

Special-occasion Clubs

Special-occasion clubs require a guest to register information regarding his or her birthday, anniversary, or other special occasion. An invitation, which offers a discounted or free meal or item, is then mailed to the guest in time for his or her "special day." Not only does this type of promotion build a mailing list, but additional sales are generated as well – rarely do recipients dine alone. At least one other person usually accompanies the "hononred guest", generating additional sales at regular prices.

Gift Certificates

Gift certificates can be issued in a variety of denominations or for specific meals (free dinner, etc.). As with special-occasion-club promotions, recipients will rarely dine alone, and, in many cases, the guest's check will exceed the certificate amount. In addition, gift certificates represent prepaid sales. In some cases, certificates are not redeemed, providing pure profit.

Sampling

Offering samples of new or speciality products is an excellent way to generate interest and build sales. Free samples give guests the opportunity to taste new items without having to pay for an entire dish. This type of promotion is especially effective if it includes some form of showmanship. Employees giving out samples of Swiss mocha cheese cake can be costumed in colorful Swiss outfits, for example.

Food Festivals and Other Special Events

Themed events, ethnic nights, and other promotions, such as a "Meet the Chef" night or a "Chocolate Fantasy" festival, are excellent ways to generate interest and business. One restaurant staged a "Price Roll-Back" promotion to celebrate its 25th anniversary. Prices were reduced to reflect those on its first menu, and, while the promotion was initially costly, it generated tremendous crowds, and many guests returned after the promotion.

Planning ahead is the key to successful in-house promotions. Generally, major promotions should not run for more than four to six weeks and should be spaced with minimal intervals of two to three months. Maintaining a promotions calendar can help managers organize their promotions ahead of time, keep major holidays from sneaking up on them, and spark ideas for new promotions. April 29, for example, is celebrated as "Zipper Day" in Dunedin, New Zealand, to commemorate the invention of the zipper in 1913. Prizes are awarded for the most zippers on an outfit, and for telling the most outrageous "my-zipper-was-stuck" stories.

Outside Promotions

Outside promotions fall into two general categories: paid advertising and supplemental promotion.

Most restaurants, whether they are hotel outlets or free-standing facilities, make extensive use of a number of forms of paid advertising—both print (newspaper, magazine, direct mail, and so on) and broadcast (see Figure 6.3). Paid advertising offers the advantage of controlling the message to the consumer.Provides examples of the types of creative advertising that can be used to promote restaurant to both new and repeat guests.

Figure 6.3
Types of Advertising Used by Table Service Restaurants (by Check Size)

Types of Advertising	*Check Size in 2000*			
	Less than Rs. 320	*Rs. 320–599*	*Rs. 600–999*	*Rs. 1000 or more*
Radio	55%	55%	55%	48%
Newspaper	81	80	81	75
TV	24	22	25	16
Restaurant Guide	42	59	66	63
Magazine	18	37	64	68
Billboard, Outdoor	44	29	27	18
Team Sponsorship	57	58	50	16
Community Event				
Sponsorships	56	58	61	55
Handout, Flier	40	49	54	40
Direct Mail	31	34	49	65
Press Release	17	25	36	57

This chart shows how the types of advertising used by restaurants differ depending on average check size. High-check restaurants, for example, reported using magazines, direct mail, and handouts or fliers as advertising vehicles, while making little use of the team sponsorship that is popular with many table service restaurants.

Source: National Restaurant Association.

Supplemental promotion includes the use of sales materials—discount coupons, fliers, offers of giveaways, and so on—and promotional pieces such as news-letters. A newsletter *not* only provides information about the restaurant's latest promotions or special offers, it also serves to keep the restaurant's name in front of the public. Since nearly everyone has an interest in food, this type of promotional literature is likely to be kept and referred to a number of times. And newsletters are usually extremely cost-effective in comparison with other print advertising.

Supplemental promotion also includes publicity. Publicity can play an important part in public awareness of a restaurant, and opportunities to receive free publicity are almost everywhere. Local newspapers may eagerly snap up news of restaurant expansions, special promotions and offers to local patrons, and feature stories about employees or special recipes.

Planning Effective Promotions

While sales promotions are used by many restaurants today because they stimulate sales, sometimes long-term guest loyalty may be sacrificed for short-term profit Guest and faced with a myriad of discount options, may be more inclined to switch I the restaurant offering the best deal or postpone dining out until there is a "sale" (substantial discount rather than stay with a restaurant that has been satisfying the past.

In order to combat this danger, sales promotions must be carefully planned and supportive of the overall marketing effort. To ensure that sales promotions a planned in a systematic way, management should:

Analyze Business Patterns

You should analyze records by volume and profit as many ways as possible to determine areas that need promoting. Liquor versus food sales, lunch versus dinner volumes, and business by days of the week can be analyzed, for example.

Identify Profitable Current Business

The direction of promotions will often depend on which areas are already most profitable; perhaps the gourmet restaurant is enjoying extensive local patronage or the coffee shop is attracting large crowd for its Friday night clambake. Can profitable areas be expanded? Are potentially profitable areas being promoted to best advantage?

Identify the Audience

What target market segments will the promotion reaching? What types of promotions will appeal to the targeted segments?

Set Objectives

Once you've identified the areas of greatest opportunity, you can set specific objectives, whether in terms of rupees volume, percentages, number of covers or items sold.

Evaluate Promotion Techniques

A promotion may lend itself to publicity, paid advertising, internal merchandising, personal selling, or combinations of these techniques. Each of these techniques should be evaluated for possible before actually creating a promotion.

Determine an Offer

What type of items might be offered in a successful promotion? Prizes? Free meals? Discounts? Special dishes?

When considering a promotion or offer, it isn't always best to offer discounts. If Tuesday is typically a slow night for a restaurant, simply lower menu prices may not generate additional business. Instead, it might be a better idea to offer something special—a gourmet night, an ethnic night, or other themed event—at a higher price, which will still be perceived as a good value for the money. It is important to remember, however, that new promotion sometimes take several weeks to catch on; a promotion shouldn't be drop just because it wasn't as successful as anticipated during the first week or two.

Develop a Budget

The costs of the suggested promotion should be considered printing costs, advertising costs, costs of incentive gifts for staff members involved in the promotion, costs of special offers, and so on. If not enough money is available to meet these needs, you may need to trim the promotion to ensure effectiveness. A well-done small promotion is usually more effective than a poorly financed, half-hearted large one.

Monitor the Promotion

An ineffective promotion can be discontinued if provisions are made to monitor results on a timely basis. If a restaurant is offering a half-price dinner special, for example, it is important to know the number of specials ordered, the number of regular dinners ordered, and the cost per person of the promotion. *Involve the staff.* While this item has been listed last, it is certainly not least in its importance to a promotion's success. An enthusiastic staff can make an in-house promotion more successful than can paid advertising, and at a substantially lower cost. But the staff must be totally familiar with and sold on the promotion, especially if it involves special costumes or extra effort.

Building Repeat Business

Repeat business is a significant factor in the success of hotel restaurants. Therefore, it is important to cultivate guest loyalty.

The Importance of Employees

Guests do not buy just a meal or a few drinks; they buy a social experience as well. Social experiences always involve people. Food and beverage employees can help make dining or relaxing over a drink a pleasurable occasion. Well-trained employees dedicated to serving guests can make the difference between a highly successful operation and empty seats.

A good manager will make sure that his or her staff not only serves guests but makes friends of them as well. Managers should start with personable employees who are truly interested in each guest and eager to give guests the three free "gifts" that can make each visit memorable and build guest loyalty: recognition, recommendations and reassurance.

Recognition

Recognition of guests is one of the most effective tools for building guest goodwill and repeat business. Almost everyone likes to hear his or her name and feel valued.

Name recognition should begin as soon as a guest walks in. This important part of guest relations can take a number of forms. In some restaurants, guests are greeted personally by the manager. If this is not feasible, a host can make guests feel welcome and introduce them to their food server, or give the food server the names of the guests before he or she waits on them. Food servers should use the guests' names often while greeting and serving them.

Recommendations

Recommendations are another part of the server's job that can help build repeat business. Good recommendations depend on both food and service knowledge. Servers should be fully informed about each item on the menu and should be ready to respond when guests ask for suggestions. Far too many servers are inadequate in this area. They answer questions about what's good on the menu with an evasive "Everything", and, if pressed about a personal preference, reply, "It's all good. I like everything."

These replies do not help the guest or increase the size of the check, so it is important that each food server know the ingredients in each dish, the method of preparation, and the approximate preparation time. In addition, each menu item should be taste-tested to enable the food server to answer questions about the dish's flavour, spiciness, consistency, and so on. For even better results, the restaurant's staff should occasionally eat at the establishments of competitors. If the server has dined at a competitor's restaurant, he or she can honestly tell the patron the difference between the French onion soup offered by the competitor and the French onion soup served in the hotel's restaurant.

When food servers have this extensive knowledge, they find it far easier to assist the restaurant's guests in making selections, which helps build guest trust and loyalty.

Reassurance

Reassuring guests means making them feel at home. Food servers can use conversation and personal observation to tailor their service to each guest. A leisurely diner, for example, has time to talk to the server and taste-test different foods, linger over a meal that took time to prepare, and enjoy a dessert. A business person, on the other hand, may want to place an order immediately and may prefer foods that can be prepared quickly. A group of guests engaged in an animated discussion may not want to be disturbed. In this case, the food server should simply take the order and interrupt as seldom as possible.

Food servers should be sensitive to the special needs of certain guests. Diners eating alone, for example, may feel conspicuous, or families dining with small children may feel uncomfortable if the children become restless or cranky. In these cases, the food server can become a public relations ambassador by meeting the unique needs of these guests.

If a lone diner apologetically says, "There's just one today," for example, the host or food server can project a friendly image, be sure that the lone diner is not seated in an out-of-the-way location, and check back to make sure that everything is all right. Some restaurants offer a daily newspaper to guests dining alone, or (as previously mentioned) offer to seat them at a "Friendship Table" for company and conversation. Providing these special touches can prove to be enormously profitable for the restaurant. Lone diners who are treated well are more likely to become repeat guests and may bring their friends to the restaurant as well.

In the case of a family dining situation, the food server can be friendly and attentive, and assure the family that the children are welcome. The food server should take the order promptly and, if possible, offer a light complimentary snack to the children to help prevent restlessness. Most children are satisfied when given a cracker, a piece of fresh fruit, or some type of "finger food" to occupy them while they wait for the meal. A little extra personal attention helps keep children (and parents) content.

Food servers can make all guests feel at home by engaging them in conversation, truthfully answering questions, and involving them in the restaurant by sharing "trade secrets" or asking for feedback about the food or service. This usually

Michael E. Hurst Owner 15th Street Fisheries Restaurant Fort Lauderdale, Florida:

Mike Hurst is currently a professor at Florida International University's School of Hospitality Management in Miami, Florida, and is a director of the National Restaurant Association in Washington, D.C. He is a former regional (Southeast) chairman of the Culinary Institute of America and is past president of the National Restaurant Association. In 1991, Mr. Hurst received Industry Person of the Year honours from Pennsylvania State University and was the recipient of the Distinguished Alumnus Award from Michigan State University.

For food service students, there just could not be more exciting opportunities than at this time. You should prepare yourself to capitalize on these opportunities. If you lay the proper foundation, you should have an exciting and satisfying career.

My own foundation is based on five lessons I learned during my years in the food service business:

1. *Focus on people:* Early in my career, I was influenced by Ed Mirvish, then owner of Honest Ed's department store in Toronto, who achieved phenomenal business success due to his focus on people. Not only should you focus on your customers—you should also focus on the staff that serves your customers.
2. *Manage for your customers:* Another influence on my career was Paul Shank of the Tiffin Inn in Denver, who delivered food with runners to get the product to the guests hotter and faster. I asked Paul if he thought the runner system accounted for his success. Nope-his success was because he managed for customers: "Provide more service and you create customers."
3. *Dining is an experience:* WM Schuler's philosophy that guests thrive on recognition and friendliness was another important lesson. I learned that what people buy when they dine out is a pleasant experience, not just food. From remembering guest names, to remembering their favorite tables, to creating "Lover's Salads" and special appetizers and desserts, the philosophy of "giving to get" means exceeding customer expectations.
4. *Food can be fun:* The Coral Trout Restaurant in Brisbane, Australia, provided lesson number four: a specialty item-"Moreton Bay Bugs"—appeared on their menu. This fun dish proved to taste like lobster. I borrowed the idea and now serve a similar entree at my restaurant in Florida—"Palmetto Bugs." I gave samples away and asked people to guess what was actually in the dish, creating a fun experience. Customers are willing to try a tasty, unusual item if you introduce it in the right way. Next time they will buy it because fun is precious at any price.

5. Treat your employees as if your business depends on them—it does. The guest experience is determined by the performance of your employees, and that truth has geared the way I manage. While recruitment and selection are important, I focus on making work exciting and fun, and on imparting a sense of worth to my employees. Giving the gift of friendship is as important or even more so than the good food, the decor, and so on. The lesson I took so long to learn is that the greatest compliment I can get is, "Where do you get the nice people who work here?"

These five principles, my "lessons of yesterday," are my game plan for tomorrow. Never forget that business is people. Playing the "game" of satisfying customers can be a non-stressful, fun game that, as a pro, you can win again and again. Enhances a guest's restaurant experience, and provides an excellent reason for the guest to return to "his" or "her" restaurant.

Guest Follow-up

One of the easiest and most inexpensive ways to build guest goodwill and loyalty is with a follow-up telephone call. Telephone numbers can be obtained from the reservations book or a guest survey card provided at each table. The call should be brief, but should express the fact that the guest is valued by the restaurant. Asking if everything was satisfactory can give guests an opportunity to express themselves and can provide the caller with the opportunity to handle complaints and obtain information to help serve guests better.

Keeping in touch with past patrons through the mails also helps to build repeat business. Personal notes or mailings are an excellent way to provide guest follow-up; notes may be sent after a telephone call or may be used to thank a guest for completing a guest survey. Another way to encourage guests to come back is to print a monthly calendar of events. This type of general mailing can be used to announce special promotions, new menu items, or upcoming events.

Guests can also be given incentives to return, such as free meals after they have purchased a required number of dinners, prizes (food or merchandise) to frequent guests through drawings or special contests, and discounts on guestrooms or other property facilities for regular patrons.

Other properties make use of display items to recognize frequent visitors. Lounges may provide engraved mugs to regular patrons. Restaurants may even name a dish after a patron who has suggested the item or who is a frequent consumer of the selection.

Making sure guests are satisfied through guest follow-up is one of the most effective ways to build a loyal guest base and promote the restaurant. Satisfied guests are repeat guests and excellent sources of word-of-mouth referrals.

Other Food Service Operations

Room Service

Many properties, in addition to restaurants and coffee shops, offer room service for the convenience of their guests. Many managers consider room service a costly amenity because of the long and odd hours of operation and the impossibility – predicting the volume of business. Labour shortages and soaring overhead cost have also had a negative impact on room service operations. In terms of labor, for example, additional staff is required, including preparation cooks, steward, order-takers, and delivery personnel, who must be willing to work the often inconvenient hours associated with room service operations. In addition, room service operations cannot take advantage of quantity cooking; meals must be prepared to order, which means a greater per-meal cost.

Nevertheless, many properties feel that room service is a key to keeping guests over the long-term. To maximize effectiveness, room service operations, like other profit centers, require an individual budget and action plans to increase profitability.

Some of these action plans have brought about dramatic changes in the room service operations of today. The U.N. Plaza Hotel, San Francisco, for example, offers guests the opportunity to order food from a local McDonald's (the food is delivered on a silver platter by a bell person). Other properties are opting for contracts with local pizza outlets, providing guests with a favourite food in the convenience of their rooms.

Other alternatives to traditional room service include:

- The addition of guestroom mini-bars with snack foods.
- Microwavable items in guest rooms with mini-kitchens.

*Hotel" delis," where guests can choose favourite foods and prepare them in their rooms.

- * Speciality kitchens that offer a single item, such as pizza, fried chicken, burgers, or sandwiches that can be ordered and delivered to the room.

Limited Service Operations

Limited service is a popular food and beverage option, especially with mid-priced properties and all-suite hotels. In a limited service operation, one meal, typically breakfast, is offered to the guest at no (or a nominal) cost. In some cases, there is no table service – guests get their made-to-order breakfasts at a counter. At other properties, such as Budgetel Inns, a free continental breakfast is delivered to each guest's room.

Hotels have found that guests are enthusiastic about the free breakfast concept, both in terms of price and convenience, and many properties are featuring this option. But there are pros and cons to breakfast give aways. The advantages are obvious: the guest saves money and time and receives an added value for the price of the room, the hotel can save money by providing meals or other food service without the overhead of a full-service restaurant, and free breakfasts enable mid-priced and budget properties to better compete with upscale properties that offer more amenities.

On the downside, the property may have to raise room rates to cover food expenses, additional workers may be needed to run breakfast bars or delivery services, and extra costs may be incurred for cleanup. But, overall, properties are finding that the benefits of serving "free" breakfasts far outweigh the disadvantages, and the "Breakfast Wars" may well continue through the 1990s.

In terms of generating guest relationships, free breakfasts are an ideal promotion. At Hampton Inns, for example, breakfast is served in a living room-type environment that brings guests together as "one big family." Mark Wells, vice-president of marketing for Hampton Inns, states that guests not only get a high quality breakfast, but camaraderie is built among the people staying at the chain and the staff members servicing the breakfast – creating the potential for repeat business.

Breakfast Wars

Some hotels are going to ex-traordinary lengths to retain guests. The following hotels are among those competing in the free-breakfast market.

Budgetel Inns—Free continental breakfast (sweet roll and orange juice) is delivered to each guest's room; guest rooms are equipped with coffee makers.

Hampton Inn—Free continental breakfast, cereals, and fruit.

Hilton Suites—Complimentary cooked-to-order breakfast.

Embassy Suites—Complimentary cooked-to-order breakfast and express service (individual stations for coffee and hot and cold foods).

Park Inn International—Free continental breakfast in lounging area featuring giant screen television.

Holiday Inn Express—Free continental breakfast at limited locations.

Hilton Hotels and Resorts—Free continental breakfast as part of its "Bounce Back Weekend" programme.

Quality Suites—Complimentary cooked-to-order breakfast, including eggs, meats, juices, coffee, and hot and cold cereals. Source: Edward C. Achorn, "Food Fight: The Free Breakfast War," *Lodging*, December 1990.

MERCHANDISING FOOD AND BEVERAGES

Food and beverages can be merchandised by special packaging and pricing, promotional materials such as posters and table tent cards, and suggestive selling by food servers. But perhaps the most important merchandising tool is the restaurant's menu. A good menu, through the types of items offered and the presentation of those items, can enhance the image and increase the profits of any food and beverage operation.

Creating Menus That Sell

A menu must reflect the restaurant's positioning or image, provide information, and serve as a suggestive selling tool. While this may seem like a monumental challenge, it is actually quite easy when food and beverage managers follow a menu development cycle that includes image, price, message and design.

Image

The menu development cycle begins with the restaurant's positioning or image. What image does the restaurant create? What type of ambience or atmosphere does it have? When people visit the restaurant, do they expect a romantic atmosphere or a casual dining experience? In other words, the restaurant's image refers to how the restaurant is perceived by its patrons, and the restaurant's menu must live up to their expectations.

Since a restaurant's image is determined in part by the type of clientele the restaurant attracts (or hopes to attract), it is important to determine whether patrons are coming from inside or outside the property (or a mixture of both), and what market segments the restaurant serves. Does the restaurant cater primarily to the health-conscious? Do business travellers, who usually prefer rapid service during their lunch hours, make up the largest number of patrons? Or does the restaurant serve a great number of families and therefore need a more varied menu?

Price

Price information is a critical menu consideration. What prices do guests expect to pay for menu items? Will items be priced individually (3 la carte) or as full meals? Will prices appear at all? Pricing strategy must be determined long before the menu is designed, and must correspond to the restaurant's positioning.

Determining Prices

Unlike free-standing restaurants, which operate with established overheads, hotel restaurants often share facilities (kitchens, store-rooms, etc.) with other arms of the food and beverage department, making it difficult to determine operating costs or to properly price menu items. For this reason, hotel restaurants price menu selections primarily on a cost-of-merchandise basis. Since cost-of-merchandise can vary significantly, it is impractical to use.

Menus should be designed to reflect the character or image of the restaurant. The headings in this menu from the Beef Barron are reminiscent of the Old West. Imporant dishes are encircled by lariats, and line drawings reinforce the Western theme. (Courtesy of Hilton Hotels Corporation) general percentage for all items. Common cost of merchandise targets are 30 to 40 per cent on food, 17 to 22 per cent on bar drinks, and 33 to 50 per cent on wines. Therefore, to determine the selling price of a menu item, you must divide the cost of the item by the desired cost percentage. Labour costs for certain items (oysters must be sucked, for example) should also be considered.

It is important to remember that you "can't bank percentages," and that a lower cost of merchandise percentage does not always mean higher profits. Figure 6.4, which lists Tuesday and Wednesday covers, foods costs, and revenue, shows how average gross profit per guest can differ substantially. Even though Tuesday shows the lower food cost percentage, it was the less profitable of the two days.

Menu pricing is also difficult because restaurants face the problem of changing market conditions, including fluctuating wholesale prices for merchandise and alterations in what the competition is offering and charging. Menu prices in most establishments must be monitored constantly and adjusted for seasonal and competitive changes.

Figure 6.4 : Menu Price Analysis

	Tuesday			*Wednesday*		
Menu Item	*Covers*	*Food Cost*	*Revenue*	*Covers*	*Food Cost*	*Revenue*
Chicken	550	66,000	1,98,000	150	18,000	54,000
Prime Rib	200	48,000	1,12,000	400	96,000	2,24,000
Crab Legs	150	54,000	1,08,000	350	1,26,000	2,52,000
Total	900	1,68,000	4,18,000	900	2,40,000	5,30,000

Food Cost %	1,68,000/Rs. 4,18,000 = 40.2% 2,40,000/5,30,000 = 45.3%
Total Gross Profit	Rs. 4,18,000 – Rs. 1,68,000 = Rs. 2,50,000 Rs. 5,30,000– Rs. 2,40,000 = Rs. 5,70,000 average.
Profit/Guest	Rs. 2,50,000/900 = Rs. 277.60, Rs. 2,90,000/900 = Rs. 322.

The following factors should be studied in order to properly price menu items for hotel restaurants:

1. *Type of operation:* Is the hotel restaurant a coffee shop, a multipurpose dining room, or an elegant supper club? Does the restaurant offer a varied menu or are selections fairly consistent? Offering a consistent menu may keep costs down.

If the restaurant caters primarily to hotel guests who stay for an ex-tended period of time, however, a varied menu that could keep extended-stay guests interested in on-property food facilities may be more cost-effective.

2. *Guest perception:* How do guests perceive the restaurant? Do they expect to pay high prices for superior service and menu selections, or do they see the restaurant as a casual dining room and expect to pay low prices?
3. *Competition:* How many restaurants are nearby, and how do their prices compare with the hotel restaurant? How do their food, service, and atmosphere compare? When a patron has a special occasion for dining out, does he or she have only a few acceptable restaurants to choose from or are there many high-quality restaurants in the vicinity?

Message

The menu's message—the written information it contains—is an important part of a menu's appeal. Will the menu simply list the foods and beverages offered, or will it also include the size of the item, the cooking method, the main ingredients, and methods of service? In addition to describing menu selections, will the menu be used to provide information such as restaurant hours, methods of payment, special dietary information, and cross-selling messages for other property facilities? A restaurant with historic significance may opt for menus featuring background stories; a "fun" restaurant (a restaurant that features zany decor or that involves guests in sing-alongs, for example) may feature offbeat information.

Menu copy should describe food in an honest and attractive manner. It is important that guests know exactly what they are getting ("served with your choice of soup or salad, vegetable of the day, and dinner roll or garlic toast"). The menu should feature the actual name of the item. "Steak and eggs," for example, is too vague; is it a sirloin steak, a T-bone steak, or a minute steak? Menu descriptions should also include:

- The cooking method ("deep-fried in vegetable oil," "broiled to your specification").
- Other main ingredients (descriptions can be kept brief, but should focus the freshness and quality of additional ingredients).

- Descriptions of any sauces used ("brown butter sauce," "white clam sauce" etc.).
- Information about unusual presentations ("wrapped in parchment," stir-fried at your table).
- Health-related information (information about fat, cholesterol, sodium, calories is especially important to today's health-conscious consumers).

When writing menu copy or checking menu copy written by a menu specialist or advertising agency, it is important that the restaurant's image not be tarnished by the use of sexist language, negative restrictions ("Your credit card welcomed here" is far more diplomatic than "Positively no personal checks"), or poorly designed promotions. One of the most common errors—and a striking example of poor taste is the lumping together of a senior citizens' menu and a menu for children: "For those under 12 and over 65."

Design

The menu's message is only part of the presentation. An attractive design will enhance the copy and draw guests to featured items and specials (see Exhibit 5). There are many styles of menus, from a simple blackboard on the wall to parchment paper tied with gold cord. The factors previously mentioned (image, price and message) will play an important role in determining the menu's design. A restaurant with contemporary positioning and an emphasis on fresh foods, for example, may select a menu enhanced by color photography. A family restaurant or coffee shop that caters to a variety of tastes may prefer using a menu divided into categories: a breakfast section, a light-lunch section, a "hearty fare" section, a desert section, a "for the youngsters" section, and so on.

Good menus, no matter what the format, share the following design characteristics:

1. *Effective use of space.* The menu must be clean and uncluttered. Wide borders, space between selections, and large type are effective ways to increase menu's readability.
2. *Effective layout.* The most popular items, or those that the restaurant wants to promote, should be placed at the head of a list, boxed, featured graphically or otherwise set apart. Items listed first in each category sell best. If a two-page

menu is used, the right page gets the most attention; with three-panel menu, the middle panel should be used for special promotions. And last but certainly not least, prices should be placed at the end of each item (this can increase the check average by as much as 6%).

3. *Eye appeal.* Good menus are attractive. The choice of paper, type style, and art work is important. The colour of ink and paper affects readability. Dark ink on light-coloured paper is best, especially if restaurant lighting is dim.

Supplemental Menus

In addition to its regular menu, a restaurant may provide supplemental menus such as drink menus and wine lists, children's menus, and dessert menus. Children's menus are often designed as colourful take-home items, and may feature games or stories to keep children occupied while waiting for the meal. Dessert menus are an effective addition to the regular menu; by the time the meal is over, guests may have forgotten which desserts are available.

Clip-ons are used to avoid expensive reprinting when restaurants supplement the regular menu with daily specials, theme meals, or special menu items in season. If a restaurant plans to use clip-ons, appropriate space should be allotted in the menu's design. Perhaps a blank inside flap or a blank space in the center of the menu can be set aside so the clip-on does not obscure other entrees.

Other F&B Merchandising Methods

In addition to menus, restaurants can use merchandising methods such as the following to increase sales:

- Product packaging
- Added-value alternatives
- Point-of-purchase materials
- Suggestive selling
- Special promotional items

Product Packaging

In order to sell, product packaging relies on an appeal to the senses. Product packaging—both table setting and the garnishing of the food or beverage—usually involves producing a special visual impact that can turn something ordinary into a special delight.

Product packaging can begin at the restaurant's entrance—a display of wines a tempting dessert cart, or an attractive display of fresh produce are all effective sales tools. A display of fresh produce not only whets the appetite but also convey the message that the restaurant uses only the freshest ingredients. This message can be carried throughout the restaurant through salad bars and table decor.

Product packaging can inspire promotions that generate additional business. One restaurant featured an apple promotion that included theme posters, recipe brochures, bushel basket displays of apples, special menu items such as baked apples and apple bread, and a free apple with each delicious soup and sandwich lunch.

Many food and drink items can be made special through product packaging. Colourful garnishes of fresh fruits or vegetables create a feeling of quality and abut' dance and can make even simple food and beverage items more appetizing and salable. A bowl of dry cereal, for example, becomes a more memorable breakfast when served with a choice of colourful fruits (bowls of bananas, strawberries, raisins, and so on). A simple salad can become a work of art when enhanced with skewers of fresh fruits or vegetables.

Unusual presentations can also be used for eye-appeal. A hollowed-out avocado can become a unique bowl for homemade guacamole, an impressive pineapple half may showcase a special chicken curry or salad, and a fresh, crisp tortilla bowl can hold a taco salad. Drinks, too, whether alcoholic or non-alcoholic can generate impulse sales when presented in unique ways. An unusual glass; the addition of attractive garnishes, whether as simple as a few grapes placed in a glass of wine or as elaborate as artistically arranged skewered fruit in frosted glasses; and the use of speciality items (tiny umbrellas, unusual stirrers, or even clay parrot or sombrero attached to a wooden skewer) can generate interest and sales.

Novelty service-ware might also increase food sales. Eggs served in cast-iron skillets, bread warm from the oven and offered on miniature breadboards, and soups brought to the table in small covered kettles are all examples of creative merchandising that sells.

Creativity is equally important in how the food is offered to guests. When every restaurant in town is serving prime rib, for example, why should a guest choose the hotels? One answer might be the hotel's unique way of serving the meal. Perhaps the ribs are rolled to each table on a serving cart and the guest chooses his or her cut and watches it being sliced to order. Or, rather than making salad in the kitchen, dousing it with salad dressing, and setting it unceremoniously on the table, a food server can prepare the salad at the guest's table, spinning the salad and sprinkling dressing over it as it spins. In either case, the difference is entertainment value, and dining becomes more than satisfying hunger. It becomes an experience to be enjoyed.

Sales can be increased by presenting a spectacular dessert early in the evening. A complimentary dish such as bananas flambé can be presented to one table of guests (the guests can be told they have been chosen to receive the dessert for any lumber of reasons), and sales of that item are almost guaranteed to increase as other guests are impressed by the flaming presentations. The ways that creative product packaging can be used to boost sales are almost endless.

Added-Value Alternatives. Not all guests are influenced by showmanship, however; there will always be guests who are most interested in getting value for Heir money. The principle behind added-value alternatives is simple – the guest is given an opportunity to purchase the greatest value among several alternatives. The ways in which to offer greater value are limited only by the imagination of the restaurant manager.

One way to provide value alternatives is to offer various sizes of items, whether the item is a cup of coffee or a steak. Salad items can be sold on different-size plates; teak can be sold by the ounce to appeal to those with small appetites. When large sizes are offered, it is important to note that although the cost-of-merchandise-percentage rises, the contribution margin or profit per guest also rises.

Another option that will appeal to value-conscious guests is offering price alternatives – the choice of full meals or a la carte entrees, for example. Other examples of price alternatives are salad bars priced both with and without a dinner entree, pie offered with or without icecream, and drinks offered with or without appetizers.

In order for this method to be effective, guests must see real value—an alternative that appeals to their lifestyle. Guests who never eat ice cream on their pie, for example, will appreciate not having to pay a higher price.

Prices also figure into another way to provide added-value alternatives: package pricing. This technique is often used in restaurants, and involves including a number of items in one selection; the price of the items, of course, would be higher of purchased separately. Examples of this type of alternative include offering a glass of wine with dinner; a sandwich served with a choice of soup or salad and beverage; a dinner entree that comes complete with a choice of salad, vegetables, breads, and dessert; and so on.

Point-of-Purchase Materials

Sometimes guests are not influenced by either product packaging or value factors, and must be coaxed into making selections. Point-of-purchase merchandising can be used to promote speciality or high-profit items to best advantage. Merchandising at the point of purchase makes extensive use of display advertising such as posters, tent cards on tables, and additional graphic reinforcement such as strategically placed salad bars, displays of vines, and dessert carts.

Some properties also use tabletop selling—for example, a bottle of wine labelled with a tag identifying it as the "wine of the month," or complimentary samples of appetizers or entrees that the restaurant is promoting. When using tabletop, selling, the restaurant must make it clear whether the item is complimentary or for ,ale. If a bottle of wine is for purchase only, it must be clearly identified as such and

Figure 6.5: Sample Point-of-Purchase

Some point-or-purchase displays are as elaborate as this six-panel, full-colour tent card promoting exo drinks. Point-of-purchase materials are used to encourage impulse sales. (Courtesy of Flamingo Hilt (and Tower, Las Vegas, Nevada) guests must not feel obligated to buy. If a fruit basket contains complimentary in and is not on the table strictly for decoration or for sale, a simple banner ("With 0 compliments") can clear up any confusion and make guests feel more at home.

Point-of-purchase merchandising can lead undecided guests into making impulse decisions but, like menus, it has a limitation: it is a one-way communication medium. There is still a missing ingredient: people.

Suggestive Selling

Food servers and other restaurant personnel play an important part in merchandising food and beverages. One of their most effective merchandising tools is suggestive selling. Suggestive selling can begin from the moment a guest is seated. The food server can suggest a cocktail from the bar or a special appetizer to begin the meal. A group can be offered an appetizer sample plate, and the food server can suggest several appetizers that can be ordered various members of the group and shared. Entrees may be suggested or upgrade with a few suggestive-selling phrases. After the meal the food server can suggest choice of desserts rather than just asking if anyone would like dessert. The chances of sales success are enhanced with the use of an attractive dessert cart.

Suggestive selling can also be used in a lounge. The bartender or cocktail self can suggest appetizers or specialty drinks: "We have a terrific new tropical drink *Dessert trays are often used by food servers to enhance their suggestive selling presentation*. That I know you'd enjoy. It's made with a blend of fresh pineapple juice and orange juice with our quality rum, and is served in a tall, frosted glass.

Suggestive selling responsibilities should be part of a food or cocktail server's job description, and wait staff should be trained in the proper use of suggestive sales. Suggestive selling should never be perceived as an attempt to railroad guests into accepting items they really don't want, or as an effort to "bump up" a check. Instead, suggestive sales should be viewed as a part of good service, a way to servet he best interests of guests and make their visits more enjoyable.

Management should make sure that the staff understands the principles behind suggestive selling and the audiences that are most receptive to this sales technique. Leisure travellers, for example, may be more receptive to taking their time and trying new dishes than guests having a business lunch.

Special Promotional Items

Some restaurants use special promotional items such as recipe cards, postcards depicting drinks, and souvenir menus. If a menu is expensive to produce, a smaller-scale souvenir version can be designed to take home). If the property is part of a chain, special promotional items may be available through corporate headquarters. They can also be specially designed by an advertising agency, freelance artist, or menu specialist. If outside sources are used, However, the food and beverage manager should approve the final design and ensure that the copy and design accurately reflect the positioning of the property.

FOOD MENUS AND BEVERAGE LIST THE MENU AS A SALES TOOL

Your menu is one of your most important sales tools. There are many adverting techniques you can use to attract guests into your food service establishment. Once they are inside, your main sales tool is probably your menu. It lists and describes what you offer for sale. Everything that goes on in your food service operation has a direct or indirect effect on your menu. It is a very important central factor.

Before a food service operation is opened to the public, owners and/or management should have made plans concerning what type of food to offer on the menu. The items you offer for sale directly affect the prices you will charge. The prices you charge directly affect the market you will cater to. This in turn affects the atmosphere of the establishment, the skills your employees will need, and so on. They are all interrelated. The menu is basic to everything else.

Suggestions for Your Menu

You should consider a number of factors in planning your menu to mark it your most important sales tool. Some of them are discussed below.

1. Ease of Reading

The menu should be easy to read. Except for foreign food specialty establishments, the tendency today in the United States is toward English wording. If you do use foreign terminology, consider including a translation and/or explanation with the menu listing. For example, if you list "Filets de Sole Poches au Vin Blanc," you might add a description: "Filets of Sole Poached in White Wine."

2. *Cleanliness*

The menu should be clean. The use of plastic-coated menus is a good idea for many operations. Plastic coating is relatively inexpensive, and it makes menus durable and easy to wipe clean. When a menu gets worn or permanently soiled, throw it away.

3. *Size of Menus*

You can order practically any size menu you want. Menu can be so large that they cover half the table or so small that they are appropriate only for use at a counter. Larger menus are more expensive to buy and are usually used in luxurious establishments. Choose a size that will fit the general atmosphere of your establishment. Be sure that the size of the menu you decide on gives you enough space thing you want to offer for sale.

4. *Size of Print*

You may want to use a variety of type sizes—perhaps large type for entrees and smaller type for accompanying items. Your printer gives you the great varieties of styles and sizes of type that are available. Try to make your menu easy to read but also interesting to look.

5. *Colour Photographs*

Colour photographs printed on the menu are a good types of food service operations. Use of colour photos substantially increases the cost of the menu, but good pictures can be very you do use colour photos, try to be sure that the food you served look good as the pictures.

6. *Souvenir Menus*

If you use large, beautiful, or unique menus, some guest may want them for souvenirs. If any guests want to keep them expensive menus, you could consider selling them to guests.

Some restaurants print miniature copies of their menus. They are usually not printed on expensive paper stock and can be quite inexpensive—especially if you order them in large quantities. You might use miniature menus for sales promotion and give them to guests can buy (or receive free) and mail to friends copies of your menu.

These souvenir menu ideas probably apply mostly to expensive, luxury food service operations which develop exotic or unusually interesting menus.

7. Gimmick Menu

Some food operations use gimmick menus—pumpkin-shaped Halloween menus, turkey-shaped for Thanksgiving, Christmas—tree shaped for Christmas, and so on. These are specialty promotion item operations also develop their own ideas.

Some use special children's menus. These may convert into hats or masks, have children's games printed on them, or use other features meant to amuse children.

Other restaurants may use a regular menu layout terminology. If people get a big enough kick out of a silly menu (and if the food service operation is also a good one), guests may bring friends along to enjoy the amusing menu (and the good food). If you are interested in trying the humour menu, make sure that it is funny, not a forced try at being funny.

Whale Stuffed with Yacht..Rs. 55,00,87,920
Unflamed Cherries Jubilee...Rs. 400
Flaming Cherries Jubilee..Rs. 15,02,640

(Waiter is a pyromaniac)

Breast of Boiled Peasant..Rs. 10,000

The examples will give you the general idea. Your guests' reactions will tell you what they find funny.

In some operations outrageous joke items or subtly amusing comments are inserted right into the serious menus. In others, both silly menus and separate real menus are used; the staff is trained to present both menus to guests in a planned way so that all guests see a silly menu for fun but also get a copy of a menu that really tells them what food is available.

How Many Menus?

The number of menus you will need will vary depending on what type of operation you have and what type of menu you use. Luxury restaurants may use elaborate menus that are expensive to print.

Family restaurants are more apt to use less expensive, plastic-coated menus. Most fast-food operations use menu boards posted on the wall listing items and prices.

It costs you less per menu when you order large quantities. The major expenses of menus are the design, the artwork, and the printer's setup work time. The printing and the paper stock used are usually inexpensive compared to the other costs. As a result, you can order 1,000 menus for not a great deal more than you would pay for 500. But if you need only 300, there is no point in ordering 1,000.

You could consider buying paper stock for 1,000 menus. You could have the name of your establishment, standard decorations, front page, and so on printed on each and leave the rest of each menu blank. You might be able to have your printer hold these in storage for you or store them yourself. When your 300 menus have been printed, there will still be 700 pieces of the paper stock, already partially printed, left over. If you want to change your menu item offerings and get new menus, it is a simple, fast matter to have the printer make them up on the paper already there. And you have saved some money by buying paper in quantity and doing some preprinting. Flexibility and ease of reprinting are strong arguments for having fewer menus printed at one time and being prepared to print new ones whenever you should.

Do not be afraid to reprint your menus if you need to adjust for price changes. Many operators refuse to do this and it is usually false for example, because of rising meat prices, you should now sell your steaks for Rs. 40 more than the price printed on your menus. Suppose you sell about 250 steaks a week. The revenue you will lose because of the improper pricing of steak on your menu could be Rs. 10,000 a week. Say that it costs Rs. 8,000 to reprint menus. In this example, if you reprint menus to adjust the price of the steak item alone, you recover the cost of printing the menus plus another Rs. 2,000 in just one week's sales of just the one steak item. You will probably have other item too, that could use price adjustment at the same time.

Do adjust menu prices when necessary. If you absolutely cannot afford to reprint all your menus, paste tape over the incorrect prices and write new prices on the tape. Or, if there is no other way, cross out old marking pen and write in new ones. Do not leave a price on a menu if it is not right. Fix it.

How Guests Read Menus

Fig. 6.6

3	1
4	2

Figure 6.6 is a very simple diagram of a two-page menu. It shows how most people naturally tend to read a menu. When they open a menu most people glance first at the right-hand side. They look first at the top area the chart, then down to area 2. Only after they have looked at section 1 and 2 will their eyes naturally range up to section 3 and down to section 4. Take advantage of this normal reading pattern when you make up your menu.

Consider listing appetizers in section 1 and entrees follow accompanying items in sections 1 and 2. You might promote wines in section 3 and use section 4 for listing desserts and nonalcoholic beverages. Mostly these ideas, or work out your own arrangement. But it is smart to use section 1 and 2 to list items you particularly want to sell. Specialty items or specialties of the house, which give a good average check and good profit, should be listed in sections 1 and 2. That is where most guests will look first, and you do not want them to miss these, many people will not the entire menu.

TYPES OF MENUS

Basic Menus

There are three types of basic menus used in food service operations:

1. Table d'hote menu
2. A la carte menu
3. Combination menu

Table d'Hote Menu

Table d'hote means "table of the host." This type of menu originated with innkeepers and is hundreds of years old. When travellers stayed at an inn, they ate with their host, the innkeeper, and they ate whatever foods the innkeeper happened to be having for dinner. All guests ate the same dinner for the same price.

Today a table d'hote menu lists complete dinners. Each dinner generally includes appetizer or soup, entree, potato, vegetable, salad and dessert. There is usually an asterisk and a note saying, "The price of the entree is the price of the complete dinner." Since accompanying items (or choices of them) are the same for all dinners, the only variable cost is the entree. It costs a food service operation less to buy turkey than steak, so you charge less for a turkey dinner in for a steak dinner.

The table d'hote menu is not as popular as it used to be. Many guests seem to feel that there is too much food and that it costs too much.

A la Carte Menu

A la carte means that each item is individually priced. Usually, the only thing included in the price of the entree is the entree's own garnish (lettuce, parsley, watercress). Each entree, vegetable, salad, dessert, beverage-every item – is listed separately with its own price.

Because of individual pricing, an a la carte dinner is more expensive for the guest than a comparable table d'hote dinner. But the dinners are not usually comparable. From an a la carte menu, guests select only what they want. They do not have to pay for a several-course meal, part of which they may not want. For example, from an a la carte menu, guests may choose clams an appetizer, a chefs salad, a sirloin strip steak, and coffee. If that is all they choose, that is all they get and all they pay for. They will not get a baked potato included, for example, and they will not pay for it.

A la carte prices may be higher than table d'hote prices because most of the items are prepared and cooked to order. This can mean a higher labor cost. A la carte menus usually offer a wider variety of items than do table d'hote menus. The a la carte menu tends to be used in expensive, well-appointed restaurants catering to couples and business people. The table d'hote more apt to be used in medium-priced restaurants catering to families.

Combination Menu

This is a combination of the table d'hote and the a la carte menu styles. Certain items are grouped together for a set price (like the table d'hote menu) and other items are priced individually (like the a la carte menu). The combination menu became popular in the 1930s with the so-called blue plate special. For one, all-inclusive set price, you received, for an entree, bread and butter, choice of potato, and choice of vegetable. No appetizer or dessert was included in the set price. The combination menu reduce cost for the customers because they did not have to buy items they did not want or could not afford or pay the higher price of ordering each individually.

The combination menu has gained popularity for the following reasons:

(a) Changing Eating Patterns of the Public

The public no longer wants heavy, complete meals. People are more weight conscious today. During the 1930s the blue plate special became popular because it was all that people could afford and it usual a filling meal. Now many nutritionists tell us that many American eaten too well, too much, too often, and not healthfully.

A lot of Americans are not satisfied with their weight. A few are underweight and want to gain, but most people want to be thinner, and this affects their ideas about eating. Some may splurge and eat they go out for dinner, but many try to stay with a diet even eat out.

For whatever reasons, guests today are not usually complete meals. Many do not want an appetizer or dessert. We have through cycles of smaller steaks, larger steaks, and greater demand for seafood. Some operations simply offer an entree and salad bar combination, with other items extra. The public's eating patterns again, of course, keep yourself current on what the public because preferences can alter at any time.

(b) Increased Costs

By switching from a table d'hote menu to a combination service operations found it possible to raise their prices with to do so. Years ago they could afford to serve a complete steak dinner for Rs. 200. As inflation increased, they could no longer do that. But many food service operators felt that they did not want to charge more than Rs. 200. So they changed from a table d'hote to a combination menu by pricing appetizers and desserts a la carte. Perhaps they listed steak, potato, and salad for Rs. 195, staying just under the Rs. 200 price. They would start juice and soup appetizer prices at about 12 rupees extra a la carte price and go up to Rs. 40 or more for shrimp cocktail.

Desserts probably would start at about 14 rupees extra a la carte for a dish of ice cream and go up to 24 rupees extra or more for pastries and other items. They probably set beverage prices at 6 rupees and up.

In the past, many food operations offered a complete (table d'hote) meal for Rs. 200. Later they offered a combination of steak, potato and salad for Rs. 198 but anything extra was priced a la carte. If guests chose to add other items to their meals, the bill could go up to Rs. 240 or more. Since this trend to combination menus began, more and more establishments have converted to this type of pricing. Even though the combination steak-salad-potato price is now much higher than the Rs. 200 mentioned, the idea of using combination menus prevails.

(c) Combination Menu as a Means of Building Total Guest Check

Instead of serving just a hamburger, for example, for Rs. 100, the food service operation may offer a hamburger plate, which might include hamburger, French fries, and cole slaw, all for Rs. 158. At a la carte prices, the hamburger might sell for Rs. 100, the French fries for Rs. 38, and the cole slaw for Rs. 38, for a total of Rs. 176. But the combination plate can be sold for Rs. 158 combination menu price instead of Rs. 176 a la carte menu price. The amount of cole slaw and French fries served would usually be slightly less than an a la carte portion of either. The average check, however, has increased. It is less expensive for the customer to buy the total hamburger plate package. More people will probably buy the hamburger combination plate because they feel it is worth the Rs. 158 price and is less expensive than the same items priced a la carte.

Many other combinations of foods have been developed and offered to customers at a combination price (lower than individual item price) in an effort to increase the amount of the average check. An example would be the businessperson's lunch. This may include entree, potato or other vegetable, and salad. Guests can buy this for a lower price than the same food would cost if they ordered the same items separately from an a la carte menu.

The businessperson's lunch has gained in popularity with customers. Guests pay a reasonable price for the food they receive. And it allows operators to prepare larger quantities of fewer items, which they can serve quickly. This can help to increase guest turnover, increase volume, and give operators a better chance for bigger profits.

Standardized Menus

Standardized menus can be any of the three types of menus just described. When you set your menu prices, the three types of menus—table d'hote, a la carte and combination—are the basis for arranging what you offer for sale.

A standardized menu is exactly what it sounds like—it is standard; it does not change. This menu has become very popular. Put a special amount of effort and thought into the preparation, design, and layout of a standardized menu. It lists on one menu all the items you offer for sale, but you do not change this menu often. You use the same menu day in and day out, over and over again for at least several months without changing the selection of food item offered, although you may have to adjust some prices.

One advantage of the standardized menu is that it helps to control costs. If you do not sell an item today, you can probably sell it tomorrow because it is on the menu both days. You only have to purchase the food for the items on your standardized menu. You do not have to have other items in stock. This reduces your inventory.

The standardized menu has gained considerable popularity as a dinner menu. Dinner business has declined for many food service operations, particularly for those located in the downtown sections of many cities. Transportation costs, parking problems, and crime have contributed to this situation.

Many people work downtown and eat out for lunch there, but many of them live in the suburbs. If they do decide to eat out at night, they generally go home to the suburbs first and then go to an establishment closer to their homes—one that can be reached easily and offers plenty of parking spaces. Parking is a major concern to the guest, and many downtown food service operations cannot provide it. Dinner businesses for a downtown operation may have wide fluctuation because suburbanites may come in unexpectedly and unpredictably, or you may get convention business from ho during the tourist season, and the like.

The standardized menu lists the same foods day after different people each night with not much daily repeat business. Most items are cooked to order. This works out well because guests dinning out in the evening are more apt to want a leisurely meal and are less apt to mind the extra time it takes to have foods cooked to order. Preparing entrees to order means less waste for the food service operation.

The luncheon menu may also be standardized except for one, two, or may be three daily specials you can change. The luncheon me composed of cooked-to-order items plus a variety of sandwiches. Specials can add variety to the menu. This is especially important where there is much repeat business, which you may have at lunch time.

The breakfast menu is almost always standardized. It usually offers eggs (prepared in a variety of ways), ham, bacon, sausage, pancake specialties, French toast specialties, hot and cold cereals, and variations or combinations of these. You might have a different "hot cereal of the day," but break menus normally do not change much.

Cyclical Menus

A cyclical menu (like the standardized menu) can be any of the three basic menu types (table d'hote, a la carte, or combination). With a "cyclical menu" you use a different menu in one cycle every day for the duration of cycle. Then you can start the same cycle over again, or you can begin a different cycle (or you can repeat the same cycle several times in a row, then switch to different cycles).

A cycle may be for seven days-a different menu for each day of the week. Then you repeat the same seven menus, starting the cycle again with Monday's menu. The cycle can apply to the whole menu or to only a few daily specials, for which you attach flyers to your standardized menu.

There are 14-day cycles, 28-day cycles, 35-day cycles, or any other cycle you want. Some restaurants use a 5-or 10-day Monday through Friday cycle with standardized menus for Saturdays and Sundays. Cycles are usually based on sevens, and there is a reason for this. Foods that are appropriate Monday through Friday may not sell well on weekends, and vice versa. Saturday and Sunday have a different effect on the cycle. Saturday may be a day to increased or reduced business for you and can call for different menu offerings. Sunday will almost always call for different types of food items. Use seven days as the basis for cycles.

For a cyclical menu, you put certain items together on your menu for the same day, but you do not put them together again in the same combination in the same cycle. Individual items will be repeated, but not with each other. For example, there may be hamburger steak, calves liver, and breaded pork chop. Each of these can be repeated during a cycle but not in combination with each other. Menu cycles are especially useful for institutional food services where the same clientele are served day after day. You can build variety into the menu and still control your costs.

The concept of a cyclical menu can be used for daily specials. For example, a restaurant may use a standardized menu but offer three or four new specials each day. The daily special could be set up on a rotating cycle for, say for example, 14 days. On the 15th day, the cycle starts over again. This allows for planning and ordering and helps to control costs. But you can still offer variety for customers who come to your food service operation regularly.

Cycles of 28 and 35 days are popular in institutions (hospitals, university food services, penal institutions). Usually, one cycle is repeated three times and then a different cycle is started.

Make adjustments for seasonal changes in eating habits. People usually want heavier foods in cold weather and lighter foods in hot weather. Ideally, you should change cyclical and standardized menus at least twice a year, perhaps in the spring and then again in the fall. Menu items and appropriate price changes could be adjusted at these times.

MENU FACTORS

Guests come to a food service establishment to have needs satisfied. They want food, of course, but they want other things, too. These can vary and may include specifics such as a relaxing atmosphere, pleasant service personnel, clean and attractive surroundings, or prompt service. These factors affected your menu. The following factors affect it, too:

Market

As a food service operator, you should know what your own market is and cater to it. (We discussed market and how it affects terms in Chapter 4).

Changing Eating Patterns

We have mentioned the changing food habits of increased demand for seafood, decreased demand for desserts appetizers). These attitudes may change again. Be aware of current tastes. Consider changes in the types and quantities of foods that guests want when you make up your menu.

Regional Preferences

Be aware of regional food preferences and cater to them. Some food are very popular in one part of the country (or world) unknown in another. Consider that some regional foods can transfer well and might bear introducing to different geographical areas.

Employees' Skills

You have to evaluate and conform to the skills of your employees-unless you are prepared to train them or hire others with different level of skills. It is foolish to put an item on your menu cannot prepare it well, or if preparing it is so complicated or difficult that it would disrupt production of other foods. If your employees do not know how to prepare something and it is too much of a problem to train them to prepare it well, do not insist on that item. Adapt make changes.

Physical Layout of Kitchen

The physical layout of your kitchen affects your menu and what kinds of foods you can offer. A well-designed kitchen results in simplified production and fewer wasted motions for employees. Food service managers usually have little or nothing to say, however, about originally designing or later changing the layout of the kitchens at their operations. Making big changes in an existing kitchen is a major cost and owners will seldom approve. If you are an owner or an owner/manager, put great. forethought into kitchen design before you buy or build a food service operation. Get the help of kitchen design experts if you can. If you are manager, study the existing physical kitchen layout and plan the work and the menu accordingly. Plan the menu and the work so that your kitchen layout does not make production formidable. Keep it as easy and fast as you can. This will take some serious study and analysis of your layout. Observe and arrange objects and work routines so that things are easiest. Be your own efficiency expert if you cannot hire one.

Balanced Work Load

Plan your menu so that the work load is sensibly balanced. Do not, for example, put a fruit plate and a shrimp salad plate on a menu as the two daily specials and expect one person to prepare both if the same person also has to produce all the cold sandwiches. And definitely do not do this to anyone on a hot day! Assign someone to help. Keep the work load fair. You (and your supervisors) should balance the work load so that all departments and all employees in the kitchen perform a fair share of work.

Labour Cost

When you write your menu, keep labour costs as well as food cost constantly in mind. Some items require very little labour, some a great deal. Steak, for example, is usually just taken from a refrigerator, cooked (on a grill or broiler, and served. But preparing stew means a lot more time and work for your employees. Specialty items "made from scratch" can give you a wide menu offering but they can also increase the work load so much that you might have to hire extra personnel. This is where convenience or pre-cooked entrees have proved exceptionally useful. Watch your costs closely for these, however. Pre-cooked and/or frozen entrees can be used to give variety to the menu without overtaxing your labour force and usually without increasing production costs or waste if you are careful.

These are some of the factors that affect your menu. Plan a menu taking sensible account of all possible factors.

Separate Menus

Today most food service operations have a separate menu for each meal period – breakfast, lunch, dinner and supper (very late evening meal). This is generally the recommended procedure. Some operations, however, use one large menu with separate sections for breakfast, lunch, and dinner and notes specifying what times you can order which items.

Each meal period is different. At different times of the day you will serve different foods, and you will probably be catering to different customers eating out for different reasons. For many people in the United States, lunch is just a food break. Or it may be more important to them if it gives then promote a business deal. Lunch is many things to many people. Dinner is apt to be more special to your guests. People use selecting a place for dinner.

You may be dealing with different markets at different meal periods. So you will probably find different menus appropriate for different meal periods.

Menu Format and Content

Format and content means what foods (and food combinations) you sell and how you write them on the menu. You should consider each item you put on your menu with reference to the other items in the same category and in all your other categories. Say, for example, you decide that for lunch eight entrees, two vegetables, two salads, and four desserts. Establish a menu format so that you get enough variety to appeal to many people. Avoid monotony or duplication, which are not appealing to anybody.

Of the eight entrees, you might select one fish, one egg, three extended meat (meat plus other ingredients – such items as beef stew, Salisbury steak, chili), and three solid meat items. You might decide to offer French fried potatoes and one other potato dish prepared by another method (mashed, boiled, scalloped); one green vegetable and one vegetable of another colour; dessert of pie, cake, ice cream, and so on. Put things together for balance as you select, classify, and categorize food items on your menu.

Your dinner menu should probably be different from your lunch menu. A luncheon menu may include a standard selection of sandwiches same day after day, with only entrees and their accompaniments changing daily. You will probably want to list more entrees for dinner; especially cooked-to-order entrees that can help you cut waste.

When you have decided what items to offer and which one you want to emphasize and sell most of, it is time to consider the physical written arrangement of the menu. Some food managers like to list the entrée with specific vegetable, potato, and salad all together as a unit. Others prefer to list all their entrees and let guests choose the vegetables, potatoes, or salad they want. The first method has the advantage of balancing the entree with its accompanying items. The second method has the advantage of flexibility and more choice in selecting food.

Varieties of Menus

You should be aware of how many different kinds of menus there are when you decide what suits you. Some food service operations-cafeterias, for example—may have nothing more than a big menu signboard posted on the wall. Some establishments have no written menus whatsoever. Their service persons tell guests what is available. Other establishments may use a photocopied menu, perhaps produced daily. A few may have a separate printed menu for each day of the week. Some use a partially standardized menu with insert to list items that change daily. Still others may list their daily special by the use of a table tent, which is a small, folded card set on the table. Use a menu that helps you to sell foods most effectively and at reasonable cost to you and your customers. Use menus that induce guests to buy.

MASTER MENU INDEX

When you have decided on the type of menu you want and the contents, the next thing to do in the process of making up your menu is to develop a good master menu index. This is a time-consuming undertaking, but when you have a good one in working order, it is an invaluable tool. A master menu index is a listing by separate classification of the food items you will offer for sale. Just list foods, no prices.

The master menu index is most useful for establishments that change menus daily. It is also useful for those that use standardized menus, but the need not be as complete.

As soon as you get an idea about your menu, try to take time to write it down in your master menu index right away. You are a fortunate (and rare) person if you can remember all those good ideas you get without writing them down.

In most establishments the breakfast menu is standardized and used day; after day. The luncheon menu may be standardized, but the specials will probably change daily. The dinner menu is apt to be standardized, although can vary, depending on the type of establishment. A steak house may have standardized menu for dinner. A college dormitory would probably have separate menu for each night, and so on.

If you use a standardized menu, you may want to change it in the future. A master menu index can help virtually every type of food service operation.

Classifications for a Master Menu Index

Here is a suggested list of headings you could use in setting up your, master menu index. Adapt and expand the list to suit your own needs.

1. Appetizers
2. Soups
3. Entrees

    (a) Meat
    Beef
    Lamb Pork
    Veal
    Variety
    Extended (beef stew, Salisbury steak) 170 *The Menu Chapter 10*

    (b) Fish and Seafood

    (c) Eggs

4. Sauces
5. Potatoes
6. Vegetables
7. Salads and Dressings
8. Desserts
9. Beverages (nonalcoholic)

If you have a computer, put your master menu index in it. If your master menu index in it. If you don't, use a loose-leaf notebook. Set up the notebook with all the heading you want. Use a separate section for each category and a separate page for 1 subheading. Then list all the items you might serve. You should probably have two separate master menu indexes—one for lunch and one for dinner. Many of the items will be the same, but it is better to have things list forget them or have to shuffle back and forth trying to find something.

To illustrate how the master menu index might be set up under "Soups" for example, you might have a list of between 20 and 35 types soups you may want to serve (depending on your type of operation).

Soups

1. Broth
   (*a*) Chicken Broth
   (*b*) Beef Bouillon
   (*c*) Lamb Broth

2. Cream
   (*a*) Cream of Chicken Soup
   (*b*) Cream of Tomato Soup
   (*c*) Cream of Mushroom Soup

3. Chowder
   (*a*) Corn Chowder
   (*b*) Manhattan Clam Chowder
   (*c*) New England Clam Chowder

You could also list under each type of soup details of variations you will use in addition to serving it plain—for example, Chicken Broth with Rice, Chicken Noodle Soup, Chicken Egg Drop Soup.

For another example of a heading for your master menu set up "Potatoes" as follows:

1. French Fried Potatoes
2. Creamy Whipped Potatoes
3. Creamed Potatoes with Cheese
4. Hash Brown Potatoes
5. Baked Potatoes
   (*a*) Baked Potato
   (*b*) Baked Potato with Sour Cream Topping

(c) Special Baked Potato with Ham, Onion and Cheese

When you write your master menu index, use the same words you will use when you actually print the item on the menu. For example, do not just list your vegetables as "peas," "corn," and so on. Write down exactly what you intend to print on your menu — "Buttered Peas with Mushrooms," "Green Peas with Tiny Whole Onions," "Creamed Peas," and so on. Write the entire, exact descriptive phrase just as you want it to appear on your menu. Then just copy it when you write your menus.

The brief sample master menu index lists above illustrate only a couple of categories. You need a complete listing (without prices) of every item you know you will offer, plus anything you think you might ever want to offer in the future. Keep adding new ideas. Make revisions. Cross out items that are not successful. Write it all down. It is impossible to remember all potential items.

Put real thought, time and work into developing your master menu index. A good one will greatly simplify the actual mechanics of menu writing. You will not forget ideas because you write them in constantly. You will have everything at your fingertips. It is efficient and it is a good management menu control tool, which will make it much easier for you to attain variety on your menu. Once you have your master menu index in working order, you will use it from then on. It will save you a great deal of time and energy when you plan and write your menus. This is especially true if your operation uses cyclical menus.

MENU WRITING

In talking about menu format and content, we discussed the types, number, and arrangements of entrees and accompanying items on the menu. We have also discussed a master menu index and making comprehensive lists of food items you might offer for sale. When you actually write your menus, you apply all these ideas and make real use of your master menu index.

To assure good variety, try to plan several days' menus or daily specials simultaneously. Better yet, plan a complete cycle (7, 28, 35 days) all at once if you possibly can. When you set out to plan and write a menu, the first thing to do your master menu index. Copy the wording you used in the master menu index.

List the entrees first. List all the entrees you will offer for several days or for a cycle. Many of these entrees may be the same day after day, will probably be some variation. (Put items together on the menu so get some that you get some range and variation in prices).

When you have listed the entrees, go back to each separate classification and list all appetizers, soups, potatoes, vegetables, salads, and desserts that will best accompany these combinations of entrees. This process will achieve balance of your menu items for colour combinations, variety and costs.

Wording

Be careful how you use descriptive words in your master menu on your printed menu. How many times have you seen a menu listing "Garden Peas?" Does the phrase mean anything? "Garden" is a silly descriptive word for peas. "Field-Grown Peas" would be more accurate, less picturesque, but just as silly.

Take, too, the menu that promotes "Half-Fried Chicken." These words mean literally that the chicken is a bit raw. It has been fried for only much time as it should have been. Pessimists can interpret this to half the chicken is raw. Optimists may believe that half the chicken is fried. Customers will know what you mean. Some will catch careless wording and laugh. They will hope your cooks cook better than you write. "Fried One-Half Chicken" does the job accurately.

Menu wording should be accurate and it must be truthful. California has a "truth in menu" law. Other states are considering putting such a law into effect. No one will sue you for your "half-fried chicken." But be sure you correctly list exactly what you are offering for sale. For example if you say "fresh," be sure that the item you are serving is fresh and has frozen or processed. Don't say Roquefort dressing and then serve your customers blue cheese dressing. Roquefort cheese comes only from certain specific caves in France. These are just a few examples of the types of thin be careful about. Be very exact and truthful in your menu wording. Restaurants in the industry should police themselves to avoid having legislatures do it for them.

Listing Accompaniments

When people go out to eat, most expect to receive some sort of accompanying dishes. List the accompaniments you are going to serve. Do accompaniments and do list them on your menu in appetizing (lavish if you wish) but grammatically correct terms. Failure to serve adequate sauces, accompaniments and garnishes and to list them on the menu is a major mistake. Many operators make it, though.

Preparing Food

Of course your job does not stop when you have written a menu. You cannot just hand the menus to your chef or food production specialist or chief hamburger frier and say: "Here's the menu. Fix the food." You have to tell (and maybe shown) your employees how you want the food prepared, what time you want it ready, and how much of it you want. You should also prepare and use standardized recipes.

Overproduction and Underproduction

When you write your menus, you must pay attention to potential problems of overproduction and underproduction. If you prepare too much of an item, leftovers may have to be discarded. If you have or prepare too little of an item, you can run out of it too soon. Do not be like the manager is implied to be in the old restaurant joke: "A restaurant opens for lunch. One customer comes in, looks at the menu and orders liver. A few minutes later the second customer, comes in, looks at the menu, and orders liver. The waitress says, 'Sorry. We're out. Someone just ordered it." Not much of a joke. Not much of a manage either.

Plan for reasonable runout times, particularly for foods that are expensive to prepare. For example, if you anticipate and forecast that you will probably sell 100 orders of Swiss steak for lunch, you might want to *try* to run out of it at about 1:30 although your dining room will stay open until 2:00. You do not want Swiss steak left over because it may be a comparatively expensive entree in relation to others you are offering on that menu. Swiss steak takes time to prepare properly, and there is not much you can do with it profitably it is left over. Leftover Swiss steak probably won't have a satisfactory alternative use. You might put it into stew or croquettes, but neither of these alternative uses will bring you the price that Swiss steak should.

Try to sell all of everything you prepare that is not cooked to order. This may mean that you will run out of some items. But try not to run out too soon. It is acceptable to run out of one or two items toward the end of the meal period. Most customers understand this if it is toward the end of a mealtime. But if an item is listed on your menu for lunch and a guest orders it at noon, she or he may well be irritated if you have "run out."

If you do unexpectedly run out of items early, or if you plan purposely run out during a meal period, you had better know what foods you will have ready to substitute in their places and what prices you will charge for them. Try to have substitutes ready which at least have a fighting chance of pleasing.

A guest who wanted what you ran out of. If you run out of Swiss steak, for example, you might plan to substitute one of your regular menu items such as cube steak at the same price. Perhaps a cube steak portion cost you a few cents more than a portion of Swiss steak. But you can cook the cube steak to order. And you are substituting one of your regular menu item (used, for example, on a cube steak platter or in a cube steak sandwich), which makes the substitution much easier for you.

Consider problems of overproduction and underproduction for every item you have to cook ahead of time. Foods cooked after a guest has ordered them do not pose these real overproduction and underproduction problem unless they have to be partially altered or partially altered or partially prepared ahead of time also a problem.

Always try to figure out in advance what uses you can make of leftovers. It is impossible to be totally accurate all of the time in your forecasting. All food service operations will have leftovers. If you possibly can, use leftovers so they will produce revenue for the operation. Food service managers who consistently permit leftovers to be thrown away are throwing away money, and maybe their own jobs, too.

Perhaps you can use leftovers in employees' meals, but about this. Employees' meals must always be of good quality relatively inexpensive for the food service operation. If your employees are not good, the psychological-not to mention gastronomical—effects on employees will not be conducive to happy employees. You may intentionally plan for some extra production of a item, planning to use this for employees' meals because it is low in cost.

BANQUET MENUS

Food service establishments with separate banquet dining rooms should have separate banquet menus. There are two ways to write banquet menus:

1. Group certain classes of items together. The person who is making banquet reservations can choose from these. For example choice of appetizer, vegetable, potato, salad, chicken or chopped steak, and a sundae for a certain set price. Steak or prime rib higher prices than the chicken or chopped steak even though the rest of the accompanying items would be the same. Usually vegetables offered for banquets will be the ones you are serving in your regular dining room that day.
2. Price each item individually (a' la carte) and let the booking select the specific i tems they want.

Booking Banquets

Several typed or printed copies of the complete banquet menu should be made up and available at all times for use by the manager, assistant manager, catering manager, secretary, sales manager – any personnel who book banquet parties and meetings. Your personnel should be ready at all times to give firm price quotes, menu selections, and complete information whenever anyone inquires.

Too often people call food service operations to make arrangements (or just ask about making them) for a banquet and are told to call back because no one is there who can give them the information. They should not be told to call back. Someone at the restaurant should call them back. But this should very rarely be necessary because you should always have someone available who does know about banquets and can provide information. If you do not, you are almost sure to lose some banquet business.

Along with the banquet menu, you might consider having a notebook made up for your sales personnel to show to potential banquet and business meeting customers. The notebook could have colour photos showing your banquet rooms with various seating and table arrangements, different table setups, china setups, service setups, and so on. The notebook should indicate the number of occupants the room can accommodate with different types of room setups. Complete menus and prices should be included.

A complete descriptive notebook on your banquets and meetings facilities could be an extremely useful sales tool. You might make up several of these notebooks for interested customers to look at. Have at least one always available on the premises if others are being used elsewhere in attempts to get banquet business. You might also consider having less expensive brochures made up to give or mail to prospective banquet and business meeting customers. The main thing is to be sure that you have complete and valid information ready at all times when potential banquet or meetings customers inquire in person or by phone.

Explaining Your Banquet and Meeting Facilities to Customers

Private parties, business and club meetings, and banquets can be a good sales bonus for you above and beyond regular business. Prices you charge and foods you offer should be appropriate for your food service operation. You should probably decide on a minimum number of guests for a banquet or meeting and a minimum dollar amount to be sure that your costs will be covered.

Sometimes a person calling to make banquet reservations will say: "We are all ordering the same thing (the roast beef dinner or the chicken dinner, for example), so will it cost us less per person than it would in your regular dining room?" It will usually cost them more. The following are examples the factors that can contribute to making it necessary for you to change more for banquet facilities than you do for your regular dining room service:

1. You have an extra investment in your private dining room and facilities.
2. Your private dining rooms are not used continuously. When they are idle you are still incurring some costs (rent, some cleaning) and paying some utilities for them.
3. You may have to hire extra personnel to take care of service for a private party, banquet or meeting.
4. Guests can have private dining rooms set up in any way they want.
5. In your private dining room, guests can all sit together, have privacy make noise, give speeches, and conduct meetings. They cannot do these things in your regular public dining area.

These are just samples of factors that mayor may or may not apply to your operation. Make a list of factors that do apply to your banquet facilities and make sure that any of your staff who may be asked about banquets not the facts. Do not under price your banquet facilities. Some food service establishments sell their banquets at their regular menu price but charge rental for the private dining room. Others charge higher prices for the banquet menu and any room rental price is included in this higher banquet menu price.

Menu Engineering

The term "menu engineering" was conied by M.L. Kasavana andD.I. Smith, two American authors who published who published a book entitled *Menu Engineering: a Practical Guide to Menu Analysis* in 1982 (Hospitality Publications, USA). The book represents the most important contribution to pricing through cash gross profit. Our treatment of menu engineering is based on this American soucre but it places the essential problems involved in the wide context of gross profit control and menu profitability.

Menu engineering represents a major break with past attitudes to menu pricing: We no longer accept the percentage approach, which has been used for several decades. Instead we recognise that:

(a) the principal aim of menu pricing is to secure the right level of cash gross profit, and

(b) each menu item should make a sufficient contribution to overall profitability in terms of cash gross profit. In order to achieve satisfactory menu profitability the following are required:

1. An analysis of the probularity and profitability of each menu item. In this context popularity is measured by the number of items (protions) sold. Profitability is measured in terms of cash gross profit.
2. A continual reappraised of the choice of menu items. Those which are unsatisfactory (unpopular, unprofitable or both) are examined in detail. If adequate improvements cannot be secured, they are replaced by other items which are more effective in terms of cash gross profit.
3. Finally, there is a continual reveiw of menu prices, protion costs and sometimes menu design.

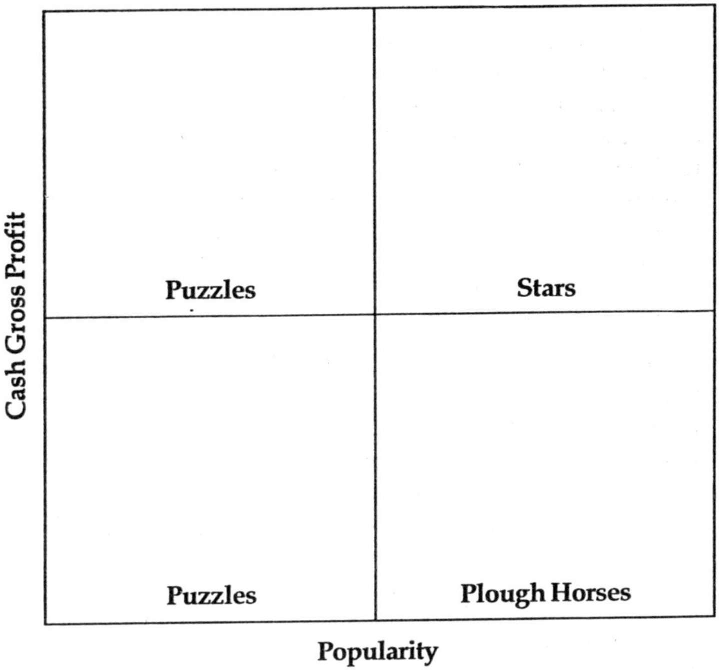

Figure 6.7 : Menu Item Categories

Menu Engineering Terminology

We group all menu items into four separate categories:

1. A star is menu item which is pouplar and profitable.
2. A plough horse is an item which is popular but does not atttract a high gross profit per item sold.
3. A puzzle is an item which is profitable, but for some reason (which is a puzzle) is not popular.
4. A dog is a menu item which is neither popular nor profitable.

A diagrammatic represenation of the four categories is show in Figure: 6.7.

Menu Engineering Worksheet

In Figure 6.9 overleaf we show the Menu Engineering Worksheet. In this example we have only the main dishes: separte worksheets would be completed in respect of the other parts of the menu, i.e., starters and desserts.

Figure 6.8 : Menu Engineering Worksheet

Menu item	*No. of items*	*Menu mix %*	*Item food*	*Item SP cost*	*Item CGP*	*Total food*	*Total sales cost*	*Total CGP Amount*	*%*	*Rank*			*Notes*
	1	*2*	*3*	*4*	*5*	*6*	*7*	*8*			*9*	*10*	
1. Sole Veronique	560	14.0	114	340	226	63840	190400	126560	16.5	2	H	H	Star
2. Grilled Trout	500	12.5	106	318	212	53000	159000	106000	13.9	3	H	H	Star
3. Chicken Kiev	630	15.7	102	238	136	64260	149940	85680	11.2	5	L	H	Plough house
4. Calves Liver	180	4.5	94	290	196	16920	522000	35280	4.6	7	H	L	Puzzle
5. Leg of Lamb	210	5.2	84	190	106	17640	39900	22260	2.9	9	L	L	Dog
6. Irish Chops	540	13.5	78	260	182	42120	140400	98280	12.9	4	L	H	Plough horse
7. Lamb Chops	190	4.8	74	250	176	14020	47500	33440	4.4	8	L	L	Dog
8. Irish Steak	240	6.0	78	170	92	18720	40800	22080	2.9	10	L	L	Dog
9. Sirloin Steak	280	7.0	124	358	234	34720	100240	65520	8.8	6	H	H	Star
10. Entrecote Steak	670	16.8	126	378	252	84420	253260	168840	22.1	1	H	H	Star
	4,000	1,000				409700	1173640	763940					

The essential aim of the Menu Engineering Worksheet is to analyse the popularity and profitability of the menu items, and to slot each item into one of the four categories already defined.

Notes on the Completion of the Menu Engineering Worksheet (by Column)

1. In Column 1 we show, in respect of each menu item, the total number of items sold during the period under review.
2. Here, in Column 2, we show the percentage composition of the total of menu items shold.
3. The food cost per portion would, of course, be obtained from the estabishment's standard recipes, costing sheets, etc.
4. The time selling price is the menu price less the VAT element.
5. In Column 5 we show the cash gross profit per menu item. This is obtained by deducting the cost per portion in Column 3 from the item selling price show in Column 4.
6. Here, in Column 6, we show the total food cost of each menu item. Each figure in this column is obtained by mutiplying the relevent number of menu items sold by the cost per portion show in Column 3.
7. Total sales in Column 7 is obtained by multiplying each number of menu items sold by the appropriate item selling price shown in Column. 4.
8. Under the heading "Total cash gross profit we enter three figures for each menu item. The amount of cash gross profit is, in each case, the difference between the relevant figures in Columns 7 and 6. Such Figures many also be obtained by mutiplying the appropriate amounts in Columns 1 and 5. In the next column we show the percentage composition of total cash gross profit. This is a most useful part of the Menu Engineering Worksheet in that it shows the respective contribution of each menu item to total cash gross profit. Finally, in the third column, we show the ranking of the ten menu items in terms of the contribution they make to total cash gross profit. Finally, in the third column, we show the ranking of the ten menu items in terms of the contribution they make to total cash gross profit.
9. In Column 9 we catgorise all menu items in terms of their cash gross profits. This is done by reference to the weighted average cash gross profit. In this case the average cash gross

profit per menu item is Rs. 7,63,940 divided by 4,000 Rs. 1,908. Menu items with a cash gross profit loading of 4.77 or more are classified as high cash gross profit items (H); those with less than Rs. 1,908 are classified as low cash profit items (L).

10. The function of Column 10 is to classify the proularity of menu items. With a menu consisting of ten items one would expect—other things being equal—each item to account for 10 per cent of the menu mix. Any item which reached at least 10 per cent of the total of menu items sold would be classified as enjoying high popularity (H); and, conversely, item which failed to reach their rightful share of 10 per cent would be categorised as having low popularity (L). With this approach, half the menu items tend to be shown as being 'below average' in terms of their popularity. This in turn may call for rather frequent and fundamental revisions of the menu. It is for this reason that American food service operators use the 70 per formula. and regard all menu items which reach at least 70 per cen of their 'rightful share' of the menu mix as enjoying high popularity. With this approach, where a menu consists of 20 items, which reached (70 per cen of 5 per cent) 3.5 per cent of the menu mix would be regarded as enjoying high popularity. Whilst there is no convincing theoretical support for choosing 70 per cent rather than some other similar percentage. Common sense tends to sugget that there is merit in this approach.

Remedial Action

After an appropriate analysis of a menu, the right corrective action is required.

Stars—These are menu items which make a significant contribution to menu profitability. These items desrve a lot of attention. We must not do anything to prejudice their success. Also we must ensure that we ingredients, their quality through the pruchase of the best possible ingredients, comnpetent food preparation and attractive presenatation.

Plough horses— these menu items do not generate a lot of cash gross profit per item sold, but they frequently contribute, in total, an amount of profit which is very reasonable indeed. Whilst it is tempting to increase their prices and convert them to stars, there may be a singnificant minority of guests who favour these menu items because of their low prices. Ajdustements to protion costs may be possible in certain circumstances.

Puzzles—a variety corrective action is possible. In some cases a lower price may incerease their popularity. Some of these menu items do not sell because they do not appear attractive on the menu: A possible solution then is to rename the menu item. An important consideration here is the shelf life of the item concerned. As a genernal principle, the longer the shlef life the stronger the case for retaining the menu item, and vice versa.

Dogs—as a gernal principle, a dog should be removed and replaced by a more successfull food item. Whilst their removal should not ncessarily be automatic, it must be remembered that there is a dual problem here: both profitability and popularity are unsatisfactory.

Some Problems and Limitations

Elasticity of Demand

One of the most important practical problems in price level adjustments is that we do not know enough about elasticity of demand. However thorough the menu engineering analysis, we can never be sure of the effect on demand (number of covers) of any one change in the general level of menu prices. What applies to the menu as a whole applies equally to particular menu prices. What applies to the menu as a whole applies aqually to particular menu items. Also there is the problem of—to use economics terminology—'cross-elasticity of demand'. This is defined ad the change in the demand for one commodity (say menu item A) which would result from a given change in the price of another commodity (say menu item B). We know even less about cross-elasticity of demand for individual menu items than we do about the elasticity of demand for the meau as a whole. Therefore when we adjust the price of menu item B, any benefits arising from the ajdustment may be more than offset by the change in the demand for menu item A. There is of course the knock-on effect in terms of the resulting choice of desserts, etc. It is essential to remember, therefore, that price level ajdustment decisions must be underprinned by a lot of common sense, experience and knowledge of the particular circumstances of the operation concerned.

Labour Intensity

In menu engineering the most critical element is cash gross profit. Whilst no one would dispute its importance, we should not ignore the related aspect of labour intensity. The cash gross profit on a Banana Flambee may be higher than that on Poire Belle Helene. When we taken the cost of labour into account—and particularly during peak periods—it may well be that Poire Belle Helene is the more profitable menu item to well.

Shelf Life

Menu engineering in its crude form doesnot take the shelf life of menu items into account. Amongst the strarters we may have on the menu (canned) Fruit Juice, showing a cash gross proft of Rs. 1.20 and a Seafood Salad with a Cash gross profit of Rs. 1.40. It may well be that, especially during slack periods, the Fruit Juice is more profitable than the other starter.

Potential vs. Actual Costs

Many of the figures used in menu engineering ananlysis are potential rather than actual figures. Thus all item food costs (and all figures of item gross profit, total food cost and total cash gross profit) are potential rather the actual figures. Whilst one should not expect under discrepancies between potential and actual costs, it is important to realise that we are analysing intended reults rather than facts. Readers will of course appeciate that any such discrepancies between potential and acutal figures will depend on the size of the operation as well as the extent of the menu. Whilst in the case of a large industrial canteen the overall actual food cost many well differ by 2 – 3 percentage points from the potential cost, individual menu items may show more substantial discrepancies. A small up-market restaurant with an extensive menu may well find that its 'gross profit gap' (difference between potential and actual gross profit) is much higher, and that in consequence some actual portion costs maydiffer quite considerably from those used in its menu engineering analysis.

Operating Standards

A related problem which tends to detract from the validity of menu engineering analysis is the use of incorrect operating standards.

When calculating potential portion costs we have basically two possibilities:

(*a*) to use 'ideal standards', when we divide the total cost of ingredients by the projected number of portions;

(*b*) to rely on 'attainable standards', when we make an appropritate allowance for unforeseen losses during food preparation, bad portioning, leftovers, etc. The majority of American food service operators use attainable standards by adding a small percentage—frequently up to 10 per cent—in respect of 'unporductive cost'. Portion costs thus calcuated are more realistic and contirbute significantly to the validity of menu engineering analyses. Unfortunately most British hotel and catering companies tend to use ideal standards with the result that actual portion costs differ somewhat from potential portion costs.

Conclusion

Earlier in this chapter we said that the percentage approach is unsafe because of changes in the sales volume and sales mix. When we use the techniques of menu engineering we still face these problems but, most certainly, we are more likely to succed in achieving the right cash gross profit for the following reasons:

1. We plan for and continuously monitor our cash gross profit, and this activity is not distracted by other considerations such as percentages.
2. We give prominence to and control, on an ongoing basis, the determinants of menu profitability, i.e. the number of the items sold and the item cash gross profit.
3. We control not only total results but also the separate contribution to total results of each menu item.
4. Finally, we think more anlytically about menu items. This new analytical approach means that the menu offerings are not just 'menu items', but distinctly dissimilar groups which have different characteristics and require different handling in the context of gross profit control.

Bibliography

Bob Stein, *Marketing in Action for Hotels, Motels and Restaurants,* Ahrens Publishing Company, Inc., New York, 1971.

Carl H. Albers, *Food and Beverage Cost Planning and Control Procedure,* Educational Institute of American Hotel and Motel Association, East Lansing, MI, 1974.

Charles Levinson, *Food and Beverage Operation,* Prentice-Hall, Inc., Englewood Cliffs, NJ., 1976.

Costas Katsigris and Mary Porter, *Bar and Beverage Book,* John Wileys Sons, Inc., New York, 1983.

Douglas C. Keister and Ralph D. Wilson, *Selected Readings for an Introduction to Hotel and Restaurant Management,* McCutchan Publishing Corporation, Berkeley, CA, 1971.

Douglas C. Keister, *How to Increase Profit with Portion Control,* National Restaurant Association, Chicago, 1966.

Essentials of Good Table Service, rev.ed. School of Hotel Administration, Cornell University, Ithaca, NY., n.d.

Harold J. Grossman, *Grossman's Guide to Wines, Spirits, and Beers,* rev.ed. Charles Scribner's Sons, New York, 1955.

James Keiser and Elmer Kallio, *Controlling and Analysing Cost in Food Service Operations,* John H. Wiley and Sons, Inc., New York, 1974.

Jerome Vallen, *Art and Science of Modern Innkeeping,* Ahrens Publishing Company, Inc., New York, 1968.

Joseph Brodner, Howard M. Carlson, and Henery T. Maschal, *Profitable Food and Beverage Operation,* Ahrens Publishing Company, Inc., New York, 1962.

Leroi A. Folsom, *Professional Chef,* 4th ed. Institutions/Volume Feeding Management, Chicago, 1971.

M.C. Warfel and Frank H. Waskey, *Professional Food Buyer,* MC Cutchan Publishing Corporation Berkeley, CA, 1979.

Marketing for a Full House, C.De Witt Coffman School of Hotel Administration, Cornell University, Itkaca, NY, 1972.

Meat Buyers Guide. The National Association of Meat Purveyors, Mcleon, VA, 1983.

Michael M. Cottman, *Cost Control for Hospitality Industry,* CBI Publishing Company, Inc., Boston, 1980.

Micheal L. Kasavana and Donald I. Smith. *Menu Engineering,* Hospitality Publications, Lansing, MI 1982.

Micheal M. Cottman, *Food and Beverage Cost Control,* Prentice-Hall Inc. Englewood Cliffs, NJ., 1977.

Pat Levings, *Profit from Food Service,* Cahners Books, Boston, 1974.

Paul R. Dittmer and Gerald G. Griffin, *Principles of Food, Beverage, and Labour Cost Contorls for Hotel and Restaurants,* 3rd ed. Van Nostrand Reinhold Company, Inc., New York, 1960.

Peter Dukas, *How to Plan and Operate a Restaurant,* 2nd ed. Hayden Book Company Inc., Rochelle Park, NJ, 1973.

Peter Van Kleek, *Beverage Management and Bortending,* Van Nostrand Reinhold Company, Inc., New York, 1983.

Raymond B. Peddersen, *Increasing Productivity in Food Service,* Cahners Books, Boston, 1973.

Thomas F. Powers and Jo Marie Powers, *Food Service Operation: Planning and Control,* John Wiley and Sons, Inc., New York, 1984.

William J. Morgan, *Supervision in Management of Quantity Food Preparation,* Jr. Mc Cutchan Publishing Corporation, Berkeley, CA, 1974.

William L. Kahrl, *Introduction to Modern Food and Beverage Service.* Prentice-Hall, Inc., Englewood Cliffs, NJ., 1976.

Index